östberg™

The title of the book should have been Rules of the Game. Ed Friedrichs, in great detail, engrosses the reader and reminds him of the complexity of the objective. *Reach Higher: Long-cycle Strategies for a Short-cycle World* should provide a foundation for anybody with serious objectives. Well worth the read.

—Samuel Zell, Chairman, Equity International

Ed Friedrichs' *Reach Higher* is a timely guide to improving business performance in the modern, global marketplace. It makes the argument as well as any that a company cannot succeed without empowering its employees and unleashing their creativity, maintaining a long-term view on the business—not being short-term slaves to quarterly results. Further, it recognizes the critical notion that people and relationships, not the latest technology or stock market play, are the key to success.

—Bob Lutz, GM Vice Chairman, Global Product Development

How do you transform a small design group into the world's largest architectural firm? Ed Friedrichs reveals the strategic moves he followed to accomplish just that. By redefining company goals, differentiating the firm and creating an in-house culture that attracted the best and brightest talent, he was able to confound competitors and achieve world wide expansion while maintaining the creativity and energy of a small company. Everyone who plans to manage or transform any business or organization must read this book. It adds an essential new dimension to understanding what makes any organization thrive. Moreover, it makes anyone wish they could work for a guy like him.

—Phelps Dewey—founder and President (retired)—Chronicle Books.

Ed Friedrichs has provided a fascinating read on the accumulation of wisdom and business accumen, and then most generously shares both with his readers. He also has, perhaps unintentionally, provided insight into the thoughts of a person possessed of uncommon ideals and character. Read and absorb his book to become a more enlightened person."

—Ray Anderson, Founder, Chairman and CEO Interface, Inc.

Ed's insights into the business cycle are a perfect antidote for the "What have you done for me lately?" mentality in today's business world. Any leader who is focused on building customer loyalty, attracting talent and building shareholder value will benefit from this book."

—Jim Hackett, President and CEO Steelcase, Inc.

In his book, Ed Friedrichs provides an insightful and valuable perspective on leadership issues and techniques. Each issue is broken down chapter-by-chapter and illustrated with examples from both the real world of business as well as from Ed's extensive reading. The reference list that Ed has compiled is a key resource for any leader.

—Arthur Gensler, Chairman, Gensler

REACH HIGHER

LONG-CYCLE STRATEGIES
FOR A SHORT-CYCLE WORLD

REACH HIGHER

LONG-CYCLE STRATEGIES
FOR A SHORT-CYCLE WORLD

Ed Friedrichs

Greenway Communications

östberg

REACH HIGHER © 2006 by Ed Friedrichs

Östberg Library of Design Management

ISBN-10: 0-9755654-7-8
ISBN-13: 978-0-9755654-7-6

Cover design: Austin Cramer
Layout: Dan Downey

Published by:
Greenway Communications, LLC
A division of The Greenway Group
25 Technology Parkway South, Suite 101
Atlanta, GA 30092
800.726.8603
www.greenway.us

With my deepest gratitude to my wife, Pat, without whose untiring support, reflections, and rich insights, this book could not have been done.

Contents

Preface

This book is dedicated to my father,
Edward Charles Friedrichs, Jr.

How do your ideas about business, leadership, ethics and values come about? When we arrive at that point in life where we begin to support ourselves, our behavior patterns have been set—but how did this happen? We see behavioral patterns in business ranging from kindness to commanding, from gentle and supportive to downright mean-spirited. Some enterprises evolve into great places that people want to be a part of, and others experience high turnover or rapid failure. Which ideas, behavior and actions make a difference, and how do you learn about them? Many of mine were formed early. You'd almost say they were absorbed by osmosis. I really didn't begin to understand them until much later in my business career. But when I did, I found many of the roots of my philosophy, approach and values came from my childhood.

My father, born in 1905 the son of German immigrants, modeled great instinctive leadership behavior. Although I didn't begin to realize it until a few years before he died in 1978, he has been an inspiration throughout my life. It's only as I reflect back on my career that I recognize how many elements of his style I've incorporated into my own business life. To this day, I puzzle over how he became the leader that he was.

My grandfather died when my father was 12. A baker by trade, he had come around the tip of South America on a wooden sailing ship for the Alaskan gold rush in the late 19th century. My father and his mother were left with a tiny bakery in a 25-foot-wide storefront in Hayward, California, a then rural town across the bay from San Francisco. Together, living above the bakery, they kept the business alive. His education was limited. He finished high school but had only a few college-level courses at the Chicago Institute of Baking to guide him in shaping his business. I was born late in his life for that era—he was 39 and my mother 38. By then, his business was strong and growing.

I remember most my father's fascination with everything new in the world and his entrepreneurial spirit. The speed with which technology was evolving thrilled him (if he could only be alive today). In his early 20s, Dole, a major pineapple grower, sponsored the first solo flight from California to Hawaii departing from Oakland, a few miles north of Hayward. He simply had to be there to watch the preparations, which went on for weeks, but his strong German work ethic demanded a business purpose. The airfield was like a carnival with people coming every day to watch the planes being prepared and to meet those brave pilots.

His only transportation was a Model "T" delivery truck, so he contracted with the food vendors at the airfield to deliver hotdog and hamburger buns. But the truck would hold more than what he sold to them, so he filled it with bread and pastries and started knocking on doors in a nearby neighborhood, Alameda, starting a house-to-house bakery delivery business. By the time I was in my teens, he had more than 250 trucks delivering bakery goods from Sacramento to Monterey.

I started working in the bakery when I was five and continued on weekends and summers until I was 19. I did every imaginable job from folding donut boxes and making pastries to repairing machinery and trucks. I joined the Teamsters to drive a 40-foot semi in college, delivering bread as far north as Fort Bragg and as far south as Monterey. I worked not because it was needed, not because

I was told to; I worked because my father worked. And I was lucky enough to be able to trail along behind him and be given things to do.

I believe that no one as a child knows his or her father well. When we're young, our fathers are just there; we don't think about who they are or what they're like. If we're fortunate enough and they live long enough, we may gain a sense of them as a person by the time we're adults. But being able to see them in the full richness of their personalities, with their values, their dreams and their fears, is rare.

Through my continuous relationship with the men and women who worked for my father, I saw a man of exceptional integrity, one whose highest ambition was to create an environment in which people found satisfaction in what they did and pride in what they made. Through their eyes and their observations of his behavior, I watched him deal with the brutality of unionization, men being beaten, bones broken, arson at the bakery, and I saw the dreams of new products and markets being realized. I learned what it felt like to be proud of the enterprise you were a part of and to have an employer who was accessible, interested in your welfare and driven by quality for the customer. I also saw the value that his approach to business built for all stakeholders—for the ownership, the people who worked in it and the community in and for which it existed.

As college years approached for me, the space age was upon us. From the time I was 12 years old, I knew I wanted to be an architect, but my father and his friends would hear nothing of it. As in the film, "The Graduate," a word was whispered in my ear—it wasn't "plastics," it was "engineering." They considered architecture a dumb profession with high risk and low reward. "You'll never make any money," they said.

I began college at Stanford University in 1961, reluctantly entering the undergraduate engineering program, migrating quickly into industrial engineering, which, in those days, meant product design so that my course work would parallel the architecture program. For my senior year I returned to Palo Alto, having spent six months at Stanford's German campus immersed in wondrous and timeless cities and an architecture of permanence. I shed slide rules and vinyl pocket protectors—the badges of an engineer—to pursue my passion. My father's advice then, as it had been throughout my life and as it had been to everyone in his organization, was: "Whatever you do, be the best at it."

I owe a great deal of my success as an architect to an overwhelming drive to do just that, a value deeply instilled by my father. I have to add, though, that in reflection there was another motivator—a bit of a desire to prove my father and his pals wrong about architecture, to create a model for a design enterprise that made money and made sense, as my father had done in the bakery business for his customers and employees.

The real learning and the premise of this book is that there are no dumb businesses. Every enterprise has the potential to build value for its stakeholders, to be successful in the context of the world in which it exists, to be an enterprise that people want to be a part of and to have customers who seek the products and services it offers. These are the lessons I've learned about how to do that. I've structured them into five sections—designing a business strategy, attracting and retaining great people, building strong and loyal customer relationships, nurturing the networks that allow them to do their best for themselves and your customers and leadership and design.

I dedicate this book to my father.

Introduction

Early in my career, I began to wrestle with a question - how do you build an organization that continues to grow in value over time? I had begun working with a small architectural firm in San Francisco—M. Arthur Gensler, Jr., & Associates, Architects. We were a merry band of about 20 people doing a wide variety of architecture and interior design projects. It was a young practice, but even then we were puzzling with some very basic questions about what sort of business we would like to be in. We were asking questions like what constitutes value and to whom? Which characteristics of the fundamentals of the firm and the business would yield highest value to our clients? Value is delivered to those clients through the people in the firm, so we also had to ask which characteristics would attract the very best people. Since architectural and even many interior design projects last a long time and we knew that the continuity of the information carried in the heads of the people who worked in the firm constituted high value to our clients (or, conversely, discontinuity through turnover of staff was very costly to us and to our clients because of lost information and relationships), we wanted to know which programs and what environment would keep people engaged with the firm for a long time. What would attract people to make a career at Gensler?

Every enterprise has numerous stakeholders—the people in it, those that own it, the customers that it serves and the community of which it's a part. Truly valuable organizations have optimized the value to each of these stakeholders. Their structure, values and culture foster sustainable growth in value to each over time. They are sustainable in a human sense as they build healthy and supportive relationships among people. They are also sustainable in the environmental sense in that they do no harm to the world around them—they make that world and the communities they serve a better place.

As I searched for a grounding principle for sustainability and value in an enterprise, I became fascinated with the cycle times of things that affect our lives. While this may seem to you like a lengthy digression, I think you'll see how this exploration began to anchor many of the organizational design elements that I've found most successful over the years.

So many of the decisions we make, priorities we set and strategies we employ are responding to the rhythms of the world around us. Some of these cycles are natural. The length of a year is determined by the earth's eccentric orbit around the sun and seasonality is enhanced by the slight wobble in the planet's axis. Tides move with the moon's orbit around the earth. Some cycle times are biological such as the nine-month gestation for a fetus.

But many are imposed by our social institutions. The Gregorian calendar that we follow today was introduced in 1582 by Pope Gregory XIII as a revision to the Julian calendar. It was adopted in Great Britain and the American colonies in 1752. Months coincided roughly with the lunar calendar and the seven-day week set a pace for work comprised of six days of labor followed by one day of religious observation, the precursor to the pattern our lives follow today, although we've made a little alteration, substituting one day of penance for two days of leisure activities.

Other cycles have historical roots and are not necessarily in synch with contemporary life, such as the primary and secondary school year that was devised in an agrarian era to allow children to help their families in the fields during the peak growing and harvesting seasons. This thoroughly institutionalized cycle has proven incredibly resistant to change despite the shift to an era where, in most families, both parents work and have great difficulty caring for their children during the extended summer break.

Universities continue to rigidly adhere to semester or quarterly segments even though modules of learning may be more appropriately taught in different units of time—a week, a month or a year or two. Military contracts are generally awarded for a one-year period following the passage of a congressional appropriation even though different cycles might be more appropriate to the procurement at hand.

In business, we observe and respond to a number of cycles. Sales cycles can range from impulse buys like the National Enquirer and Altoids in the grocery store checkout line to the sale of a major computer or software system to an insurance company or financial institution that may take years to close. And multiple cycle times are built into many business processes. The prescription of a pharmaceutical is fundamentally a doctor's specification with sales following the incidence of the ailment for which it is prescribed and only somewhat affected by direct marketing to physicians or patients. But many other cycles are buried in the process of bringing a new drug to market including research, several stages of clinical trials and FDA approval, often totaling up to 15 years. In construction, the cycle time to obtain a building permit can require many years following a circuitous path through regulatory and discretionary reviews and appeals.

Yet we are driven by performance metrics that measure weekly sales reports, monthly financial statements and quarterly earnings and projections. For publicly traded companies, harsh punishment to the stock price is meted out to those who miss their quarterly estimates. I've watched the effects of these very short-cycle drivers on business for many years, fascinated by the aberrant behavior that has taken place simply to make quarterly numbers look good. In fact, the recent spate of doctored reporting in public companies like Enron and others has landed more than a few executives in jail. The most painful aspect of the focus on short-cycle reporting, however, has been the short-sighted business decisions that organizations have made losing enormous value as a result.

Government is no exception to the aberrant behavior patterns of business. Incumbents make decisions in election years to endear themselves to the electorate. During a politician's tenure, policies with long-ranging impacts are implemented because of ideological beliefs, in response to polls or simply due to pressures from lobbying groups. For instance, during the Clinton administration, in a focused effort to reduce deficit spending and balance the budget, wholesale cuts were made to research and development programs and infrastructure, causing a setback to our competitiveness in the world market place. And, of course, the wholesale change to much of the bureaucratic leadership as each new administration assumes power dismantles the functioning networks that allow the work of government to get done.

When we moved from a hunter/gatherer to an agrarian society, our culture shifted its cycle time focus. When your strategy is hunt, kill and eat, you're opportunistic. You move with the herd or toward more easily accessed naturally occurring food and shelter. Short-cycle thinking pushes us to organizational behavior that follows this pattern. As our societies adopted farming techniques and domesticated animals and plants for food and clothing, our cycles began to follow a pattern of sow, nurture and harvest. Long-cycle strategies began.

As our civilization has moved from agrarianism through industrialization to knowledge work, successful organizations have adjusted the cycle times for many aspects of their businesses to respond to changing characteristics of work and human behavior. Industrial enterprises thrived with command and control structures, breaking tasks into small units of work to maximize the efficiency of human labor which was treated as a commodity to be shaped and organized to the benefit of the company. Now, knowledge work enterprises expect people to think and respond independently based on a range of carefully nurtured skills and talents changing the nature and value of a worker in an organization. Rather than a person representing an interchangeable labor commodity, an individual's value continues to grow as their embedded knowledge and wisdom increases.

A grossly overlooked aspect of this value is the network of relationships an individual builds as part of an organization. Knowledge work has migrated rapidly from individual effort to group- or team-based work, and teams often extend well beyond the bounds of the enterprise to incorporate the knowledge and actions of subcontractors and vendors, government officials and consultants to accomplish the task at hand. Mergers and acquisitions have been the perennial enemy of networks, often leading to wholesale disruption of key elements of a network as companies downsize and streamline to achieve efficiencies. Social networks and norms in an organization determine the performance of a group and when they are lost, can destroy the most important intrinsic value to the combined enterprise that is also the most difficult and time consuming to replace.

Some newly evolving aspects of contemporary society, a society that places ever higher value on creative work, suggest that we must redesign our institutions and decision-making processes, looking at issues that simply don't respond in neat quarterly blocks of time or to organizational structure design as moving people around like chess pieces. The natural human tendencies to seek opportunities for socialization in an organization and to be doing meaningful and purposeful work have been amplified. Individual goals have shifted from a job to a career that fulfills deeper needs, achieves both physical and symbolic satisfaction in life, a place in the community and a sense of purpose.

The case for a participatory culture was made long ago when Elton Mayo, in a now-famous experiment at Western Electric in the 1930s, observed an increase in productivity when workers were asked for input on how to do their jobs, now known as the Hawthorne Effect. Today more than ever, knowledge workers expect to have a participatory role in their enterprise. When denied, performance suffers; when involvement becomes an embedded characteristic of an organization's culture and processes, productivity flourishes.

Liars, Lovers and Heroes by Steven Quartz and Terrence

Sejnowski describes how much of an individual's intelligence is a result of his or her socialization, placing some strong evidence found in new brain science squarely in the "nurture" camp in the perennial nature vs. nurture argument about how our personalities and intelligence are formed. In a conversation with Terry, I confirmed my conviction that not only organizational value but also actual intellectual development takes place in a well socialized enterprise. To the degree that your company builds and supports durable and well-socialized teams and network-based units, you're building very real value for the individual and for the organization, actually increasing the individual's and the organization's intelligence.

These are all processes that demand a long-cycle look at business decisions and practices. Yet, we're living in a world where more and more actions are driven by short-cycle reporting and the reactions of those to whom the reports are made. Since so much of my career and experience was spent in search of a balance between short- and long-cycle business drivers, I decided to document those that I found created the highest long-term value.

This book is intended for all enterprises, public or private, that are interested in enhancing the performance and value of their organizations and the people in them. In the chapters that follow, I propose a series of strategies that transcend periodic reporting cycles, looking to the long-cycle nature of business today to create real value for all stakeholders. These strategies share a common denominator, a tight and difficult to achieve focus: creating value through nurturing individuals and their networks in your organization.

Much emphasis is placed today on creating and growing shareholder value; but so often, that "value" is defined as the price of the stock in each succeeding quarter with little note taken of the long-cycle effects of short-cycle actions. Since the stakeholders of any enterprise include not just those with an equity ownership interest, but also the employees, customers and community, in fact, everyone associated with the enterprise in any way, long-term value and high-level performance cannot be measured by quarterly returns. They are built over time, incorporating decisions and actions appropriate to each aspect of business design. That can only be done when the interests of all stakeholders are balanced, aligned and attended to regularly. This will ultimately yield the highest return for equity shareholders as well.

While I recognize and occasionally refer to capital and research and development investments, I focus far greater attention on investments in people and networks. The value is higher and, when these programs are deeply embedded, well-considered research, development, plant and equipment decisions follow as a natural course. But not always. These types of investments must be separated from quarterly reporting and performance pressures as well. How many times has a major research program or capital expenditure been shut down as a response to concerns that analysts will punish the stock price if word of a program appears in the quarterly report?

While senior leaders in any organization have a greater opportunity to apply these strategies, enterprises responding to the trends in work design noted above will, by nature, have a degree of participation that draws ideas from throughout the organization, giving additional voices a hand in shaping the enterprise. So, I encourage those of you who are not part of the leadership team of your company and who recognize characteristics that you'd like to see incorporated into your business to phrase the strategies I set forth in words that fit the unique characteristics of your enterprise and begin to build a constituency for them. That's what I did in my career. Was it rebellious or even treasonous? When I was young, it often seemed so, but I was blessed to be associated with a group of people who always had the patience to listen. If that's not a characteristic of your organization you probably belong somewhere else anyway.

I must insert a disclaimer here. I'm not an academic. My ideas and observations are not the result of the type of research that might accompany the work of a university professor. I'm an architect who learned by experimentation. The basis for what I've written comes from a sample of one, but a rather remarkable one—my tenure with an architecture and design firm which grew from a handful of people in the mid-60s to the largest design firm in the world by the 90s. It could no longer be considered in the context of conventional architectural practice. We became a big business, billing in excess of $300 million per year at the peak of my tenure. We found that the business decisions we were making about the deployment of people, capital, facilities and equipment demanded parallel considerations to other types of business including manufacturing, sales and service-based companies.

Along with what might still seem like a rather provincial view, however, is the incredible depth of observations I've been able to make throughout my career in my close working relationships with hundreds of corporations and institutions, large and small. The architect/client relationship is a highly personal one and the senior executives of these many companies, from tiny start-ups to Fortune 500 enterprises were gracious enough to speak freely and openly about their thoughts and strategies for the management of their companies as well as the difficulties they encountered, providing me with a wealth of comparative thinking about the issues they faced and the strategies they employed to address them.

For 34 years, I was part of a wonderful organization, Gensler Architecture Design & Planning Worldwide. I began my career in 1968 shortly after completing a Master's Program in Architecture at the University of Pennsylvania. I returned to my home to find the San Francisco Bay Area deep in a recession and, despite numerous interviews could not find a job in an architectural firm. Penn was a "hot" degree, and I had expected to have numerous job offers from large prestigious firms. None were forthcoming. What did I end up doing? For a year and a half, I worked for a housing developer designing tract houses and customizing kitchens for the housewives who would inhabit them. My classmates were appalled.

I refused to be an employee of the developer, though, working instead as a consultant. I wanted to maintain the flexibility to join an architectural firm if an opportunity presented itself. Without an apprenticeship under a registered architect, I could not obtain that all-important license to practice architecture. In retrospect, the experience I had was better than any apprenticeship with a conventional architectural practice could have been. My work included land planning, designing homes, presenting to planning commissions and architectural review boards, negotiating subcontracts and working through funding requests with lenders. I learned more about how things really got done in the development and construction industries than I ever could have in school or on a conventional career track in the profession.

In a bar in Tiburon (a small town in Marin County on the San Francisco Bay) following a successful presentation to the city council of a house I'd designed, I ran into a big guy who had liked what I had presented and asked what I did. I explained my circumstances, and he handed me his card suggesting I call him for an interview. He was an architect with a small firm he'd founded in San Francisco and was hiring. His name was Art Gensler. In August 1969, I became employee number 22.

During my tenure, the firm grew beyond any of our wildest dreams, reaching nearly 2,400 people in 25 offices around the world. Unusual for any business today, we accomplished this organically, without merger or acquisition. I served on the firm's board helping to shape policy and direction, became its president in 1995 and its CEO in 2000.

Leading a design firm has been likened to herding cats or butterflies, an analogy I find frighteningly close to the truth. Design firms are filled with creative people who must balance art with craft, pursuing an inner higher calling while exposing themselves to enormous liability. I never thought the day would come when an architectural practice might serve as a model for business, just as I never thought a landlord would look at an architectural firm as a "credit tenant." But that's just what happened when we leased 50,000 square feet of space in San Francisco at the depth of the recession in 2001 and found that many of our clients were encountering the same problems managing creative people that we had.

Now I'm more convinced than ever that, as we move into the 21st century, the forefront of the new wave of business and social endeavors will be creative enterprises that will design their businesses in response to the same challenges that a design practice confronts. In the chapters that follow, I describe strategies we developed and put into practice, extending their application to other types of organizations. They're based on many years of evolutionary thought within Gensler as well as my long and deep associations with many clients. I owe a tremendous debt of gratitude to the talented professionals in the firm and the many colleagues outside Gensler whose patience with my endless redefinition and refinement of these ideas resulted in the firm we built and, ultimately, in the experiences I share with you in this book.

The challenge to any great body of thought is to move an organization into alignment, testing theories, making them broadly applicable and then actionable, finally getting those butterflies to fly in formation. During my tenure as president of Gensler, I used our monthly newsletter, InsideGensler, to communicate our strategies in a way that gave substance to these ideas. Much of this book is based on those editorial essays and the points of view that we translated into action. Cumulatively, they became the culture of the firm. While this is, to a great degree, a book based on one company's journey, the lessons are broadly applicable. I ask for your patience in adapting these ideas to the particular circumstances of your organization and hope that, in so doing, you'll find them helpful.

Ultimately, though, accomplishing cultural alignment in an organization goes far beyond taking an idea, shaping it into the perfect solution for your organization and writing an essay about it. It happens when you and the people in your organization live the models, day in and day out, "walking the talk." I had many responsibilities in my role as president and CEO, but none was as important as working on this alignment. Achieving it was never seen as an "end," it was simply hygiene, like flossing your teeth. It required daily energy and focus in everything I and the principles in the firm did to maintain organizational health. Backing away from that commitment, even for short periods, caused almost immediate erosion.

Don't read this book looking for a quick fix, a few platitudes to throw around in your organization as "ideas du jour." The value that accrues to long-term enterprises is about doing it, not just talking about it. I spent my career trying to make ideas actionable. Dedication brought enormous rewards in business growth, profitability, client satisfaction and shareholder value. But most importantly, it brought a fine sense of accomplishment and pride for the people who made it happen. That value and satisfaction can't be driven by weekly, monthly or quarterly reporting. It's born of patience, focus and commitment to the long-cycles of your business.

PART
I

DESIGNING A
BUSINESS STRATEGY

Understanding the Market Drivers for your Enterprise and the People in it

I began my career in design with at least some perspective on how a business is structured. I'd experienced every imaginable aspect of my father's bakery business and saw it not as an artisan's work but as a fully evolved corporation dealing with finance, bank borrowings, legal and contractual challenges, personnel problems, union negotiations, sales, marketing and manufacturing. But it was a family enterprise where decisions could be made with an eye to future ramifications that were often years ahead, rather than responding to the quarterly demands of outside shareholders.

As I got further into my professional life, dealing frequently with publicly held companies, I began to see the impacts of the marketplace and how brutally a company's stock value could be punished based on quarterly performance. As the years went by, the influence of stock analysts on corporate decision making set me to thinking about this conundrum of acting to drive quarterly results when those actions were frequently antithetical to long-term performance. I began to ask what might be done to transcend this pressure.

But first, I had to ask, "Are businesses supposed to be long-cycle structured? What are the market forces driving businesses today, and should they be evolving toward long-cycle thinking?" In design, the business I know, product and customer relationship cycles are exceptionally long. But I found the broader world of business evolving toward long cycles as well. The products of more and more companies take longer to bring to market. A new bio-pharmaceutical is in design and testing for 15 years at a cost often exceeding $1 billion before the first dose is sold. While automobile product cycles have certainly been reduced in the last 20 years, it still takes roughly three years to bring a new model from concept to the dealer's showroom, and as rapidly as consumer tastes change, this is a risky proposition.

Businesses have a longer and deeper relationship with their customers. This is not just true of service enterprises but of product manufacturers as well. The investment in fiber optic cable or cell phone broadcast towers means a need for long-term customer relationships to recover capital costs. Calloway wants you to buy not just that one Big Bertha, but to acquire a whole set of clubs, changing your entire golf game over time. In fact, the Holy Grail of all service and product businesses today is brand loyalty, the customer for life, the long-cycle relationship.

In example after example, I found this true of every sort of enterprise, not just in private sector businesses. Your church wants to see you engaged much more deeply than just the Sunday service. They'd like you in a bible study class, a men's or women's group, a senior's group, and wouldn't your children like to be schooled there? The army no longer relies on conscripts. It deals with the same recruitment and retention issues as private enterprise to build a professional force of career soldiers.

So I concluded that these and many other market forces were leading inexorably to a world driven by long-cycle forces, demanding thoughtful strategies, decisions and programs that were quite different from our command and control, short-cycle history. But the quarterly scrutiny by third-party investors of financial results is not about to end any time soon. To be successful in the markets of tomorrow and to build true value for not just shareholders but all stakeholders, we must be able to transcend these pressures, making decisions and building programs with time frames that extend long into the future while still responding to short-cycle financial metrics. We must be able to build the case for value creation beyond next quarter's results.

From workers to professionals

Now let's take a look at an important trend that's having a significant impact on business today. Our world of work is well along the migratory path from "doing" to "thinking." We're moving from a world of trained units of labor to a world of professionals. In this world, the people you're recruiting and the jobs you'll have available are not going to be repetitive and process oriented. Such tasks are being rapidly automated. Job descriptions of all types today require thinking and an ability to take independent action. The job is different every day and relies on workers to exercise judgment based on knowledge gained over time.

This is true in every business, from the financial industries to telecommunication, from entertainment and hospitality to construction, from government agencies and the army to insurance agencies and automobile manufacturers. The concept of a "professional"—someone educated in a body of knowledge who is expected to stay current with research and new discovery in their field and who acts independently and in the broader interest of the success of the enterprise based on that knowledge, experience and judgment is no longer limited to doctors, lawyers, accountants and architects. We've left the world of "command and control."

And the people in your business are acting on the challenges of thinking and responding independently, not just following rules or protocols or procedures. They have begun to think of themselves as professionals. They recognize that they've acquired a unique body of knowledge, they take great pride in adding to that knowledge as part of their professional careers, and they realize that they are taking risk in the exercise of independent judgment—risk to themselves with respect to their careers and risk to the organizations of which they're a part.

They've also found that, as professionals with the significantly longer education and training they've acquired in their field, they have a different value, one sought by employers. While their professional knowledge and skills certainly have value, their actual work is much more complex, relying heavily on a network of relationships to accomplish what they do. This conundrum, the developed professionalism that makes them desirable commodities, has limited value without connections to a broader network of relationships, creating a challenge to the individual as well as the long-cycle enterprise. In the marketplace, your most highly developed professionals are in great demand, but their value to you and to themselves in the deployment of their professional skills is linked to the relationships they've developed. This is as true for an architect as it is for a car salesperson; for a nurse as for a lawyer.

The design business model

This book is meant for all businesses, but I use the architecture and design firm model because it's what I know best, and I leave it to you to interpolate for the market factors and customer relationship processes that drive your business. As you follow this description of the forces driving a design firm, substitute your own specific circumstances. While no two enterprises are identical, all share a common trait—they're driven by and must respond to the customer and regulatory and business practices that are part of the environment in the markets they serve.

In many ways my father was right—architecture and interior design are funny businesses. While these two disciplines are often discussed as separate professions, they have so many similarities that I'll just describe them as "design." Let's take the process apart. A designer is engaged by a client to interpret his or her needs; describe a solution to satisfy those needs; document that solution in a way that others can build it; guide the process of contracting with those that do the building and supply the materials, systems and products used; oversee the construction, fabrication and installation;

and orchestrate the occupancy and use of the resulting place while adhering to a schedule and budget. The expected result must keep water and weather out, protect its occupants from injury, deliver comfortable and healthy air, provide light to see after dark and at the same time create an emotional impact supportive of the intended use of the place being created.

The relationship between client and designer begins when a need is identified, a new building is required to house an enterprise, or a lease has expired and moving to new quarters will achieve better organizational efficiencies. It happens when people move into a community, which creates a demand for new housing, commercial structures and schools. Land must be purchased or a lease must be negotiated. Entitlements, the thoroughly regulated right to build what is desired, must be sought before real design can begin. Documents are prepared and put out to bid, a contract is awarded, construction ensues, and finally one day, the client moves in.

The total elapsed time to establish a client relationship, design a building and get it approved and built is counted in years. My wife consulted for many years in the high technology field, counseling dot.com startups whose entire life cycles from start-up to IPO or acquisition were counted in months and were often complete before land had been acquired or lease negotiations had been concluded for a client with whom I was working.

In a design practice, the highest value to a client is often embedded in a piece of knowledge gained or a relationship formed by an individual many years before that can be applied to a client's benefit at exactly the right moment in time. This is not possible without continuity of individual relationships between the client or customer and the individual with the knowledge or relationship. Turnover is the enemy of an organization's ability to deliver this value. Our organizational stability was often far greater than our clients' organizations (usually due to mergers or acquisitions), so we found ourselves often in a position to deliver a type of value that a competitor simply couldn't do.

My career allowed me to explore how to build an organization to thrive in this environment, develop and test strategies, watch what worked and what did not. I hope that you will be able to recast my experiences in the language, business drivers and issues particular to your company and that the continuity of thought about the value of people and networks will serve as a model for you as you build your enterprise.

Describe the World
for Which You're Designing
Your Business

N ow that I've discussed some reasons why business in general is migrating toward longer cycle times, let's think about the world in which we're doing that business. Using an analogy I referred to earlier, the short-cycle organization is like a hunter/gatherer society, feeding on what's available now and moving on when the herd moves. The long-cycle enterprise evaluates longer trends in the world and the marketplace, shaping the design of its business to fit the current scenario, then positioning and building for what's to come.

Looking back to look forward

One of the toughest exercises I ever did (and I tried to do it frequently) was to challenge the way we did things. Institutional inertia would grab me by the ankles and say, "Of course this is the right way to do things. We've always done them that way, and look how successful we are. Besides, everyone's going to think you're crazy if you challenge 'X'—insert whatever topic you like; each seemed so tried and true!"

Starting with a very long view of societal trends, I tried to look back to what things were like when our company started, putting the history of our organization and its evolution over time into a market context. Why was our business set in motion the way it was? Were we responding to an unmet need in the marketplace? Were we entering a competitive environment in which we felt we could deliver a better solution? If we were to start over again, what might we do differently? Try these questions for your own organization.

Follow the societal trend timeline forward and take stock of where you are at the present. Is your business well suited to the social, political, cultural and economic context in which you're operating? Take the opportunity to think clearly about how someone looking at your business might design a new enterprise to compete with you. Remember, someone is doing just that. Are there opportunities for you to shift gears today to respond better to the market you're in today?

Now look forward. Stretch out into the future with a long view of societal trends. Any number of futurists and management consultants write constantly about the future. Among the early influences on my thinking about these long term trends was Peter Drucker in his book *New Realities*. While he was (and his work still is) prescient about the future, that book is now dated. Nevertheless, many of the longer-term societal trends he wrote about helped me reorient our business at the time, and many of the trends he described are playing out even today just as he predicted.

Every day some new prognosticator is publishing a digest of the influences changing our society and the preferences, desires and appetites of our customers. Your job is to assimilate a vast amount of information, much of which will be wrong, and synthesize some likely scenarios into which your organization is going to evolve.

This is an interesting, stimulating and frustrating exercise, and the inertia of institutional resistance can leave you right where you are. But ignoring it leaves you in an opportunistic mode, susceptible to a competitor who has read the tea leaves better than you to design an offering and a process for delivering it that will leave you in the dust. A long-cycle enterprise creates value by being anticipatory, setting initiatives in motion across every facet of the organization that readies it for the changes that are coming. Here's a snapshot of this type of thinking circa 1997. Some things have followed the trends noted, some are slightly different, but these were the issues that were shaping business drivers at the time, from research and training to help staff respond to client needs to personnel policies and programs, to the cities in which business was to be found:

Comparing the firm today to my first day on the job 28 years ago is a great way to think about the period of astounding change in the architecture and design professions. I wandered into the Hearst Building on the corner of Third and Market Streets in San Francisco, in the neighborhood where the convention center, numerous museums and the Yerba Buena Gardens stand today, to join a merry band of 22 assorted architects and interior designers doing something I'd never heard of: tenant planning services. Of course, we were doing a few other things, too. But the practice represented the typical multiple-project type, small architectural practice of the time save this extraordinary interest in something which had previously been done by real estate brokers on the back of envelopes and by furniture dealers and decorators.

We set out to define and professionalize a service that hadn't existed before; to focus on design in service to our clients' business mission and to extend the layout of furniture into three dimensions; to be architects of the interiors (not just furniture space planners), addressing structural, mechanical, electrical, lighting and acoustic issues with the same skill and care expected of the architect of the building shell. We added to that the dimension of time, designing for the life cycle of a place, searching for the answers to adaptability as businesses change.

Today, we're providing a broad variety of services that continually evolve in response to our clients' needs to create and manage physical (and today, virtual) space that will enhance their business performance.

That's "what we do." How we do it may be more interesting. Lately, we've started playing around with a technique
used for many years by Royal Dutch Shell to brainstorm organizational responses to the world they serve called "Scenario
Planning," best summarized in a book by Peter Schwartz called
The Art of the Long View. It's a process of developing multiple
scenarios about all the things that are going on in the world
around us: environmental, political, social, demographic, religious and economic; and then designing a business, or in our
case, service strategies that respond to each scenario. This is new
stuff for us; we're not quite the size of Shell. But we seem to be
culturally well suited to this approach. Other than those who
become sidetracked by the Howard Roark egocentric school
of design, I think we, as architects and designers, are a pretty
empathic lot.

So, if we're doing scenario planning today to help shape
the types of services that will be most appropriate for the folks
who purchase design services, what sort of models should we
be using? Most of us have spent a generation believing that the
population around the world was exploding at an unsustainable
rate; that we would very rapidly, perhaps within our lifetimes,
reach a level that exceeded the earth's capacity to provide food,
water and natural resources; that air quality and lifestyle would
continue in a deteriorating spiral. We've lived with constant fear
of recurrent inflation or a repeat of the great depression. These
are also factors most of our client organizations have been using
as building blocks for their planning.

Some alternative models are worth analysis. Consider
Roger Bootle's book, *The Death of Inflation: Surviving and
Thriving in the Zero Era*. Roger is a renowned economist
who has served on the British Treasury's Panel of Independent
Economic Advisors and makes a compelling case that both 1929
and the inflation anomalies of the 70's and 80's are not likely
to recur. He suggests we should think more seriously about our
responses to a world economy that will cycle through a nar-

row band of inflation and deflation averaging zero and points to the consequences of deflation as experienced recently in the Scandinavian countries and Japan. It's a different scenario than our economists are using as they micromanage interests rates, or than the markets hold as evidenced by the daily skittish response to minute bits of daily news that might indicate a trend toward increased or decreased inflation.

Think about Ben Wattenberg's book, *Values Matter Most.* Wattenberg is a demographer who provides compelling evidence that the global fertility rates are trending rapidly downward. His prediction is that the global population will top out at 8.5 billion (it was 5.8 billion in 1996). His position is that we're actually at greater risk from population decrease. Consider for example that the replacement level in our population is 2.1 children per woman of child-bearing age. The U. S. fertility rate dropped from 2.08 children per woman to 1.9 between 1990 and 1996, and the trend appears to be continuing downward. Great Britain is at 1.78, Japan is at 1.48, Germany is 1.3, and Italy is 1.2. There is a real crisis of population depletion in Italy. Even the countries that have traditionally had high fertility rates are trending rapidly downward. China is now at 1.8, and the average of the less-developed countries is 3.3 and falling.

This is at substantial odds with the paradigm we've all been living with and offers some new challenges. With life expectancy extending and fewer new folks in the workforce, the workers per beneficiary (those dependent on the current work force for support) has gone from 8.6 in 1955 to 3.3 in 1995 and is projected to be 2.0 by 2035. This is fairly predictable stuff based on people alive on the planet today. In other words, our social institutions are going to go through some dramatic changes in the next several decades, and this will alter the demand for the places we create.

Finally, let's consider pollution and natural resources. Until recently, I've carried a mental model based on the precept that we're trashing our planet and exhausting our resources. But consider Julian Simon and his book, *The State of Humanity*. Simon is known as the "Doom-Slayer," and in a February 1997 issue of *Wired* magazine statistically debunks Paul Ehrlich and every other nattering nabob of negativism (I will be forever grateful to Spiro Agnew for this delightful descriptor) on issues as far ranging as world cereal yields, industrial lead pollution, species extinction and air pollution. As he points out, the most severe food-related problem in America is not hunger; it's obesity. Think about what that means for the design professions.

Throughout my career, I've been interested in everything from long-range planning of cities to furniture design, and just about everything in between. I consider anything that affects the way we use buildings—the places between them and the spaces in them—as part of design. As a result, I have been involved in the development of a practice that blends all the disciplines involved in making places, fostering an environment of inter-personal respect for each professional involved in the process, from graphics and furnishings, to engineering and technology. As designers, the quality of our work is as related to our breadth of knowledge as it is to our empathy for, and engagement of, each expert's contribution to the complex process of making the places where we work.

Interior designers must be psychologists as well as tech-nologists, understanding people's needs and desires, as well as the sociological processes of human interaction. Along with efficiency in office design, particularly with the increased impor-tance of technology, we must continually build our expertise in understanding the effects of the spaces we design on personal interaction and creativity. We must put ourselves in our cli-ents' shoes as we design, trying to live as they do, worry about the things that frighten them and anticipate the physiological responses that are fostered by the places we create.

Since I began designing offices in 1969, work methods have gone through a rapid evolution that rivals the shift from an agrarian to an industrial society that took place in the 19th century. The changing ways and places in which work is done have had a profound effect on our living patterns, as well as the office space we design. The changes are most often attributed to technology. But technology is only the enabler. It facilitated the rapid reduction of labor content in manufacturing and agriculture, dramatically increasing productivity. Compared to 100 years ago, it now takes a fraction of our work effort as a society to create the food, clothing, shelter and products we consume as a society. The length of the current strong economic cycle with its high employment and low inflation is fundamentally attributable to increases in technology driven productivity; and this includes the service sector that comprises such a large proportion of our business.

As productivity in the United States accelerated after World War II, a whole new array of business services developed. Some were part of the growing manufacturing industry; others, such as banking and insurance, law and government, entertainment and leisure activities, generated a whole new set of job descriptions loosely described as service and knowledge work. These new jobs have proliferated since the 1960s, creating a demand for space. It's the continual change in the design requirements for this work that has fascinated me as we've developed innovative and forward-looking solutions for our clients.

So much of what we did in the 1960s and 1970s preceded the influence of technology on work process design. Our clients were focused on achieving efficiency based on an industrial model of work flow. Lessons learned from industrial engineers on the factory floor were applied to office work design, a model that led to the linear flow of paper-based information and narrow, repetitive job descriptions. The goal was to design a work floor that was flexible, allowing people and desks to be moved around like machines in a factory as new service "product lines" were introduced. Our earliest efforts in anticipating the impact of technology in our designs of office space were for the insurance and banking businesses, where we introduced concepts of universal planning to accommodate change through technology and accommodate the movement of people with minimal reconfiguration of space. It wasn't until the 1990s that we saw a dramatic acceleration in the automation of repetitive work and a true break from the industrial work process analog. The manufacturing sector was actually automating repetitive tasks well before the service sector, with the rapid introduction of robotics and experiments with team manufacturing such as with Volvo in Sweden in the 1980s.

Today, we're designing in an era of continual change driven by advances in technology. As much as anything, the proliferation of mergers and acquisitions has been to achieve an economy of scale necessary to make the enormous investments in technology required for sophisticated work process automation. New equipment in both the manufacturing and service sectors is flexible, allowing rapid redeployment of capital investments as product mixes change. In fact, the progress toward the ability to deliver mass-produced custom products, individually tailored to your personal needs but with the cost advantages of mass production, has become the Holy Grail of both product and service enterprises. Several computer companies manufacture every computer to each customer's specification; many banks tailor each mortgage to a wide range of variables to suit each borrower's unique circumstances.

The work that people do is no longer bound to a single location by virtue of a linear, physical process. People today function as team members: they're mobile; they're away from the office visiting their customers; they're in meetings; they're in classrooms. The world of nine to five is rapidly disappearing. Like the large remote factory, the corporate headquarters and regional offices located in wooded suburbs no longer connect people to the work they do. Just as factories now demand "just-in-time" delivery of material and components requiring proximity to suppliers and access to an inventory of space in the area to add, subtract or change, so offices benefit from proximity to a business district offering space flexibility, services and infrastructure.

In fact, our design work must be adaptable, it must respond to clients whose mission and business structure are rarely foreseeable beyond 18 months. Nearly every organization we work with today is time driven: "How fast can I have it? Can I expand it quickly if my business grows? Can I get rid of it if my business changes? Can I alter it to satisfy a new work process?" Add to this an increasing shortage of talented and qualified knowledge workers, and some new variables enter the equation for determining both location selection and design. Locations convenient to good housing and services along with a secure environment and neighborhood are strong factors in recruitment and retention.

Since the recession of the late 1980s and early 1990s when "design" meant spending money for things to be "added on" communicating waste to customers and shareholders, we're seeing a resurgence in the perceived value and benefits of excellent design; not just good, efficient planning, but environments that are a source of pride and inspiration to the people who work in them.

These are places where the use of high-quality materials is integral to design for adaptability and an appropriate life cycle, not as a symbol of prestige or importance. The design image of the workplace communicates a distinct meaning to customers and clients, to employees and to the public at large. Good design and bad design have little to do with how much money is spent but have a lot to do with how well it is spent. The look and feel, the amenities and the technological infrastructure all impact the performance of an organization.

All of these factors bode well for the design profession but demand talents and focus that are quite a stretch from what most of us learned in school. We're certainly not designing only for the accolades of our peers despite the fact that all of us still get an enormous charge when someone whose design work we admire thinks our stuff is great. Today we're playing for the applause of the people who work in the organizations that hire us. If they're pleased, they work more effectively; if their performance improves, the people who hired us look good, and they tell their friends or hire us to do some more. That is the design firm food chain today, and the skill sets are psychology, sociology and anthropology along with a healthy dose of corporate politics.

But the time dimension is the most important and is where the opportunities lie for servicing our clients more broadly and effectively. In listening to our clients, we've learned that strategic facilities planning is a marvelously valuable service in helping a client make decisions regarding the "where, what and when" of the physical places that house their businesses. We're trying to change the paradigm of expectations in our firm from doing things right to doing the right things. Why? Because our clients' business models are in a constant state of evolution. Nothing exactly fits into a template we've accomplished before. But strategic planning only has value if our designers are "thinking strategically" as they design. In other words, they continue to focus on the "why" of the program, not just the "what."

And then there's the concern for managing the facility after it is occupied. Today's dynamics present tremendous business opportunities in creating and managing the databases that can be a natural byproduct of the work we do for tracking systems, equipment and area allocation. But the greatest potential value to the client comes from the designer who is attuned to the rigors of work process change and finds greater satisfaction from how gracefully the space responds to these demands than how terrific the photos look in the magazine. So, the future belongs to the designer who makes choices based on the life cycle of the facility based on learning that takes place through the use of these databases over time in the managing of facilities.

Finally, the time driver offers the most potential for the profession through recapturing some of our traditional turf from project management consultants who have appeared around the country telling horror stories about irresponsible designers (since many project managers came from the design profession, this approach is a bit suspect). We are on a two-fold mission: first to reestablish ourselves as responsible professionals who honor budgets and schedules. This is an imperative for the entire profession, or we will continually be cast into a commoditized role in our client relationships. The second is where the real business opportunity lies: taking responsible leadership in guiding the work of the complex array of enterprises from engineering and technology consultants to vendors and contractors to government agencies that are responsible for taking an idea to reality. The business and design opportunity belongs to the designer who accepts project performance accountability through project leadership. Leadership is not, however, worth much unless it is infused with a sense of purpose aligned with the client's business mission and a deep and abiding knowledge about good design and the role it plays in enhancing that business performance. That is why the independent project manager will never deliver as much value to the client as the project leader who is fully connected to the entire design process from strategic planning to facility management.

My call is for more education and more breadth of understanding about how the pieces that make up the life cycle of the places we create fit together. I'm a designer, but I'm convinced that good design is not even possible today until we're working in this broader definition of our profession.

Ed Friedrichs' keynote address at the IIDA [International Interior Design Association] International Design Conference in Jackson Hole, Wyoming, May 21, 1997.

My intent in presenting you with this material is not to suggest a path for the future but to demonstrate how important it is to monitor trends and evaluate your fit to the broader issues of society on an ongoing basis. Some of the scenarios described above are still valid; others have changed. I'm less comfortable today that we're making changes quickly enough to respond to environmental and population demographic trends. Jared Diamond's *Collapse* and Thom Hartmann's *The Last Hours of Ancient Sunlight* have caused me to commit even more deeply to the need for business to take leadership in sustainability.

Such an exercise isn't something you do once and put on a shelf, it needs to become habitual, a way of thinking about your business. You also shouldn't do it too frequently. Frankly, you'll scare yourself with every new sensationalist headline about how our world is changing. This effort is about building awareness, assimilating information all the time and then stopping once in a while to take stock and make appropriate adjustments. It helps you to develop sensitivity to your customers' priorities and to shape the presentation of your product or service in a relevant way.

As time has gone by, other things have shifted for me. Importantly, I learned not to hand down directives but rather to develop initiatives in a participatory fashion, engaging others in the effort. In a long-cycle enterprise, deep involvement in the direction the organization is taking infuses everyone with an awareness of why you're doing what you do, making each person's work more meaningful to them.

Here are some contemporary issues that I'm using today to guide my work and the work of firms I consult with to align with the market. After you read the following, construct your own list of influences that are shaping your specific market and ask yourself the following questions: How else might I design my business? How else might the people in my organization respond more appropriately to my customers in real time?

These are my "Top 10" and reflect the application side of the trends cited above:

1. **Time:** Change is so pervasive and rapid that no one is able to predict very far into the future, causing clients and customers to wait

until the last minute before committing to anything and then wanting it delivered as quickly as possible. Those that can foreshorten their cycle times will survive; those that change the process and redefine the product will dominate.

2. **Learning:** Continual change means continuous learning. Educational institutions, their mission and process will be completely redefined to meet today's world. Memorizing facts will be displaced by learning how to research. With the advent of search engines and the Internet, we have become nearly omniscient, limited only by our ability to know the questions to ask and the skill to search the Internet intelligently. Just-in-time learning modules will displace core curriculum. The value of emotional intelligence will displace the narrow focus on alpha-numeric and linguistic skill building. Distance learning will augment group learning. Collaborative and leadership skills will displace individual accomplishment.

3. **Technology:** Continual discovery, refinement and miniaturization will redefine communication, computation, knowledge access, health care delivery, power generation and utilization, business and financial transactions causing a redefinition of work process and location requirements. So, every industry will completely change the formulas that formed the traditional ground rules by which they made decisions. Technology will replace many types of knowledge work, not just repetitive work, through the implementation of expert systems.

4. **Demographics:** The aging population, which is a result of the migration of the baby boom generation into old age as well as the slowing of the birth-rate globally, coupled with increased longevity, will rapidly increase the health care and social service burden on the workforce. At the same time, the nature of facilities needs from schools to assisted living facilities, from retail/entertainment centers to churches and social centers, and location decisions like the migration from the cold northeast to the warmer southeast and west, will continue to change at an accelerating pace.

5. **Trust:** With the decline in integrity globally, from Clinton to the spread of corruption, as companies go global and deal with cultures

that are less honest than the U.S. and Europe have traditionally been, individuals and enterprises that build a brand of integrity and trustworthiness over time will dominate. This is the optimistic view. The pessimist says we all devolve into corruption as in the film Blade Runner. I don't buy it and will remain hopeful that a direction of integrity will survive.

6. **Instant Global Communication:** The speed with which people across the planet can learn about an idea combined with the search for meaning and stability while standing on ever-shifting sands will mean that people will continue to rally around an "idea-du-jour." This will make it difficult to predict what might come out of left field, throwing entire industries, governments and institutions for a loop. Until the world reaches equilibrium with having a common global agenda (which I think is where this leads but it's a long way off), we will have this kind of shifting equilibrium that never seems to settle down. I think the cycles between causes of the moment will shorten as global instant communication becomes pervasive and then diminish as people get used to it.

7. **Globalization:** Interdependency of companies and economies transcending national boundaries will continue to shift the power emphasis away from governments and toward enterprises with common and shared interests. The question is whether this will lead to the "gentrification" and therefore incorporation of third-world countries into the global economy or whether the result will be further alienation. As long as companies pursue cheap labor in the world market, the prognosis is good because with jobs comes prosperity, social reform and, ultimately, a leveling of quality of life. When social degradation, corruption and starvation are prevalent, hope dims. There's good news and bad news here as global companies don't operate with great social consciences, at least less than prosperous governments have in the past. On the other hand, there is a growing globalization of volunteer social enterprises (NGOs) that also transcend individual governments and may be a piece of the vehicle for the advancement of poverty stricken nations.

8. **Consolidation:** Companies and therefore your customers and cli-

ents will consolidate and realign their organizations and the markets they serve to optimize their global competitiveness.

9. **Tribalization:** People will continue to move away from global homogenization, resisting sameness everywhere and searching for identity and affinity with like people and values.

10. **Balance of Life:** Quite independently of job loss due to corporate restructuring (the "push" side), more people are choosing to work independently in a quest for a more balanced and meaningful life (the "pull" side). The manifestation is more small enterprises, consultants and other independent business forms. Many women reach a point (glass ceiling, children, and frustration with large company politics) and go into business on their own or with small groups of other women. Men also experience the desire for better balance. What effects does this have on career choices, job location, job performance, job satisfaction? This is leading to a shift into work-at-home or within a village atmosphere (in order to maintain the socialization of work life), even in major urban areas.

This may seem a lot to digest, but the business decisions we make today in response to these and other trends will dramatically affect our future success. That's why we must think about and act on the changing trends in our global society.

Getting specific

Specific events or localized trends can require more immediate response. Regular updates on the progress of the world are important to your leadership team as they shape the strategies and tactics that drive your organization. It's critically important that the people in direct contact with your customers who are expected to make informed decisions in real time on a daily basis understand these market drivers. This is the difference between a trained employee and a professional.

But how do you and your leadership team assimilate this knowledge to develop a context for your business? How do you stay current? The patterns are similar for most leading organizations I've observed. The leadership not only reads broadly but participates in a variety of forums; some related to the business they're in, some covering a much broader context. But invariably, the leadership of long-cycle, high-value enterprises, those that have been able to consistently emerge ahead of the market and their competition, is exceptionally well informed about the world around them. This is not a job to be relegated to a management consultant in strategic planning or a paper you commission about the future. It is the job of the leadership of your organization.

Sharing this information broadly in the organization helps your people understand why you do what you do. People are always a bit suspect of management decisions. Successful enterprises build trust and confidence among their constituents through open and thorough communication about what's going on in the world and how it's affecting their livelihood. For those of you involved in real estate in any way (and most of you are whether you choose to admit it or not) here's a news report based on the mid-May 2003 Urban Land Institute meeting in Baltimore. While I'm always suspect of this sort of information in a contemporary book, I've been tracking these trends since then and as of this writing find them to be still worthy of consideration.

I enjoy the ULI tremendously. I have an opportunity to spend time with many real estate industry executives but, most important-ly, I gain great insight into the financial markets for real estate and the implications for my clients—therefore, I get a glimpse of how business is going to be shaping up over the next several months and years. It's one of those forums in which I participate to keep current on evolving trends.

I belong to the Office Development Council within the ULI. The ULI meetings in the spring and fall are structured with a full day of Council meetings followed by a day or two of workshop pre-sentations, all of which are highly educational. We had two terrific economists speak at our Council Spring 2003 meeting: Ray Torto of Torto Wheaton Research, affiliated with CB Richard Ellis, and Susan Hudson-Wilson of Property & Portfolio Research, Inc. Some of their views offer insights that will help you form a vision for the future of your enterprise—at least your real estate strategy. How do you gather and share this type of information in your organization? Since this information will not be of much use a couple of years from now (although I hope someone reading this book at that time will still find it helpful), I offer this as an example of the type of information your organization needs to put the things they do with their customers in their customers' context. As an architecture and interior design firm, our clients expected everyone in our organization to be thoroughly up-to-date on this range of knowledge and to be acting on their behalf accordingly.

Ray Torto suggested that the economy is in what he termed an extended jobless recovery, noting a parallel between 1990, 1991 and 1992 to 2001, 2002 and 2003 where a continuing increase in productivity and stable demand are leading to lower employment. On the positive side, he noted that money is still flowing into real estate driven by inexpensive interest and a view among investors and pension funds (which are the major driver in investment economy) that real estate is a safe long-term play.

He noted that lower interest and higher demand with an acceptance of a lower return on investment have led to higher prices for real estate, often bringing buildings back to values close to replacement cost (it's hard to justify building a new building when there is so much inventory of vacant space that can be bought at prices cheaper than building new space). So real estate is being bought and sold at a high rate with one shift in attitude about what is being bought and sold—high-quality buildings with "credit tenants," those with a credit rating of "A" or above are selling well at favorable rates. If the building is not prime and/or the tenant's credit is suspect, forget about it! This is a great lesson as you consider how hard to pursue a new customer, client or line of business, how lenient to be with your receivables or how much "speculative" work you may want to do to curry favor with a new prospective customer or client. I recommend following the lead of the real estate market—just say "no" unless the customer or client is a very high-grade credit risk. And take the time to check your customers and clients out thoroughly.

This condition is set against a 16.9 percent vacancy rate, which, with "shadow" vacancy (space that someone is paying rent on but is not being occupied and has not been put on the sublease market) could be as high as 23 percent, causing new rental and sublet rates to continue to decline. The good news is that new construction throttled way back prior to the recession, reducing the rate of new supply in the market (three cheers for discipline within the development community unlike what happened prior to the last recession), and sublet vacancy is now beginning to come down. In fact, rates in some cities are actually starting to rise.

Susan Hudson-Wilson continued with a refinement on the economy. Much has been written about whether we're going to experience a "double-dip" recession, where the economy goes down (it has) then recovers somewhat then goes down again. Her outlook is that we've already experienced the double-dip (job growth went up from June to October 2002, then down from November 2002, through April 2003), and the economy is now coming back, albeit slowly, and will continue to do so—encouraging news.

Hudson-Wilson's observations:

- This cycle will be demand driven. That's good. Since the office supply spigot was turned off before the demand dropped, we're not faced with space continuing to come onto the market as we were in 1990-91. She feels that office vacancy has peaked and will clean up faster than we think; maybe not as fast as it did in the 90's, but at an accelerating rate starting now.

- Office worker demographics point to a slowing in growth of the working age population, and, even with people working until an older age, the demand for workers will increase. Echo boomers don't start to become a positive influence until 2022. The U.S. has an advantage over Europe and Japan, however, as we've allowed increased immigration, we are softening the demographic population dips that are beginning to be felt there. Hudson-Wilson felt that the effect of a shortage of workers on the use of office space would be a reversal of the trends toward reduced space per person and increased "hoteling" that we've felt with the economic crunch in the last couple of years, leading to a rate of absorption of office space higher than rates of growth in company populations, good news for all that vacant space hanging around. As to new construction in the office market, she projected that we'll see some new construction in some select locations in the next year or two and that things will get really good by 2010.

- It's about offices, not manufacturing. As she put it, manufacturing is "toast." It's all been moved offshore. That was then [2003, this is now. The dollar is worth significantly less against the Euro and Yen and is about to be worth less relative to the Yuan. Yes, China will feel the effects of an increasingly valuable currency, and manufacturing jobs will start to come back to the U.S. They already are with the first Chinese auto parts manufacturers buying Michigan companies and European companies outsourcing manufacturing to the U.S.

- Retail sales have continued to grow and will be a reliable source of further growth, driven by a demographic increase in the population segments in their prime purchasing years, 35 to 54, over the next 10 years. Grocery store- anchored centers are also "toast," being overshadowed by WalMart, Target and their kin. Value retail centers are the winners (have you checked out your local outlet mall lately? That's where the action is). Only the top-tier conventional malls will survive in their present form. Second-tier malls will be repositioned or adaptively reused. Department stores in these second-tier malls will be converted to multi-floor value retailers (Bed, Bath & Beyond and the like) with the advent of the "cart-veyor," an escalator that lets your shopping cart ride next to you on a parallel escalator. Because of the need for shopping carts, these "big-box" retailers have always demanded large single-level stores. Multi-story stores are now possible. This will also facilitate the conversion of dying department stores in urban areas to be converted to value retail.

- Multi-family demand has fallen while supply has increased. This is also demographically driven and will be a severe problem in real estate—a note of caution for any of you entertaining multi-family housing opportunities.

- "Owned" housing (this can be single-family houses, townhouses, condominiums, what are now thought of as second homes but, because a couple is aging, are being bought now as the future permanent residence) will grow as people moving through the demographic cycle are moving to their "next home" (the kids have left home and the dog has passed away). The market for the large family home is shrinking and should be a concern for those considering buying the traditional suburban house. Prices are going to erode in the coming years even though single-family housing does not appear to be the "bubble" that the dot.coms were.
- Warehouse space has not grown as rapidly as GDP because of well-managed (too well?) just-in-time inventories. She noted that a strike such as we had last fall on the West Coast, increased security at our borders or a terrorist incident at a port would cause major disruption. She feels that inventories have been brought down too low and will be rebuilt. This won't help our GDP much because most manufacturing is offshore. But it will affect our ports, which are terribly constrained. Regional distribution hubs, like what Hillwood Development in Dallas has built at Alliance, will thrive.

So there you have it—some takes on the economy at the time were a little more optimistic with a little more depth and, I think, more realistic than we had seen in "sound bite" headlines along with suggestions of appropriate actions related to specific types of real estate. I was encouraged, as I've been more and more lately, that as tough and competitive as things seemed at the time, there were still wonderful opportunities in the markets we served.

Another speaker, Fareed Zakaria, editor of Newsweek International, had much to say about Iraq, referring to it as our 51st state (in his words, we got it on the Pottery Barn principle—"you break it, you buy it"). He quipped that God invented war to teach

Americans geography (what did any of us know about the Euphrates river valley and the cities along it before March, 2003?).

Not so funny. With the elections just having been completed at the time of his talk, some thoughts on the situation: America is really not very democratic. Our constitution provides systematic protection of rights and liberties independent of the democratic process. Courts that are not democratically elected defend our Bill of Rights and constitution. Our system of governance took many years of testing, trial and error to achieve. We don't have time on our side in Iraq, and things will get progressively worse.

The situation is further aggravated by the population distribution: 20 percent Sunnis (the ruling class under Sadam), 60percent Shiite (the oppressed) and the balance Kurds and others. Democracy without human rights will almost assuredly lead to revenge. We should all be watching the new regime very closely.

Oil aggravates the problem. There is a strong negative correlation between abundant natural resources and progress in human rights as can be seen with every oil-rich country in the world. Iraq will take time to create a system of governance with checks and balances, rights and the means to protect them. We won't be able to facilitate that as America alone. It will require an international coalition and a great deal of patience.

Three years later, in 2006, we can only hope for statesmanship, thoughtfulness, patience and a long view in our government. The situation we've gotten ourselves into won't be fixed in a half-hour with three commercial interruptions.

Retail

I love to follow retail trends as I believe they are the precursor to so many other aspects of our economy. I use the many changes in retailing to help me work with clients to rethink the logistics of their own businesses. Here are some of the issues to consider:

Throughout the last few years, consumers have continued to spend for a constantly evolving array of products and services competing through an ever-expanding number of channels in a global marketplace. Emerging markets such as China and India are becoming avid retail consumers. Other gentrifying societies will follow suit.

Whether our presence in Iraq is long or short, the potential for further disruption to other governments in the Middle East is very real and the long-term cost to the U.S. through oil supply disruption, the tax burden of a long-term and expensive presence in the Middle East and the threat of increased terrorism create a real challenge for our economy. Retailers are the pace setters in wringing cost out of their products and today are so dependent on shipping for just-in-time deliveries that a disruption to a port as was experienced during a recent West Coast dock strike would be devastating. Think about your own business and where your "hot-spot" dependencies are that would be affected by such conditions.

We have become a globally integrated economy and nowhere is global connectivity more apparent than in retailing. Today's products are sourced from global product, component, material and service suppliers, linked together through a dense network of relationships to manufacture, deliver and service everything we consume. We're hard-pressed to find a product or service today that is fully delivered and supported from a single country. And, if you think you've found one, call their customer service line and ask the person you're speaking with where they are. It's just as likely that they will be in India or Ireland as in Kansas or the hometown of the manufacturer.

Let's explore the ways in which we learn about or source products. We're just as likely to find a product through the Internet or on E-Bay as we are at the local shopping center. The Web has had a profound impact on the role of physical space on establishing "brand" and engaging a customer. And how does that product find its way into our home or office? Today, Fedex or UPS are so thoroughly integrated into many retailers' supply chains that they're handling all delivery logistics including running the call center that takes the order and making and packing the boxes in which the products are shipped.

Customer intimacy is the new goal for retailers. They are solving well and efficiently for the back office and, frankly, don't want you to look behind the curtain because so little of the way they make and deliver their product is actually done by people in their own organizations. But they want you to think so in order to establish that very close personal link with you, the customer. I think about Apple and Volkswagen as brands that continue to stretch the customer intimacy concept by deeply engaging the customer, teaching them how to use the product more effectively and establishing an affiliative, almost tribal relationship with and between their customers. Other examples like ING direct with its Internet Café are fundamentally altering the role a financial institution plays in people's lives.

Consumers are seeking relevant context and authenticity in their shopping experience. They demand to be delighted and surprised, staying away from formulaic traditional malls with cookie-cutter repetition of national brand stores. Places like Third Street Promenade in Santa Monica, CA; Kierland Commons in Scottsdale, AZ; and Bethesda Row in Bethesda, MD, certainly have national brands represented but also present unique local merchants. And, the national brands have done one-off, non-formulaic stores giving the streets an authentic and contextually appropriate feel, attracting crowds from a broad geographic region, reinvigorating the local geographies they serve much as the classic "High Streets" in the UK did in the late 19th and early 20th centuries. The impact of importance of street life has driven major shopping center renovations to connect the mall more completely with a street scene.

Consumer demographics continue to evolve as baby boomers reach their 50s. Echo boomers (the large population age group who are the children of the baby boomers, which, by the way, is even larger than the baby-boom generation) effect buying patterns as their needs change through the stages of their lives. The watchword is "pay attention to the younger generation, the products they gravitate toward and the way they use them." Video games, rarely played by the baby-boom generation, somewhat embraced by Gen-

X, are a way of life for the echo boomers and now account for more sales volume than the entire film industry.

I've heard it expressed that retailers today are "chasing the cool." What makes something cool? The dominant themes: it's exciting, it's fresh but it's comfortable, I feel good there, I can hang out.

Hopefully these thoughts will help you as you design "cool" products and places for your clients and customers.

Fit Your Enterprise to the Market—Define What You Are and What You're Not

As you consider what you've discovered about the world in which you're doing business, it's time to evaluate how well your product or service array fits the market you've described. It's time to ask some careful questions about what the market really wants. Chapter 9 gets into far greater depth on understanding the customer you're serving, so let's focus now on what segments of the market, specifically, you're approaching to assess the fit of your organization as it's currently constructed. At the end of this exercise, you should have a much clearer picture of what you are, what you're not and, more importantly, what you should be.

Since the variables are so broad, I'm only going to pose a series of questions for you to consider. If you're the CEO or part of the leadership team of your enterprise, you've probably spent some time already answering these questions. If so, go back to them based on your description of the world as you defined it after reading Chapter 2. Define why you should have each particular product or service offering based on the political, regulatory, sociological, economic, cultural and demographic trends you've identified. Trends are never precise, and in many areas there may be several alternatives based on conflicting notions about the future. Run several "what-if" evaluations based on different optional future scenarios. To learn more about this type of scenario planning, read Peter Schwartz' excellent book *The Art of the Long View: Planning for the Future in an Uncertain World.*

If you've not been involved in the design of the product and service offerings of your company, take the time to think through from your vantage point whether your offerings and the way they're presented to your customers seem reasonable and appropriate from your perspective of the world. As part of the leadership of a large firm, I often found that my leadership team and I had become really myopic. We'd been doing certain things in our firm for so long and were so convinced that they were still viable service offerings that we couldn't see emerging trends that were affecting the way our clients wanted us to work with them. Some of the freshest and most provocative insights I got were from younger staff members who offered a point of view we hadn't considered.

If you're not part of your organization's leadership, don't be discouraged if that leadership resists or treats your ideas as foolish— I'm ashamed to admit that, from time to time I was so convinced that we were addressing the market appropriately, I missed a key piece of information from someone offering an idea even though it wasn't their job to do so. My attitude toward these well-intentioned and often remarkably prescient ideas finally changed at an interesting point in time. Our human resources director came into my office one morning with a big grin on her face to tell me that, as of that day, half of the employees of the firm had not been born on the date that I joined Gensler. Nothing could have brought home to me more clearly how disconnected I had probably become from the generational issues in our society that separated my point of view from not only younger people in the firm but clients as well. Pay attention, senior executives—listen to the younger generation!

Now take a look at your organization, taking each product or service offering and describing why the way it's configured is well fitted to the trends you see coming in the following areas:

- Political—What changes in political priorities and programs do you see coming, and how will they affect your specific product or service? Is there a trend toward new regulation or government scrutiny, or are there specific pieces of legislation pending that could impact (restrict or encourage) your specific product or service?
- Financial—How will trends in interest rates, savings rates or funds availability affect your specific product or service? Is consumer confidence in the economy stable or changing? What factors in the local, national or world economy or political situation might shift that mood, and how seriously will it impact your customer's buying decision for your specific product or service? What effect will currency rate fluctuations have on your products or services if you're buying or selling internationally? Even if you're not? What effect will the relative availability of capital or debt have on your business?
- Technological—What changes in technology (such as documenting the human genome, the proliferation of high-speed and/or wireless connectivity, proliferation of features on cell phones, instant messaging, nano-technology, new materials being developed and biomimicry) will impact the design and delivery of your product or service, your sales and service channels?
- Sociological—What trends in social institutions (such as religious, educational, cultural, social service, philanthropic, ethnic) will influence specific consumer groups for your product or service? Are any of your products or services designed to appeal specifically to one or more social institutions? Why? How? Should your products or services be more specifically tailored to individual ethnic or sociological groups?
- Cultural—What cultural trends (such as amount of time various segments of the population spend in different leisure activities like video games versus television, the proliferation of gambling, increased availability of time and money for travel, the growth in the cruise ship industry, shifts in how people receive current news like Internet and magazines versus newspapers and television) will

impact how the consumer of your product or service will come to know about you, interact with and purchase your product or service and find out how others feel about it? What specific features of your product or service are designed specifically to respond to any of these trends?

- Demographic—What age demographics are you serving? Are those ranges growing or shrinking? Is your product or service designed to specifically appeal to and fit the desires of your target age range? In what specific ways? Where do the target customers for each of your products or services live now and where will they be living in the future? Why?

Now step back from this exercise and imagine that you were going to start over.

- Which of the products or services you're now offering seem like they will continue to have a viable market? What specific trend characteristics that you've identified make this true?
- How would you redesign each of these lines of business to respond more fully to these trends?
- Which lines of business should you drop? (this is the most difficult question to face up to because of institutional inertia against change and the perceived personal risk to individuals whose careers or skill sets may make such change threatening)
- In what geographies should you be offering your product or service? Why?

This is not a simple exercise. To get it right, it won't be the work of a single individual or committee but is rather the building of awareness of societal trends throughout your organization, allowing each incremental discussion about each product or service to be informed by careful consideration of fit to market—the real gritty marketplace with all of its complexity not a fantasy marketplace in someone's mind. Where, specifically, should this work take place? Each organization's culture and communication style is different and the forum for the formal and informal conversations must be tailored to fit you and your company's style.

In my career, this exercise was ongoing. It included formal and informal scenario planning and frequent discussions about how broader trends were impacting the viability of each of our service offerings. Over the years, we continued to hone the mix, occasionally dropping something that had, at one time, represented a significant segment of business.

We frequently added new service areas and geographies based on our assessments of the trends noted before. Some worked and some didn't. And as clearly as we tried to stay focused, we had our own institutional inertia based on the issues noted above plus another: we were a very entrepreneurial and competitive group. When someone undertook a new service line, they were bound and determined to prove that they could make a success of it. Their pride wouldn't let them do otherwise. Several noble efforts were hard to kill and painful in the passing. But all were worth it, encouraging and supporting experimentation. Many of them reshaped the firm, and all of them contributed to the body of knowledge about which businesses we should be in and which we should not.

Each area of business had to meet a couple of key criteria: we had to be true experts in any field we pursued, not just mid-level competitors. Starting up a new practice area without acquiring the expertise through merger or the purchase of a firm or team of people established in the field was a challenge. We were successful building from scratch in areas like tenant development work, airport planning, retail and entertainment. In each case, we responded to an existing market with a new twist, an approach that was different from our competitors at the time based on our read of what the market really wanted.

Second, we had to be able to create a unique sustainable advantage, to offer something that was not easily copied. Serving clients consistently across a broad geographic area through a series of offices that behaved as a single firm without turf battles is an example. The rich network of relationships and trust that are required to support this type of national and, for us, international service provision takes years to develop and make effective. Our competitors found it easy to copy our marketing approach but devilishly difficult to deliver.

There were a few market areas in our field of business that we didn't enter, some by choice; some we missed. We chose not to pursue prisons. As large as that market was, there was something inherently antithetical to the nature of our design practice. We avoided condominiums. The risk of lawsuit was simply too high, irrespective of the quality of work we would do. A whole cadre of lawyers has built a thriving business of suing architects for their insurance limits within the 10-year statute of limitations on liability to which we're bound. See what I mean about assessing the political and regulatory environment? Adequate tort reform has not yet come about, and I'm pessimistic about any significant change in the foreseeable future. We should have pursued healthcare and schools—we missed a window of opportunity and lacked the patience and commitment to develop the depth of expertise to compete effectively according to our criteria of true expertise and an ability to create a unique sustainable advantage and were unwilling to acquire another firm to gain a toehold in those markets. And there were others.

Using this review as an outline, how would you assess the businesses you're in, not in, or should be in? Finding the appropriate venue for this assessment will depend on the unique character and culture of your organization. It seems to work best when it engages the broadest cross-section of people from across service and geographic boundaries and including people from the administrative or service side of your business.

How to convene this discussion: a case study

The following presents a case study based on my experience, illustrating how to bring this kind of discussion together. Our best discussions about fitting our enterprise to the market and for the tough discussions about what we should be doing and what we should not took place at our "Super Weekends." These intense sessions, filled with both work and play, boiled out the essence of how we would adjust our areas of practice and the systems and processes that supported them each year. For me they were also filled with all sorts of unintended consequences. The social time strengthened the bonds between people, deepening our ability to act collaboratively and interdependently, the keys to our pivotal unique sustainable advantage. And the inventiveness of people from different disciplines and geographic areas invariably led to "spontaneous combustion," new approaches that no individual or narrowly focused group would have thought of.

One particular "Super Weekend" was held simultaneously with a research group from within the firm dealing with global account relationships, allowing cross fertilization between this client service-focused team and our various practice area groups. Their final session was the capstone of a year of hard work by its 15 members. The leadership role we were playing serving numerous clients across broad geographic areas and service types was taking on increasing importance. Our strategy of providing seamless design work to financial institutions, corporations and professional services firms represented more than 50% of our practice and was growing every day. It's a thing that we could do day in and day out that other firms could promise but couldn't deliver as it required a deep culture of collaboration and interdependency. Later chapters will deal with designing your culture.

An outside speaker from IBM presented in-depth insights into their organization and how they manage global relationships. We had done extensive work with IBM in multiple locations and across many service types. They knew us well so were very open. IBM's dominant theme was the need to truly understand what they value, how their corporate culture and goals are driving their design and use of facilities and how the nature and history of the group which is commissioning and managing our work determines the style of the relationship we must develop to be successful. He gave us an in-depth view of IBM and how it has changed over the years. His clear message: stop selling what you've done or can do. Research who your client is, what their corporate style is and what measurements will be used by them to determine if the work you do is successful.

The "Super Weekend," got its name because of its sheer scale, more than 100 participants. Here's why it was so large. We had many task forces working within the firm for years in four categories: offices, design & delivery systems, firm-wide shared services, and practice areas. In order to develop a common agenda for the firm and to avoid redundant efforts, these groupings of task forces met together at some point during the year. Prior to the advent of the "Super Weekend," task forces had decided independently when and where to meet. The opportunity for cross-referencing between individuals and groups is tremendous. People who know each other's names through correspondence or e-mails or each other's voices have an opportunity to meet face to face.

The assembly of the practice area task forces represented by far the largest groupings in the firm. Each task force presented its accomplishments, strategies and goals followed by a work session to develop its agenda for the coming year. The charter for a task force calls for fostering innovation, sharing best practices and communicating internally and externally the work of the firm in each respective area.

The highlight of the meeting came with work sessions designed to foster collaboration between working teams with different priorities. Some clear strategies emerged with the clear message: our clients don't want a core service with other services added on. They want all disciplines to be truly integrated. This can only happen when project teams start out this way, with each team member respecting what the other brings in professional knowledge and skills, with a common mission to serve the client and without infighting over who "owns" the relationship. Facilitated interactivity with community interest groups, lenders and others who influence the process of approval of a project will lead to the best design solutions when done as part of the design process and not an additive service.

Administrative groups were also represented in these meetings based on a philosophy that for them to do their jobs well, they needed to be fully versed in the goals and ambitions of those who had to deliver our service day in and day out at a client level. These meetings invariably made each group, risk management, accounting, human resources, information technology and communications better service providers to their internal customers.

The platform of knowledge and support available in your organization is incredible. The question is, how do you harness it? This type of meeting distributes this knowledge and, if the task forces are well networked throughout your organization, the knowledge gained will be well disseminated.

We had long before identified a need through trends in our client organizations for an integrated body of design services across broad geographic range, able to deliver consistently high-quality design, production and project management no matter where, when or in what configuration a client may need it. Many of our clients were consolidating their enterprises, looking for single-source accountability across many disparate services they were contracting for. They were being cost reductive, shrinking their facilities management staffs and looking for an enterprise that could assume the coordinative responsibility they had once done in-house, while still offering incremental services on a cost competitive basis. We had built such a model, fleshing out many additional service products based on what our clients told us they wanted and needed. As you'll learn in Chapter 9, you can find a tremendous amount about what businesses you should be in by just talking to your customer.

Design the Enterprise to Support Your Core Mission

Decisions about size and structure are difficult for any organization. Do divisions, regional or branch offices operate independently with individual profit and loss statements? How about different product or service specializations? Organization design is based on the structure of the relationship with client or customer and includes the structural relationship with outside vendors and suppliers.

We can watch as many industries today experiment with different constructs. Financial institutions and brokerage firms are migrating toward a model of cross-selling products serviced by multiple divisions and often including many subcontracted elements of service or support causing all components to interact collaboratively in the interest of serving the customer.

As retail product sales become multi-channel, retailers are finding that isolating sales channels, retail, catalog and Internet, by measuring performance of each separately, causes in-fighting, battles over turf and who gets credit for a sale. Successful retailers are learning to integrate each of these channels to present a seamless face to the customer, designing their organization and reward systems to support this.

In the auto industry, the globally competitive environment has led to deeper partnership relationships with suppliers, integrating them into the design process. They're taking a global look at design, sourcing and procurement, thinking of their organizations as single global enterprises, no longer separate North American, European and Asian operations.

Each of these enterprise types is evolving in response to a more integrated and competitive global base of customers and suppliers. Even the smallest companies today, such as a single-store retailer, source their merchandise directly from a world market. Small architectural firms in New York, San Francisco, London, Paris, Tokyo and even smaller cities around the world, are finding and taking advantage of opportunities to compete for design assignments in other parts of the world. Size or industry has little to do today with the globalization of business. So, considerable introspection about your core mission and how to design your enterprise to fulfill it must be done in the context of globalization.

Designing to a unique purpose

While each organizational design must be unique in responding to an individual strategic mission, the purpose for being in business, I'll spend some time describing how the Gensler design came into being. I don't hold it up as a model, but rather a case study of the considerations for the macro level process by which an organizational design evolves and is actualized. I hope it will be helpful in illustrating some of the issues that should drive your own design.

We based our core mission on client service. While we felt that great quality design was important, it needed to be a result of service that was well tailored and delivered in a unique way to each customer. While design was a key value to our clients, it was not the first consideration. In fact, we felt that great design could only be achieved in a client relationship based on great service. We watched many of our early competitors focus on design, almost in spite of their clients, as they competed for each new assignment.

We felt that the very best work we would do for a client was not going to be on the first assignment, but on the second or third after a bond of trust had been formed. Design, of course, means different things to different people as you'll learn in Chapter 16. Very beautiful work is done frequently by architects doing a single assignment for a client. But real design value is delivered when a work meets the test of time, as it proves itself able to adapt well to functional changes and operate efficiently over its life cycle. To meet this goal, design moves well beyond style. As the decisions that a client makes about cost vs. benefit become more complex, the decisions required of the client become more difficult to comprehend and accept. The benefit of deep knowledge and trust between designer and client improves the quality and benefit of design that each achieves.

The corollary to this notion is that we began to focus our energies more on clients who were in the business of building things frequently, whether a corporation or a developer, finding that the client who was building all the time was professional about it and treated us as professionals. A client who built something once and maybe not again for many years, if ever, had a steeper learning curve and often had unrealistic expectations and frequently represented a significantly higher liability. So, while the specific focus of our core mission was client service, a number of other issues about the type of client for whom we would design our service shaped the configuration and priorities of our firm.

Gensler evolved from the late 60s as a multi-office practice, largely as a result of clients taking us to a new location because of the quality of service they'd received. It could be a financial institution wanting us to do a branch in another city, a real estate broker recommending us to a client who was building something in another location or simply the globalization of our clients, centralizing control of their facilities and wanting us to be able to provide service on a broader geographic basis.

As early as the 80s, through our focus on client service, we were seeing a stronger migration of practice toward multiple assignments, often in multiple geographic locations and frequently involving multiple service types such as architecture, interior design and graphics. During that time as we were doing our own introspection about the way our practice was evolving, we engaged McKinsey & Company, one of those long-term, multiple assignment clients, for some advice. While what they brought to us was certainly interesting and important, the single insight that had the most profound effect was an article by David Maister titled "The One-Firm Firm," which portrayed an enterprise that behaved as a single entity in multiple geographic locations providing a variety of integrated services to their client base.

The concepts in the article about how to accomplish this resonated for us and became the guiding principle for the design of the firm from that point forward. Incremental business unit financial statements, long the most significant barrier to collaborative behavior, were only used to monitor unit performance in order to identify problems and best practices, but reward systems were based on the performance of the enterprise as a whole. Promotions were considered on a firm-wide basis, removing local office autonomy in the interest of transferability through recognition of consistent standards for performance. We had no idea how prophetic this construct would be. It seemed like the right thing to do at the time in order to bring the best resources to bear on a client's issues, no matter where they existed in the firm. But this idea launched us on a path that benefited our clients through integration of services in a profound way.

At the same time, our clients were evolving, responding to the globalization of their businesses and consolidation in many of the industries we served. Clients were centralizing control of their real estate function and outsourcing many of their project management, design and administrative processes. They began consolidating the number of vendors they used for various outsourced functions, steering toward consultants who were structured to deliver a consistent and coordinated level of quality over a broad geographic area, including outside the U.S., and across a broad array of service lines. One of our financial institution clients went from more than

100 service providers in our categories of service to two in a period of five years.

This played marvelously for our "One-Firm Firm" construct. More importantly, it proved to be a very difficult structure to emulate. It takes a long view approach to system and culture design to put in place, giving us a long-term strategic advantage. While our competitors with multiple offices began marketing themselves as being able to deliver on this premise, they hadn't invested in designing and building organizations that could actually perform this way.

Size

As the firm grew, the ideal size of working units began to fascinate me. While every organization's leverage points are different, I hope my experiences will be useful as you work through this organizational design problem in your enterprise. We could observe the transitions in offices as they grew, noticing that below about 35 people, an office didn't have "critical mass," sufficient diversity of talent and depth of bench strength to build a compelling and sustainable body of business. Leadership and administrative support were under-leveraged. But 35 was a wonderfully magic number. Everyone could assemble in the same room at the same time to understand what each other were doing, share knowledge and pitch in to help their teammates in an overload condition.

Up to about 65, things remained workable, although communication and work sharing diminished. From around 65 to about 125, things were always extremely awkward. Another layer of management was needed as more and more time was required to simply direct traffic. But it was underleveraged until an office grew above 125. Additional administrative support was needed, particularly in finance, risk management, human resources and marketing, but the leverage problem stood in the way of professionalizing these positions.

At 125 to 150, these problems went away and things seemed to flow smoothly as issues of leverage allowed us to employ several incremental professional specialties. Above 200, communications across an office became fractured again. As the firm evolved, the offices in the 125- to 150-person size range seemed to represent a sweet spot of profitability and were the smoothest running. They were able to support a full range of developmental programs, had great bench strength to support client needs and began to entrepreneurially develop unique new practice specialties like airport planning or graphics and product design.

A corollary evolved as well, based on the 35 number. Studios in the range of 25 to 40 people within an office began to emerge as the basic business unit of the firm, providing for leadership development opportunities and creating groups of professionals who truly supported one another in their client activities.

I've since learned that these numbers were not uniquely suited to what we did, but are more universally applicable. From Steven Quartz and Terrence Sejnowski's excellent book, *Liars Lovers and Heroes*, I learned that the cerebral cortex of the human brain is sized to come to truly know about 150 people. From Jared Diamond's book, *Guns, Germs and Steel*, observations of the size of human tribes in the early era of human development place them at around 150. And Bill Gore of Gore-Tex fame never allowed a business unit to grow beyond 150.

As the overall size of the firm began to explode in the mid-90s, we really began to worry about holding the firm together under the constructs that we had designed. We learned, however, that this was an issue more related to the strength of our culture than strictly about size, which you'll learn more about in succeeding chapters. By the time we reached 2,400, we came to the conclusion that size of working teams and business units, knitted together by a common mission, shared values, open communication and transparency, was much more important than overall aggregated size.

While this case study is specific, I've since tested many of my conclusions with other business leaders and have found similar lessons learned as organizational and business units were formed. They vary a bit with the nature of the business, but the issues remain the same. Spend some time thinking through these sizing issues for your business. It's intriguing how profoundly they can affect unit performance and a customer or client's sense of quality.

Organic growth versus acquisition or merger

Every organization at some point makes a conscious choice to grow or to remain static. Each strategy has implications. For us, growth was an outcome of doing great work for clients who asked us to do more and referred us to their friends. But we made a conscious choice to respond to that pressure to grow as long as we could attract and retain professionals who would perpetuate our philosophy of customer-driven work. Growth for growth's sake, without the discipline to maintain quality will cause a reversal of fortune in an amazingly short period of time.

We often felt the pressure to stop growth. The reasons were always straightforward: either we had outstripped our infrastructure or felt we were going to be unable to recruit and swiftly integrate sufficiently talented professionals into the organization to do the quality of work on which we had built our reputation. But each time we weighed the choices, we responded to the opportunities in the marketplace and grew. Our abiding fear was that by limiting growth, we were also limiting opportunities for individuals to advance professionally and felt that this would cause the most entrepreneurial folks in our firm to seek greater potential elsewhere.

We never merged with or acquired another organization although a few smaller firms closed their operations and joined our firm en masse. In those cases we were already sharing extensive work in association. Joining two enterprises presents special risks and should not be undertaken lightly. I'll use the assumption that any firm worth merging with or acquiring is strong, and strong organizations have definitive cultures and robust networks that represent a significant component of their intrinsic value. Maintaining value after a merger or acquisition demands an extraordinary investment in merging cultures and networks as well. Addressing financial or market opportunities alone in a merger or acquisition is simply not enough. Further strategies on building and maintaining organizational values and culture will explore how to do this in much greater depth.

Maintenance & evolution

In designing any enterprise, you can never forget maintenance. Like an automobile or a house, no matter how brilliant the design or how well it's executed, it will deteriorate rapidly without maintenance. The further chapters in this book refine many of these design principles, illustrating how to maintain and refine them over time, but a few examples may help to understand the importance of this issue.

As structure evolves, it is imperative to keep the entire enterprise informed so everyone is pulling together on the priorities that maintain focus on the core mission. Transparency is key. At a point in time, smaller offices (+/- 35 people) simply couldn't offer the standards of training and education nor did they have the depth of resources that our employees and clients had learned to expect from a large office (+/- 150 people). We added a regional relationship between groups of offices to assure that everyone in the firm and, by extension, every client got the full measure of our capabilities.

Even in tight financial times, these investments must be made and delivered with clarity as they shape the future value of your organization. It's always a capital debate: how can you afford to spend money on things like training and support when the economy is bumping along with little indication of how quickly it may begin to grow again? If you believe strongly in your future, you must continue to invest in the tools and technology that will keep you at the forefront of your industry. You can cut back on some expenditures (meeting, travel and in-house costs relying more heavily on video teleconference, e-mail and the Internet), but an enterprise continues to build value by developing the many systems that help it to grow its capabilities and to work more effectively to serve its customers no matter what the economy is doing.

On the expense side it's a great time to get people thinking about the discretion they have to spend overhead money on everything from supplies to how they travel. If you're spending your client's or customer's money in conjunction with your product or service on things like reprographics, Federal Express deliveries, messenger services or outside vendors that get attached to your invoice to your client or customer, what a great time to reinforce the concept that each individual in your organization should treat it as if it is their own personal money. Imagine how your clients and customers will appreciate this attitude if the people in your organization make it visible. If finances are tight, your clients and customers are watching their costs very closely too.

Expanding geographically

Having watched the news coverage of the G8 summit in Genoa, Italy, a few years ago, I had a strong desire to sit down with each of the protestors and insist that they read *The Lexus and the Olive Tree*. Subsequent global economic summits have experienced similar disruptions underscoring the misunderstanding of the impact global financial transparency and business fluidity are having on poverty, living standards and human rights in underdeveloped parts of the world. I've recently added Lester Thurow's book, *Fortune Favors the Bold*, to my list of favorites as it offers new insights into globalization and its affects on our world. What the protesters don't seem to understand or accept are the dramatic improvements to many parts of this world, both economically and socially, that have been brought about by our globalizing economy. The availability or withholding of capital to various countries around the world based on their human rights policies has had a greater beneficial effect on those policies than all the protestors and politicians combined.

But my purpose here is not to convince you that globalization is a good thing. It is just the way the world has evolved and, no matter the size of your organization, you'll be drawn along as well so I'll offer some observations and advice based on my experience.

Leaving the security of "home" requires a point of view about why and how you're entering a new market. "Structure" is not always about lines of authority, organization charts and the

mechanics of doing business in a new jurisdiction. In fact, keeping
the underlying reason for entering a new market in the forefront of
your thinking is far more important. We found it enormously beneficial when entering a new geography to build early relationships
in the community as a local enterprise. No one wants to do business
with a branch office.

Several long term clients drew us initially into Europe and
Asia as an extension of the trust they had in us in the U.S. As each
regional office was established outside the U.S., however, it had to
become a "local" office serving regional clients as well, not just a
branch of an American firm only providing services to American
firms abroad. This follows the cultural development of our U.S.
practices where regional offices quickly assimilated into their local
communities, becoming involved in community interests as if the
firm had been founded there. Gensler folks joined charitable organizations, participated on planning commissions and helped make
each community a better place. We found that being a citizen of the
world also means being a citizen of your community.

Your clients and customers will continue to ask you to serve
them across geographies that are far broader than you ever imagined. This is truly the shape of business today and tomorrow. Your
success will be determined by your ability to think, act and work
globally. This means creating strong trust relationships far beyond
the bounds of your own organization. It means freeing yourself
from the notion that you can only solve your clients' or customers'
problems around the world the way you do at home, recognizing
and respecting that product and service delivery today is highly collaborative and requires that you seek the finest associations to work
with on your clients' and customers' behalf. It means educating
yourself on culture, customs, codes, materials and systems that are
appropriate to the work at hand, not stubbornly adhering to what
you know from your present experience.

Particularly as you consider multi-country expansion, be
aware of the marvelous opportunity for young professionals to have
a working experience in another country. It's a great time for people

from another land to be educated in one of your sites and some day to possibly move back to their home country as part of your organizational family. It's their opportunity to evolve into global citizens.

Brand

The sum total of the design of any enterprise becomes its "brand." Few organizations think much about designing every aspect of their enterprise in a way that supports a consistent brand to consumers, employees and other stakeholders, but the power of a consistent brand message is extraordinary. Since so much of the work we did crossed traditional service boundaries, we often became deeply involved with the design of our clients' brands and, of course, had spent a great deal of time working on the alignment of every aspect of our own organization as a cohesive single brand. Designing an enterprise to achieve high value demands unity of culture and purpose, expressed through every element that each stakeholder encounters over a long series of experiences.

The equity in a brand is what has been built over time that pops up as an attitude about an enterprise, its products and services. To use a film analogy, it's the "back story" on which an enterprise relies for consumer predisposition when introducing a new product or service, recruiting, seeking governmental approval or dealing with a crisis.

In ancient times (think of the Incas or the Romans), it was easy to create "brand" or "franchise;" you just killed the disbelievers. It had a strong brand reinforcing effect. The core cultural mythos had little, if any, competition.

Today's environment is filled with a cacophony of visceral input blasting at us from four-wheel rolling billboards and the Goodyear (make that Fuji) blimp to endless banner ads on the Internet causing a cocooning of the target market audience who build real or subconscious filters to screen the noise. It takes a strong and consistent brand to make a strike on the cerebral cortex.

There may even be a redeeming social value contributed by companies that develop strong brands; developing a bulwark against the random fragmentation of our culture. It's all about TRUST!

To create your brand (or to understand the brand you've created; because you've got one whether you like it or not, chaotic as it may be) you first have to inventory the following:

- Who are you (what do you make; what service do you sell)?
- What do you stand for (qualities of your people and their values when dealing with each other, vendor/supplier partners and customers)?
- Who is your audience/customer (do you know who wants your product or service; what are they like)?
- Are these factors consistently understood within your organization?
- Why do you want to be this way (the "vision" thing)?

Your brand is symbolized and reinforced by the physical and virtual iconography that represents your organization:

- The design "look and feel" of your product or the media through which your service is conveyed
- Product literature
- Advertising
- Business cards
- Website
- How the people in your organization behave and dress
- Sponsorship/philanthropy
- Physical facilities

The number of groups or departments affected by a brand design task can easily lead us to partition our thinking, keeping us from achieving optimum brand reinforcement from each of these elements. Entities within an organization (product development/engineering, manufacturing, marketing/sales, facilities) usually have focused agendas and are competing for scarce resources within the organization and want to spent them independently, leading to inconsistency in brand reinforcement.

Budgets are quarterly; the results of a consistent branding strategy are long-cycle. Positive market feedback is felt long after the fact but is extraordinarily powerful. Negative feedback to incremental tactics is often quick, isolated and can cause premature rejection of an important brand building move.

Who is the guardian of the "brand?" Is it a strong internal mythos (what would Walt—as in Disney—do)? Successful organizations have significant consistency across brand elements and achieve tremendous reinforcing effects that build the positive benefits of a brand. But this doesn't just happen. In most cases, the strongest brands come from a powerful cultural predisposition within the enterprise, not from "brand police."

The brand reinforcement from physical facilities is a key strategic performance tool. Physical environments elicit emotive responses in humans that are subconscious, not intellectual and offer an opportunity to reinforce the brand. *A Pattern Language* by Christopher Alexander is the definitive primer on this subject, describing the broad palette of physiological and emotional responses that humans have to light, color, space, sequence, acoustics, temperature, relative humidity and a wide variety of sensory inputs. This is the architect and designer's tool kit. The responses to the places we make are quantifiable and knowable.

I'll make specific mention of a new element of brand development: the creation of virtual environments either on the web, through advertising or some other immersive experience that your customer may have with your product or service. People have the same physiological and emotional responses to perceived environments that they experience in actual physical environments. We all experience this in film and television where the greatest set designers use your ability to project yourself into the place in which the action is happening to reinforce the story line. The same thing occurs when we create places and experiences such as a virtual test drive of a new car or a virtual walk through of a house listed on the internet. Such contact will strongly impact emotions in support of or opposition to a client's brand.

Understanding and using this tool set to achieve brand consistency, focus and excellence can deliver exponential reinforcement of customer confidence. I like to use Abraham Maslow's hierarchy of needs pyramid as an analog to the design process of physical spaces, dealing first with shelter, then security, pride and respect, intuitive way-finding, aesthetics, leading to reinforcement of brand, which, in Maslow's context, can help an organization self-actualize.

Understand Your Real Competition

My first "selling" experiences were unusual. I did excellent work for a few clients to whom I was assigned early in my career, and they asked me to do more for them or they referred me to their friends. Life was good. I could build a reputation for myself, and later the team of people with whom I was associated and my book of business would thrive and grow.

Before long, I found myself in my first recession. If I didn't do something different my book of business would shrink or I would have to become dependent again on someone else to feed me. So I entered the more traditional world of identifying business opportunities, placing a cold call or wrangling an introduction, pitching my services in a competitive marketplace. I had to ferret out competitors' strategies and contrast them to mine, and I had to price my services carefully to be below my competitor on a value-to-value basis, but not so low that I left money on the table. I had to be much more cautious in the design of my services to not over-promise what I could deliver at a high-quality level in order to maintain my high-service reputation.

Life got difficult. I discovered that I was a reluctant salesman. I didn't like the process. There was a certain satisfaction in competing and winning, of course, but the process reduced the likelihood that what I actually sold would be the best program for the client and, invariably, my ability to achieve good profit margins eroded in the competitive process. Did the customer get a better deal? Usually not, for what he bought was often not the best solution.

As I thought about it, I decided that I didn't like competition. Isn't it wonderful to be young and naïve? But when you don't know any better, you're more open to a creative solution. So I started spending a great deal of my marketing and selling time trying to figure out how not to compete by differentiating my offering in a way designed to be uniquely tailored to the client and containing elements that my competitors didn't have or couldn't offer. My mantra became a quest for the "unique sustainable advantage," and it was all a result of really disliking competing in a conventional sense.

Eventually, I found that I wasn't alone. In 2003, I had an opportunity to spend a few days in a workshop with Janine Benyus who wrote a book titled *Biomimcry*. She also coined the word. The term refers to learning from and replicating materials and processes found in nature. I was particularly fascinated to learn that, contrary to my impression from watching lots of animal and insect fights on the Nature Channel and reading Darwin about the "survival of the fittest," nature abhors competition. Janine cited example after example of natural systems that prove the case that competition is too expensive to all competitors. Survivors do so by learning to work interdependently with their surroundings. They develop a unique sustainable advantage and don't fight with other species for the same turf or resources. I was delighted to learn that my naïve dislike for head-to-head competition and my search for a way to thrive without it were simply a way of emulating nature.

When we were first playing with this notion 25 to 30 years ago, things were moving at a slower pace. Our competitors seemed to be the same at each encounter, the service offering requested or required by the client was reasonably narrow and could be specifically defined, and our competitors seemed to be pretty slow in adapting any unique strategy we would dream up. We got pretty comfortable using this approach as we only had to cook up a unique idea once in a while. Don't get me wrong, we still had to compete in a conventional sense for a lot of work, but our real satisfaction came in finding that new and unique approach that clients would pay for because it offered a special value they couldn't readily find under one roof somewhere else.

Now technology, global competitors who are quick to copy any unique approach you put forth, boundless entrepreneurial creativity, ever-evolving regulations and relentless time pressures from the marketplace drive a constant change in the entities with whom you compete. A marketplace with a knowable and stable customer base, where your competitors look like you, are configured as you are and remain that way long enough for you to understand and develop strategies for their approach is history. Every day a new entrant appears, ready to provide a service offering that is more comprehensive, more focused or less expensive. And they want to knock you off the block.

Some of this is competitively based: an alternative product or service provider aimed specifically at competing with your product or service offering but in a new or less-expensive way. At other times it's a lifestyle or cultural displacement in the market like the explosion of computer game play stealing time from what a person might otherwise have spent watching television and film (the game industry now generates more revenue in a year than the entire film industry—talk about stealing "mind-share") or a shift in concern about sustainability that has driven demand for clean air vehicles like Toyota's Prius.

And these challenges and shifts are proliferating and accelerating. Any enterprise that remains complacent, focusing on its core businesses will quickly stagnate. But the most difficult challenge, the one that has been the undoing of so many Fortune 500 companies in the past few years, is looking at your business as an outsider, but from the inside. As difficult as it is to look at the design of your product and service offering as if you were entering your market as an outsider and challenging your offering with something different, more appealing to a customer and more value laden, it is even more difficult to do something about it. Strong inertia against change exists in every organization. It's ingrained in us to resist change, and we do, both as individuals and as organizations.

Yet to survive, change and adapt we must. And we must do it in real time and on an ongoing basis. This is not the stuff of a strategic planning study or a recommendation from an outside management consultant. Constant scrutiny of what you're doing relative to the competitive marketplace and through the eyes of your customer must be embedded in the very core of your enterprise. The characteristic of awareness through an outsider's point of view alone will help you to adapt. But you need to do more. You need to be willing to start new businesses within your existing enterprise that may challenge and ultimately cannibalize or displace business entirely from your current lines.

So where do you start?

Relentless benchmarking

Step one is to keep your eyes open to what's going on around you. Conventional wisdom for many years said, "Institutionalize a process to drive cost out and raise quality." Today, any fixed process cannot adapt to rapidly changing market demands and customer preferences. Each new undertaking must start with a look at what's going on around you, searching for a better solution than has ever been done.

I saw a help-wanted ad a while back in an electronic newsletter for a company looking for a "road warrior." I remember finding it amusing at the time. With the travel schedule that many of us are keeping these days, it's no longer a curious phrase; it's a way of life. Those of you who are working in an office every day watching others come and go to places around the country or world imagining how exciting and exotic it must be, be careful what you wish for. There are some interesting benefits, though. One of the most important is the ability to "benchmark" on a much broader basis. I've always worked from the premise that before starting anything, I should go out in search of the place where it's been done the best and then try to do it better. Whether my observations are from real-life experience or from exploring through magazines, books or the Internet, I've found the precursor to great work is the homework you do before you start; the relentless search for examples of how others have solved a similar problem to find a platform from which to innovate.

An important part of innovation is a stretching of the limits of excellence. So, if you're not a student of the "latest and greatest," you're going to find the quality of your work slipping relative to a rapidly changing performance expectation. And to perform at the level of creativity and innovation to which we must aspire, we've got to go beyond what's known to be the best at the moment. You can't do that without relentless "benchmarking."

And it's not just architectural firms that look at their work today as a continuing series of one-off, unique client or customer relationships requiring a fresh look at each new engagement. It also holds that ongoing relationships need to be refreshed regularly since there's someone trying to steal yours right now.

Change is a team sport

The next step creates an active agenda inside the organization to constantly look for new opportunities to change your business, adapting it in real time to the ever-changing demands and needs of your customers. It always helped me to find third-party endorsements for the approaches I favored since I know that people at Gensler quite often found my ideas hare-brained. In 1997 I found a terrific book that resonated with what I'd been promoting for so long and used it liberally to validate what I had in mind. I will be forever indebted to Oren Harari and his *Leapfrogging the Competition, Five Giant Steps to Market Leadership* for providing me a voice and a format to adapting your organization in real time. I was particularly moved by a quote from the book, "half of the Fortune 500 companies listed in 1983 are no longer around." While the concepts are straightforward, the things you have to do are easier said than done. So, while it's a great how-to book, it won't be very easy for most enterprises to undertake enough of the "Giant Steps" to make a difference.

I'll focus on just one issue: Giant Step II, Flood Your Organization with Knowledge, leaving you to pursue others as the spirits may move you. In a section entitled "Challenge Sacred Cows in the Pursuit of Bold Goals" an idea was so clearly stated that it bears quoting:

> The goal is to create a corporate culture that is characterized by two attributes:
>
> • There are no sacred cows other than the most fundamental of corporate mission and values (and even those are examined periodically).
> • Everyone on board sees their charge as continually challenging the existing process in order to strive for quantum leaps in performance and market offerings.
>
> Dramatic upheavals outside the organization call for radical changes inside. Tweaking and improving the current systems and processes is no longer enough ...

From Harry Quadracci at Quad/Graphics in Wisconsin: "Change is our bread and butter. We see change as our job security [another CEO is quoted elsewhere in the book as saying, 'we eat change for breakfast']. That's why in almost every department ...there is virtually no similarity to the way things were running six months ago."

To foster this sort of atmosphere, companies that challenge sacred cows follow five '"to-do's": First, they encourage everyone to ask "why" questions. Why are we doing things this way? Why are we doing this at all? Would a customer pay us to do what we are doing? Would a customer prefer that we automate it, delegate it, outsource it, or eliminate it entirely?

What currently prevents us from doing things that we know we ought to - listening to our customer, collaborating with people in other divisions and other world-class companies, starting a project team, making a decision quickly and then holding people accountable for results?

Second, they constantly shed old goals and set new extraordinary ones. Leaders in these companies set broad decision boundaries (financial, strategic, ethical 'rules of the game'); then within these boundaries, they insist that people regularly set new goals and standards that are bold—even impossible—by today's standards ...

Third, companies that challenge sacred cows liberate people to take action. Liberating people means enabling them to act, which means getting out of the way and, when necessary, helping people overcome organizational hurdles that currently prevent them from taking immediate action. If employees lack the power to ask tough questions, form an exploratory task force, or visit outside the organization to search for more facts, the idea pool shrinks. Companies that liberate try to get people to adopt a start-up, entrepreneurial mentality when they look at the business, asking themselves: 'what would I do if this were my business?'

Fourth, these companies teach everyone business literacy ...employees throughout these companies learn the fundamentals of running a business: strategy, cost accounting, systems applications, computers, income statements, market research, statistical process control, how to run a meeting. Whatever the organization's purpose and vision, people must have the expertise necessary to move it toward that end...

Finally, companies that expect people to challenge sacred cows on behalf of bold goals make certain, in return, to challenge their own sacred cows of compensation. Brain-based organizations do not simply pay people to come to work in exchange for a set wage or salary. Significant performance-based variable pay—gain sharing, profit sharing, equity ownership become a key part of compensation.

In an era where your competition is going to come from a whole new array of enterprises, not just other companies in your business sector, you need to be constantly redesigning your business. No matter what you've done for the last decade, the pace is picking up. Harari suggests a method called "naïve listening." From Harari's *Leapfrogging the Competition*: "Insist that everyone on the payroll get involved with lots of 'naïve listening' to customers as an official part of their job requirements. Then provide mechanisms - from open dialogues to newsletters to groupware—that allow people to share their impressions and come up with ideas for product and service innovations. The key to 'naïve listening' is not to ask a customer, 'Would you buy this?' or 'Would you buy that?' The key is to hang out with them on project teams, on-site visits or over a beer after work listening to their issues and problems, noticing what frustrates them on the job, staying alert to what they get excited about and observing what they wish they had to make their lives easier. By doing this, you'll get plenty of food for fresh creative ideas; you'll know what they'll respond to before they themselves do."

Cannibalize your own business before someone else does

The most difficult concept to put into action in any organization is a new approach to a product or service that threatens an existing product line ... and the people whose livelihoods and career paths depend on its continued existence. The only driver that seems to get people's attention is an outside competitor doing what you have the capability to do yourself but lack the will because it is threatening in some way. Vehicles to overcome such inertia include setting up a separate business unit, staffing it with at least a few of those who are most threatened. With the assurance that they have organizational support and a safety net to return to familiar turf if the venture fails, they are often your most effective change agents, offering the added benefit of diffusing the uncertain and fearful atmosphere that they would foster from their position in the traditional business unit or if they were truly an outsider.

Another method is to partner with someone with a competing idea. In the construction industry, one of the major long-term threats to conventional architectural practice is design-build, a single entity taking complete responsibility for delivering a finished building, including hiring and managing the architect, interior designer, contractor and all other vendors. Will that entity be the architect, the contractor or a third party? Many models are being tried with advantages and disadvantages to each. But clients are increasingly demanding single-source accountability, the market force that's driving this change.

Here's a case study of how to put your toe in the water with a new market competitor, showing how to learn about your future without making a full commitment to a new business enterprise. A few years ago, Steelcase announced a new venture in which they shared ownership with Gale & Wentworth, a New Jersey-based developer, and Morgan Stanley, their financial partner, called Workstage. This entity was formed to develop and deliver a fully furnished building as a product aimed at housing the knowledge worker of the future. The prototype building, in Grand Rapids, hosted 1,700 Steelcase dealers from around the country (a formidable sales force for this new venture). The Steelcase jet made continuous round trips between Chicago and Grand Rapids during the annual furniture exposition, Neocon, shuttling prospective clients to see the building. This was a daunting new entry into the design-build marketplace.

The prototype was an 80,000-square-foot, two-story, steel frame building with a raised floor, under-floor air delivery and indirect lighting integrated into a Steelcase furniture system. The steel frame was exposed, creating high, open, loft-like space. The systems were of very high quality, and the feeling of the building was light, fresh and energized, the type of place our technology clients were seeking.

We could have sat around licking our wounds as they sold projects against us. We chose instead to join the team in an ongoing role in the roll-out of this concept including development of alternative skins, core elements and building systems. Workstage was taking a manufacturer's approach to the building process, pre-negotiating elements and systems that comprise the "chassis" of the building. Things like toilet cores and coffee/copy stations were to be completely fabricated in a factory and plugged into the structure.

To paraphrase a conversation I had with one prospective buyer, "Let me see, if I buy one of these buildings, I won't be separately hiring an architect, an interior designer, a contractor and a furniture dealer and then paying them to fight with one another?" There were numerous reasons for us to be involved with Workstage on this venture, but the most important were the lessons we learned about industrialized building processes, designed to streamline building delivery, that we could apply to our other work. We also had the opportunity to listen very closely to prospective clients' perceptions of the construction industry from a completely different vantage point, allowing us to be much more sensitive to what they really wanted to buy. We'd commented for years that our competition in the future would not be from other architects. This was a great way to learn about that future.

Standardize infrastructure; change its application

Streamlining and making your infrastructure consistent throughout the enterprise allows you to experiment with new approaches and simplifies the process of launching an experimental business line. It is entirely possible to start up whole new business ventures, entrepreneurial pursuits with relatively low risk, if you've built a structure of common protocols that are understood, accepted and practiced throughout the organization. Parochialism is the enemy of change. Standardizing infrastructure is also a great way to stay focused on cost reduction in your processes and to allow people to work fluidly across broad geographic and service boundaries. I was relentless about structuring such a platform to allow continuing experimentation.

Things like computer protocols, purchasing and contracting

forms and intranet-based knowledge platforms are common tools. There is no need for each business unit to reinvent the methodologies or approaches to any administrative platform, whether in financial reporting, risk management, human resources, information technology or communications. In fact, one of the great advantages of a large, diverse organization is to professionalize the design and development of these elements of business. One of the great risks of mergers and acquisitions is the independent development and support of legacy systems that came with the acquired company. The same risk accrues to growing businesses that allow independent business units to develop their own unique systems for these platform services.

I've always referred to them as "plumbing" and have been fascinated by how fiercely protective business entities can be about decisions that have so little gravity relative to the business at large. It's a little like deciding to drive on the right side of the road or that the gas pedal goes on the right and the brake on the left. Once you've gotten these things settled, there's no reason for a business unit to deviate. It allows them to more fluidly share human and intellectual resources by talking a "common language" and using common tools.

The caveat is not to stifle creativity or lessen your ability to be agile. You must remain flexible and fast to keep pace with smaller, aggressive competitors. In fact, the strongest organizational culture is centered on a certain amount of autonomy among business units to help react to local forces. At the same time, working with common tool sets allows work, knowledge and experience to be shared by everyone. It's a balancing act.

Technology continues to drive change in business process, automating many tasks and dramatically altering job descriptions. Making global changes is mandatory to keep pace with your industry and is much easier to accomplish if the people in your organization are focused on the work they're doing for your customer but basing that work on common platform tools. Adapting to changes usually creates additional effort in the short term and is often resisted. Not without good reason—if it takes longer to do something and you're being measured by your immediate performance, why would you want to invest in learning a new process if in the early adopter stage it's going to negatively impact performance?

A terrific example of this can be seen many years ago, before the advent of CADD (computer-aided design and drafting). I could see it coming and knew that one of its key strategies was to work in layers—one layer contained plan elements such as walls and doors, another contained ceiling elements, another had plumbing fixtures, and so forth. In the short term, I introduced a drafting system utilizing a pin-bar to align physical drawing layers, isolating specific information on individual layers that could be stacked together for drawing or printing. While this process took a little more time initially, it built in a quality control process that people weren't budgeting for but performing anyway. So the real cost impact was minimal.

The benefit, however, was realized quickly when CADD technology became available since people were already thinking in layers. I watched people who had no experience with the pin-bar system struggle with CADD while those that had adopted this methodology were able to start using CADD systems almost immediately. I used this story often as an allegorical reminder as we implemented many advanced infrastructure systems to illustrate how accepting and making the investment to learn a new system can allow you more time to perform the core service you really want to be doing for your customer. It certainly allows you to adapt your enterprise quickly to the new competitor you don't see coming.

PART

II

ATTRACTING AND RETAINING GREAT PEOPLE

Shape Your Enterprise Through the People You Hire

As trite as it sounds, your people are you organization. Their character, integrity, presence, personality and emotional intelligence form a composite personality of the enterprise itself. Whether you like it or not, your company has a very distinct personality to the outside world. It is as likely to be schizophrenic as it is to be cohesive and positive. Have you ever taken the time to ask the people who interact with your organization what it is? Have you ever thought about what you want it to be? Is it collegial and collaborative or is it made up of loners and introverts? Are the people in your organization thought of as nice or tough, cooperative or stubborn, fair or mercenary?

Much discussion takes place today about an organization's brand, focusing heavily on brand consistency, but most of it focuses on product design and marketing collateral. The people who make up your company are as important a factor in your brand as the product or packaging of the services you sell. Whether you like it or not, that cumulative behavior pattern is establishing the quality and character of the interactions you have with your customers.

Trust

Product literature can be written by the most gifted wordsmith, but if it's inconsistent with the behavior of the people in your company, your brand will wilt. Person-to-person contact sets relationships in motion. Most importantly, it establishes or diminishes trust, not just in the person but in the product or service of the company. And the quality of trust may indeed be the most important ingredient in the level of success your organization enjoys.

I grew up in a world in which a person's word was their bond. If someone told me they were going to do something or represented that their product would perform in a certain way, I was confident that it would happen. This is simply no longer the way of the world. Without any attempt to explain how the world has evolved in this fashion (which would require another complete book), today we enter the world and our interactions with the people in it with suspicion. We write contracts for things that a few decades ago were simply understood, for which people felt honor bound to perform. If they didn't, their reputation, and with it their ability to obtain future business, would be severely tarnished.

Given this business environment, the personality of your organization must, by its very nature and through every type of interaction that takes place, establish bonds of trust with everyone with whom it comes in contact. As we've moved toward an environment where contact with an organization is often computer mediated, a whole new set of barriers to establishing trust is erected. How often have you hung up the phone in anger or despair after navigating your way through an endless maze of prompts, never able to find the answer to your question or to reach a live human being? Does the company sponsoring that website have any idea the damage that it's done to its brand and trust relationships? I'll discuss building trust in greater detail in Chapter 10.

Where do your people come from?

How do people become part of your enterprise? Do you find them or do they find you? Your reputation in the marketplace can be a major attractor. It can be equally damaging to your recruiting efforts. Your reputation in the employment market is built a voice at a time by the people in your organization, your customers, vendors, in fact everyone with whom you and your people interact. The reputation that you have established will determine the type of referrals you'll receive.

We depended heavily on referrals, finding that the strongest people joining the firm learned about us from someone who already worked there. But we also received a great number of referrals from contractors, furniture dealers and manufacturers, product representatives, even building and planning officials.

This network runs circles around any headhunter and makes ads in a paper or trade publication all but useless. Even where recruiting is on a large scale, companies like Cisco Systems rely heavily on internal resources, linking people who express an interest over the Internet with people in their organization at the prospect's peer level to filter and recruit. They figure that people already in their organization are better judges of who will fit and are better able to get someone excited about joining Cisco than an outside resource would be.

Despite the fact that a number of very talented people found their way into Gensler through an ad, we found help wanted solicitations, whether newspaper or Internet based, to be an extremely low productivity channel. Each time we placed an ad in desperation, we were inundated with resumes, each of which required a response of some sort. The yield to an actual interview was minimal and rarely resulted in a hire. Your return on investment will be much higher if you take the time to build a reputation in the marketplace that has people calling you.

If your reputation is strong, the Internet has become an increasingly important channel through which people reach you and learn more about you. In fact, for service-based organizations that don't conduct commerce on the Internet, recruiting may be their website's most important function and yet most Internet sites reveal very little about the personality of the organization or what it's like to work there. Those who understand this principle and design their website accordingly have a noticeably higher yield of applicants, and those applicants are more likely to be consistent with their recruiting profile.

Becoming proactive

Many organizations today depend on universities as important recruiting sources. But the connection is often tenuous, varying from industry to industry. Two decades ago, architecture schools moved away from professor/practitioners to full-time academic faculty, causing a dramatic shift in the attitude graduating students carried as they left school. Suddenly, large firms were represented as bad places where a young professional would be swallowed up and abused, never able to do meaningful work; small firms were good, offering a variety of work experience and more design fulfillment. Ten years ago, the reality had become quite different. Most large firms had begun to offer extensive internship and continuing education programs and often gave young graduates exceptional opportunities early in their careers. Work was often more stable, particularly during the 90s and again today than in a small firm dependent on a handful of small clients where workload had much greater volatility.

We set out on a broad campaign to change that perception by hiring summer interns, giving them a rich and variegated experience during their tenure and then keeping in touch with them after they returned to school. The results in a few short years were astounding. The word of mouth at the schools we focused on yielded long lines at the career day recruiting tables each year, providing us with access to the brightest and best graduates.

It's fascinating how long impressions made during a person's academic career last. When we had a strong need for intermediate professionals in the 90s, we were fighting the word spread to those who graduated in the 80s. Conversely, we benefited greatly from the word that was spread during the 90s to people who now have a decade of work experience and think positively about the firm today.

What they learn about a company in school from first-hand experience or through a friend who had a wonderful intern experience lasts a long time.

The reputation of your organization is built over time, a person and an experience at a time. And people have long memories. So, I'll provide an answer to an earlier question: people find you and will seek you out or reject you according to the reputation you've built.

To understand how proactive you'll need to be, you must answer several questions. How deep is the market? Is it an employer's market or an employee's (who's buying and who's selling right now)? How well trained or experienced is the candidate pool from which you can draw? How much will you have to invest in education and training?

The short-cycle organization is opportunistic, recruiting from what's available with little thought about how it may be shaping its organization in years to come. The long-cycle enterprise takes a long and broad look at these questions, deciding how to expand and deepen the available candidate pool, often investing in educational institutions at an academic level to help shape the curriculum that will deliver more qualified candidates in the future. They spend time with the schools and faculty to assure access to the brightest and best coming out of the academy.

In cases like architecture, the institution involved is at a postgraduate level. But for many organizations where their candidate pool is retraining to respond to new knowledge and technology, the community college has become an exceptionally important place to help shape curriculum and to look for recruits.

Shaping the future

From the beginning, we committed a great deal of time to understanding the market from which we were recruiting. It helped us know where to look and how to be attractive to the candidates we sought. But what was there was there. We could understand it, but we weren't doing much about it. So, I began to take a keen interest in architectural and interior design education. After all, the universities were shaping the candidate pool we would have available to us in the very near term, and, as we looked at the course structure and attitudes about the profession being portrayed by the educators, we realized that we needed to take a hand in shaping our future. By being proactive, we could help improve the quality of candidates we would have available to us within a few short years, and in so doing, we would be a visible positive force for the future in the eyes of the brightest and best in the academy at the moment.

As a member of the American Institute of Architecture's (AIA) Large Firm Roundtable, made up of the CEOs of the 50+ largest architectural firms in the country, I initiated a series of dean's forums, convening a dozen deans of prominent architectural programs and a like number of CEOs from the roundtable to evaluate the alignment (or lack thereof) among education, practice and client expectations. I pulled together a similar program for the deans of a like number of interior design programs through the IIDA. These initiatives described the world into which future professionals would enter. They were highly successful, leading to some important changes in approach and curriculum by a number of institutions.

I offer the following case model for those of you who might want to take a similar proactive position with the channels that will feed your future recruiting market. A couple of years ago, I participated as the keynote speaker at the CCAIA (California Council of the AIA) Educational Summit. The background reading was Lee D. Mitgang's book entitled *Building Community: A new future for architecture education and practice*. Well, I love to read, but I couldn't imagine that this was going to be overly stimulating despite positive reviews by the AIA. After all, the institute has a vested interest, so of course they're going to give it two thumbs up. At the CCAIA meeting, I was asked to present "the challenge" to the participants to help focus the day, I felt obligated to read the book, since I doubted seriously that the movie would ever be made.

Building Community provoked some serious thinking for me about a firm's role in the profession as did a workshop I held to discuss what a group of young professionals in an office would change about their curriculum to better prepare them for real life in a firm. Here are some of the issues that came out and some excerpts of what I said:

How often do you think about why you became an architect? Buckminster Fuller was an inspiration to me as a student. During a lecture, he said something I never forgot: "The old world of architecture was simply self expression. We have the task of making man a success." Much of the profession is still making urban sculptures as opposed to being practitioners of making humanity successful. I think of architecture as an art as well as a craft. Architecture has the ability to both sing for us as an art form at the same time that we create rational, real-life functional places.

What should we do and teach at this time? Can we respond to our changing society fast enough to meet the challenge of making man a success?

Remember, it is not what we as architects want to do but what our clients want to buy that drives what we will be hired to do. Too many architects don't understand that aspect of our profession: that someone has to pay the bills before we can do something of merit. Numerous factors drive the demand for services.

- Demographics: Population growth and composition are keys. Schools ought to teach about demographic shifts.
- Tax laws: In the 80s, tax laws favored office construction. It certainly wasn't a true need for all that office space that drove the glut of construction in our urban cores in the 80s.
- Technology: This drives service demand and should be a major focus of our interest today both in academia and in practice. It is astounding how quickly we are replacing architecture with technology in the places of interaction. I spend a lot more time today interacting through technology by video, audio and data teleconference than I did in a conference room only a few years ago. Many things that I was doing that required space are being replaced by technology.

Now let's talk a bit about the practice of architecture today:

Architecture today is truly a 100 percent leveraged business. What do I mean? There is nothing we do directly as practitioners that actually constructs our work. Most of what gets built is not even fabricated from our drawings; it's completed from shop drawings and submittals based on our drawings but prepared by subcontractors. We don't paint walls; we don't weld steel; we don't pour concrete. We give design drawings and construction specifications to a building industry that documents and fabricates what we design. What are the implications of this process when we as a profession are held 100% accountable for the performance of the resulting building?

We have lost a tremendous amount of influence. A large part of what architects used to do as client representatives has been taken on by other consultants, many of whom were formerly architects. Program management, construction management and other pieces of practice that used to be part of full-service architecture are now provided by others.

We are experiencing a dramatically shortened life cycle of the predictable use of the buildings we make. This shortened life cycle is occasioned by the rapidly increasing rate of change in society's use of the places we create. It is rare that any tenant today wants to lease office space for more than a year or two because of uncertainty about their businesses. This short-cycle principle applies to churches and schools, retail facilities and factories as much as it does to office buildings. This is reducing the perceived value of design to the consuming public. What has value is our ability to cause the design to become a reality more than the design itself. Design is looked at as a short-term commodity, which will change quite often. As a result, in a hyper-competitive environment for services, we are charging fees for the design portions of our work at half the level we charged for equivalent services 10 years ago, even though our costs have increased dramatically. We have become more efficient, but even though the market is good today, we are feeling competition from other deliverers of buildings and spaces: design/constructors and other fabricators of pre-designed buildings that are competitors to architects.

The impact of technology is critical. We are going through an automation of work that is causing another glitch: the loss of connectivity between designers and those who understand the technology of how things get built. It's easy to assemble a credible set of documents without a thorough grounding in construction technology. And these documents are hidden from experienced eyes, those of the seasoned architect who used to look over the shoulder and onto the drawing board of the young practitioner, because they're in a "black box" (or gray or beige as the case may be).

Architecture has become a capital-intensive business. Today each seat represents about a $12,000 investment in hardware, software, network connectivity and training before anyone sits there. Small practitioners are facing this as well, a level of capital expenditure totally unlike when I entered the profession. Yet this technology is now essential to streamline our processes to allow us to meet competitive fee pressures and to deal with the increased complexity in the buildings we make.

Now let's look at the student base upon which our profession will depend in the very near future:

If you look at the AIA membership today, there are about 52,000 architect members of the institute. There are 35,000 students cycling through our architecture schools. Clearly, not all architecture students are going to become architects.

Starting salaries for architects are very low relative to construction tradesmen. The average career aspiration for an architect nationally is generally about the same as a skilled construction craftsman. That's not enough to attract the brightest and best into our profession in the first place, to say nothing of leading the brightest and best from each class into architectural practice. This can only be solved by us as a profession by enhancing the value we provide to our clients to the point that they will compensate us for what we deliver at a higher rate.

We took a brief survey in our office among young practitioners. They experience disillusionment with what they find when they enter the profession. They describe school as a place with all the focus on theory and design; a great opportunity to express themselves to the fullest. When they enter the profession they find time limits. They are told not to explore alternatives; to draw it up and get it out the door; that the client's budget absolutely precludes anything they might want to do. And most importantly they discover that there are only a handful of practitioners whose design talents are strong enough to find roles as designers in firms. While in school, only design was deemed a worthy career path. Real-life practice has meaningful and important roles for construction technologists, project managers and many other roles distinct and different from pure design. They finally begin to ask: "So why did I go into this profession?"

I think we do an enormous disservice to young practitioners by focusing on the theoretical without the constraints of reality; without sharing both the artistic and the craft side of our profession within the curriculum. In no way do I suggest that we should diminish the exploration, theoretically and passionately, of beauty. In fact, we need more theoretical dialogue in the offices, but we also need more reality in the schools: a closer match between the realms of study and practice.

Our young practitioners made a couple of suggestions for modifications to the academic curriculum:

1. Create a studio concept that allows the exploration of theoretical aspiration but at the same time introduces a number of pragmatic sketch studies that replicate what occurs in real practice: "The client just walked in and wants to explore one section of what you are doing a little bit differently with new constraints. You have 48 hours to explore a pragmatic solution." By using the intervention of sketch problems, theory and practice could be mixed in a way that emulates real life practice while exploring broader issues.

2. Add a second critique. How about a second jury of contractors

and engineers who say, "Okay, this is a great idea (no wet blanket comments like: 'we could never build that'), but if we wanted to build this, here is how we would do it. Let's explore together what it would take to make it a reality."

3. Finally, too much work in school focuses on urban form, as place-making for the sake of style and shape, devoid of the rigorous exploration of function (the people and use issues) and context. Too much of the way architecture students are exploring work is based on doing things for the place's sake not for people's sake. If we do not focus on people, we miss the whole point of why we do architecture, why we build buildings.

This relates to the kind of connectivity the Boyer Report suggests with allied professions. We need behavioral classes like sociology and anthropology to help us to be anticipatory of the socialization characteristics toward which society is evolving. It helps us to anticipate the way people are interacting with each other so we can create settings that enhance the kinds of experiences people are having. This has nothing to do with sculptural form but rather with behavioral science. I was taught that designing physical place is more than the creation of shelter; that its purpose is to enhance life. But who measures that?

Let me suggest some changes in the measurement of design success. For too long, architects have gauged success by their own judgment or that of other architects. The Golden Rule (Do unto others as you would have them do unto you) is egocentric. Sounds like Howard Roark from Ayn Rand's *Fountainhead*. If I think it's good, it's good! For architects, I would like to rewrite the Golden Rule so that it says "Do unto others the way that they want to be done unto." This is a completely different way of conceptualizing the success of making architecture.

Today there are five "clients" for the work that we do, each of whom want to be "done unto" in a different way. Success is the reconciliation of each client's goals in a way that makes great design. One is the owner who signs our contract. There is also the user who may not be one and the same as the owner. Of course, the lender must accept the design since none of our clients today pay to construct the things we design out of their own pockets. Then there is the community. Every building is an act of social conscience that enhances or detracts from the aspirations of a community. The judgment of fellow professionals is last. Yes, we want our work to be admired by other architects, but until we satisfy the others, in today's world we will have no building to judge.

We must look at today's marketplace and begin to recast design. We need to look at what our clients value and what they will pay for. We want them to pay for design, but design is what we do. Design comes for free as part of the service, as far as a client is concerned; that's why they came to an architect in the first place. What they pay us for is leadership: leadership within a community, leadership with the lender, the building team or in the client's own organization.

A very simple premise about leadership is "getting to yes." That's what we really get paid for: getting each of these judges of our work, lender, client and community, to say "yes." The building of trust, which is the precursor to someone saying "yes," requires superb communication and leadership skills, our most important asset as professionals.

We need to re-conceptualize our task as leaders of making the built environment to recast and recapture value enhancement for our clients. We will not be compensated well unless and until we are thoughtful leaders of collaboration rather than providers of a plan. This is the only way our insights will have real value. We are not in the business of making plans. We are in the business of leading to a solution. The way we do this is by being a participant and collaborator with our clients, not a doer of drawings. Boyer put this well in the opening of his book: "The future belongs to the integrator."

Our role as individual practitioners and as a firm is to stimulate a dialog that continues to challenge the profession and help to define a strong future for architecture and design as a career and for our society.

If you stood before a group of educators who were producing your future employees, how would you describe the world for which you're designing your business? How would you describe the role you'd like them to play in preparing your future employees? What might you do to elicit their support in delivering truly well-educated future professionals into your marketplace? Long-cycle enterprises are doing that. I spent consistent time over the years delivering this message to the academic community and have found it gratifying to see the changes in recent graduates entering the profession.

Create your profile

Now it comes time to design a recruiting profile. Talent+ (Talent Plus), a firm from Lincoln, Nebraska (more on them in Chapter 7), helped us with ours by interviewing a number of people to determine common characteristics among the most successful members of the firm. Several themes came through loud and clear, both from within the firm and from outside sources that came in contact with us. Our folks were friendly, smart, respectful, courteous and good collaborators. They were technically well grounded, but that wasn't the dominant trait cited. More emphasis was placed on their communication skills and style. What does your profile look like?

About that time, I had read the wonderful book, *Emotional Intelligence*, by Daniel Goleman. I only wish I'd read it when my son and daughter were younger. It proved as beneficial for me in guiding my actions with my kids as it did with shaping the recruiting profile for the firm. This is where I really began to focus on two of the intelligences cited by Goleman, interpersonal and intrapersonal intelligence. The former describes your ability to interact effectively with others, which embraces both speaking clearly and listening with empathy. The latter describes your ability to understand your relative position in a conversation and act appropriately; your situational awareness. Both are incredibly important in any enterprise where the development of deep relationships of trust and "getting to yes" are essential. But, I believe this defines every company today.

The subject of communication in architecture and design is

an interesting one. In the university, students with a great "hand," the ability to communicate well through drawings, are often given great latitude and accolades even if they're not skilled verbal communicators. I watched the results of this attitude as we hired many graphically skilled designers who were poor communicators, and I fought continually against promotion recommendations based strictly on design talent.

I'd watched wonderful design solutions go down in flames because the designer was incapable of making a compelling case to a client in terms that were relevant to that specific client and their circumstances. I'd seen terrific designs be endlessly compromised as the drawings developed in concert with the engineer and contractor teams, the various public review boards and building officials, because the designer was unable to build a collaborative sense of common mission within that broad constituency. This is no different than a story related to me by Talent+ about a music retailer who had hired sales staff based heavily on their knowledge of music, neglecting to filter for their interpersonal skills. They discovered that they had hired a great number of introverts in the process, and, when they changed their hiring criteria to favor extraverts (who also had a good knowledge of music), their sales skyrocketed.

I began to describe the mandate for not just good but great communication skills as a process of getting to "yes." The greatest design in the world, no matter how beautiful it looks on paper, in a model or in a rendering, no matter how "right" it is as a solution to a client's problem, will never become a reality until all sorts of people with different priorities and agendas have said "yes." In a very real sense, architects and designers and most others whose job entails selling a service or product are confronted with more than one client, all of whom must say "yes" before the sale is made, the service is sold or the building is built.

While this is mentioned above, it bears elaboration. Architects have several obvious clients:
• The person who hired you (often filled with high ambitions for the

outcome)
- The lender or financial entity who's paying for it (and their interests may be quite different except perhaps in single-family houses, and, even here it's often the wife who hires the architect and the husband who pays the bills)
- The actual occupants of the place (whose needs and desires are often at great odds with the first two)
- The contractor (who can sandbag you subtly or not so subtly with the first three if he or she doesn't like what you're doing or how you're doing it)
- Regulatory agencies, such as building, fire, planning and health departments (often at odds with one another and rarely sympathetic with the goals of the first four)
- Discretionary review panels, such as a planning commission, architectural review board or city council (who can be easily swayed by vocal citizens with wild ideas about what you should or should not be building, what it should look like and could care less about anyone else)

Make a similar list of the "clients" or "customers" who must say "yes" before a sales transaction can be closed in your business. Each of these constituents, all clients in their own right, has the ability to say "yes" or "no" to a proposed project or purchase. So you can see why building trust through intra- and interpersonal communication skills becomes of paramount importance, not only to architects and designers, but to people in every industry. Your constituencies will differ, of course, but it's likely that the people in your organization are also tasked with reconciling different agendas among a number of people and entities, each of which can help or hinder the progress of your business.

Architects, of course, are a bit masochistic and add a couple of other "clients." Young architects (and even not-so-young architects) stay in touch with their professors who, while they were in the academy, were thought of as Gods. Architects remain concerned about what those professors might think about their design work.

Finally, architects are also very concerned about what their peers think of what they're doing. It's incredibly difficult and frustrating to satisfy each one through a single piece of work because the priorities of each are so different.

In dealing with each of these clients, I use an analogy of becoming "multi-lingual" because, for all practical purposes, each speaks a different language shaped by a different culture. I've told this story over the years to illustrate the point. My children were raised near the San Fernando Valley in southern California where a unique dialect known as "valley talk," made famous through teen movies from the early 80s, became their language of choice with their friends. This concerned me as I listened to the seemingly inane patois coming from the backyard punctuated with filler words such as "umm" and "like" inserted between every other word.

I suggested, much to their embarrassment, that I was going to help them to become bilingual. While I told them that they could speak any language of their choosing with each other and their friends, they were to speak with me and their mother (and other adults, for that matter) in English. They were appalled that I would even suggest such a thing, especially when I told their friends that when they were in our house they had to do the same thing. Fortunately, their friends found it mildly amusing and they all got quite good at it. My son went on to become a molecular biology major, joined a cell phone company doing market research and is an ardent surfer and computer game aficionado. Each of these pursuits has a unique culture and vocabulary, if not language, and with each interest group he's able to speak their dialect, fluently changing from one to the other as the occasion requires.

This, in effect, is what we do when we're trying to get several different clients, all with different dialects and cultural priorities, to say "yes."

Recruiting template

After reviewing this profile, you're ready to create a recruiting template, uniquely suited to your organization and client or customer profile. I developed a series of filters that I've found very effective over the years:

Curiosity: People who are inherently curious will never stop at the immediate or expedient solution. They'll explore further to be sure the course they're pursuing is the best one. In an interview, I always ask a candidate to tell me about a discovery or how they solved a problem in a way they're proud of. I ask them how they got there. The degree to which they're able to describe false starts, dead ends, tells me a great deal about their native curiosity. If they tell me about peripheral learning that took place along the way unrelated to the course they were on but that they were able to use elsewhere at a later date, they've scored big points with me.

Skills versus interests: I'm very concerned about a person's skills, but in an interview, I qualify these carefully. Because someone has done something (learned a process, worked on a particular building type) doesn't mean that they have any particular skill at it. It may be a passing interest or simply something they've been exposed to. Real skills are based not just on experience but on an innate ability connected to a genuine commitment to continue to learn and grow. I want people who are or have the potential to be skilled, not just experienced.

Talent versus passion: I've watched many very talented people perform flatly in an organization, usually because they have no passion, and their talent never fully develops. I look for people who are truly passionate about what they do. It drives them. They lay awake at night thinking about their passions. They pursue their passions even when they're not working. I try to assign people in their areas of passion because I can depend on their relentless pursuit of excellence.

Equal opportunity

Employment laws never drove our recruiting profile. Consistency with the behavioral characteristics of our profile did. We were gender, race and ethnicity blind, not because we were required by the government to submit endless and tedious EEOC forms but because we were always on the lookout for people who fit our profile. More than 50% of our employees were women, and most of our offices looked like the United Nations because we found that passion, integrity and inter- and intra-personal communication skills were not limited to white males.

Changes

Every organization is subject to many forces of change. Let's take a look at a few:

- **Relocation:** People move (or are moved) to different locations in an enterprise from time to time. Such moves may be initiated by the employee for family reasons or a career opportunity, by the company to move a key resource to a more needed location or because of a conflict with a supervisor or other team member. When someone relocates consider carefully the network of relationships that is being dismantled and the impact that will have on the team left behind. Take into account the time frame for the person to reconnect and return to full productivity. All relocations are disruptive in some way. Great long-cycle enterprises invest to minimize the impact on organizational and personal performance.
- **Breaking up teams:** Work groups are established for a variety of reasons—projects of limited duration, work with unique technical requirements and departments with defined charters. But things change. Departments are restructured because of new technology or process change. Assignments come to an end, and people need to be reorganized or reassigned. This is commonly done by simply moving people around on an organization chart. While some consideration may be given to their skills, little is usually given to their relationships with others in the work group or to the outside world. Great value can be achieved by taking these factors into account as reassignments are made.

- **Mergers and acquisitions:** Wholesale additions of a large number of people who have been a part of a different culture represent the greatest challenge. To optimize the performance of the combined enterprise, each person should be thought of as a new hire, profiled as any recruit would be with care given to the alignment of position and teammates with talent, personal characteristics and skills. A program to acculturate each new person to the organization as described in Chapter 7, as if each is being hired into a new company, is a modest investment when compared to the disruption and loss of productivity caused by disorientation when entering a new network. A thorough evaluation of the person's outside network of relationships can yield enormous value. Shedding people who are deemed to be excess to the combined organization should be done based on these factors, not just on reducing body count. With the consolidation in the financial and telecommunication industries in the last decade, we have very few good models to look at. And the loss of value to the combined companies by not investing well in this area has been dramatic.

Saying "goodbye"

While we all like to think that our organization has only great people and that we have been highly selective in our recruiting process, every large organization eventually reaches a normalized distribution of people relative to the population at large. Some are better than others. Each can only perform as well as the way in which their role in the enterprise aligns with their skills, talents, interests and passions. Peter Drucker said years ago when discussing the forthcoming talent shortage that the best people you'll ever have are in your organization right now. So it's fruitless, particularly in large enterprises and particularly if the selection criteria you've employed are consistent with the discussion previously, to imagine that any wholesale change is going to alter your organization's ability to perform. But some individuals just aren't right for your enterprise.

While we all hope that our recruiting filters are working flawlessly, someone you just recruited with great care and welcomed with fanfare isn't going to fit. Patience is valuable; sometimes it takes a person longer to find a comfort in the context of your organization and a pace that works. This is particularly true in organizations with exceptionally strong cultures. But when it's not working, prolonging the relationship is painful to the person involved and poison to the people around. End it quickly and with grace. Use outplacement services, award an appropriate severance amount, but never be remedial. Remember, there is nothing wrong with the person, they just don't fit your organization, and their continued presence will only be toxic to your objectives and theirs.

Your enterprise is the sum of the people in it. Through consistent and continual focus on recruiting and retention according to the characteristics you determine are needed to accomplish your mission, it will become what you design, one person at a time.

Because of the continuing focus on creating an environment that would attract and retain this profile of people, in 2000 Gensler was a recipient of a coveted Best Practices Award as a great place to work from Arthur Andersen, who described Gensler as "the benchmark of its profession and a true learning organization." This didn't hurt our recruiting!

Transform "employees"
into "owners"

Our world has changed in a way we haven't paid enough attention to. Fewer and fewer people join an organization for the money. Money is very low on Maslow's hierarchy of human needs, just above survival. It has to be there and it has to be fair. It's still often a prideful measuring device that a person uses to gauge their progress or their standing relative to their peers, an ego driver somewhat higher on that Maslow pyramid, but far from the most important reasons for engagement with an enterprise.

In countless meetings with colleagues over the years, I've found consistent answers to questions about what makes belonging to an organization compelling. Invariably, people who feel they "belong" express their relationship in ownership terms. In their minds, they "own" the enterprise, take great pride in it and work very hard to keep others from screwing it up. What motivates someone to cross over that invisible line and stop thinking of their place of employment as a job and begin to embrace it as the place in which they are going to build a career? What characteristics of an organization's culture and behavior will cause a person to weather the inevitable "bumps"—a less-than-supportive supervisor, a difficult client or work team experience—and stay the course toward the desired end for a high-value enterprise—long-term continuity of people and the knowledge and network relationships they hold? Granting stock options isn't enough to bring about the pride and commitment of "ownership."

I offer the following based on many years of listening:

Affinity group: People join an organization to be with like-minded people. This is as true of a church group, a club or a softball team as it is of a place of employment. People crave relationships with people they like or, at least, respect. We learned to guard carefully the mix of people in our organization. The old folk wisdom that one rotten apple will spoil the whole barrel is pretty sound. Over time, the stronger the affinity group becomes, the less difficult it is to maintain. Its members form a kind of protective mechanism making life very uncomfortable for someone who doesn't fit in. The quality of fitting in does not mean sameness. People love variety among their colleagues. In fact, differing points of view are necessary and welcome. But a group with strong affinity will not tolerate certain behaviors that are the manifestation of an organization's values. The more the group is allowed to make visible the things that they consider important, the stronger the bond of affinity becomes.

Value system: Where are people learning values as family structures weaken (how many of your friends have relatives in their neighborhoods, let alone have multiple generations living under the same roof), schools are precluded from disciplining students (let alone teaching values or religion in a maddening desire for political correctness), and the church becomes a less-important part of people's lives? Their place of employment takes on that role by default. And with the ignominious collapse of so many major and respected enterprises over the last decade along with corruption in our government, some less-than-stellar values are being modeled. People are inherently looking for a place with consistently understood values modeled by the leaders of the organization. People seek an organization with values consistent with their own or what they'd like them to be. An organization's values can be a sought-after discipline for someone who knows what's right but has been hanging out with the wrong crowd. To the degree those values are deeply embodied in the organization's behavior, people become tenaciously loyal. This characteristic is another self-fulfilling prophecy: the stronger the values are held and lived, the lower the tolerance for deviation from those values will be.

Learning site: The rapid decay of one's ability to carry current knowledge and information caused by accelerating research and development in every industry has made the need for continual learning broadly visible. Your employees understand this. They've seen their friends lose their jobs, realizing they have to return to school in some form to be qualified for a new position because the knowledge and skills they have are decreasing in relevance. Organizations can become as ill-suited for their markets as the people in them, but organizations don't do continuous learning, people do, and it's the people in your enterprise that will keep it vital in your marketplace. The visible commitment to learning is a compelling motivator for a career-oriented professional. The deeper and richer the commitment, the more difficult it is for someone to accept a lesser commitment elsewhere.

Extended family: Whether you like it or not, the people in your organization represent an extended family to each other with bonds going far beyond just being part of an affinity group. With the mobility of our population, many of your employees are living alone or have dysfunctional family relationships. Their workplace becomes a surrogate, becoming the default venue for emotional support in times of crisis, celebration and pride in times of accomplishment. It's happening in your organization anyway. By being sensitive and supportive, you foster these bonds of friendship, binding your employees more closely to your enterprise.

Doing important work: A sense of the importance of the work being done resides at the very top of the chart for what binds a person to your organization. Every company has mundane tasks that just have to get done, but great organizations help each person understand how their task at hand is helping to achieve greatness. An organization that doesn't present its work to its employees as meaningful and important will never achieve deep loyalty and continuity. To the degree that each individual, from receptionist to accountant, secretary to principle, feels that the work in which they are involved is changing the world, the bonds to the organization at all levels become incredibly strong.

So, how does one nurture these factors and accelerate the transition from "employee" to "owner?" By developing a series of structures that bring people into the organization, helping them find their way through its complexity and helping them to accelerate their ability to take advantage of the deep resources available to them. As a person joins your organization, think of three types of relationships they're looking for.

Buddy: Everyone needs a buddy on the day they begin work, preferably a peer who has been with the company for a while and knows where things are, how to get things done, who to go to with daily questions about working here. Since people often join a company as a referral, the person who refers the new employee makes a terrific buddy. Don't try for any particular alignment with work team, studio or whatever the basic organizational unit of your company is. In fact, having a buddy in another part of the organization fosters early relationships beyond the work team and obviates concerns new people have about asking "dumb" questions of people with whom they're working every day.

Coach: Everyone needs a coach throughout their employment. This is a person who has senior knowledge in the area in which the person is working and is expected to provide technical support and direction on the specific tasks being undertaken. It is particularly important for the coach to take the responsibility for helping the new employee to see the relevance of the work they're doing, to impart that sense that the immediate task at hand is meaningful and important. Think of this not just for people in line positions. Who imparts this sense of mission to a new receptionist, secretary or accountant?

Mentor: Everyone should identify and form a relationship with a mentor in the company, someone outside their specific work assignment, someone who represents a level of professionalism and leadership as a role model. Senior members of your company should be expected to help people in your organization to grow by modeling behavior that inspires. Involvement usually means availability for ad hoc advice and participation in career development discussions of some sort.

Such programs seem to be least effective when administered by the human resources group. While this group can be helpful in making sure it happens, such programs gain greater traction when taken on by a group of mid-level staff who show an interest and commitment in creating an environment that attracts and retains great people.

Professional development

Formal employee reviews are usually undertaken once a year following a "performance evaluation" format, reviewing each person's strengths and shortcomings. Something always feels uncomfortable about these conversations, though. Most people, other than human resources professionals, aren't particularly well trained to conduct a constructive review, and most of us, reviewer and employee alike, usually find ourselves squirming or procrastinating. I certainly dreaded annual reviews, usually feeling awkward and under-prepared to provide meaningful feedback on how someone was performing.

My readings over the years brought me a different point of view, a simple concept really: each person has a unique set of talents as well as some areas in which they're not so strong—in their words, "aces and spaces." Goleman's *Emotional Intelligence*—explores the correlation between success and different intelligences than those normally tested in IQ tests and the SAT: alpha-numeric and linguistic. He reinforces the concept that if you work on things for which you have a natural predisposition, your intelligence in that area will grow. If you work very hard on things for which you aren't particularly well disposed, you'll improve, but not much.

This idea really resonated for me, making me realize that I was turned around on the whole performance evaluation protocol. It was, by its nature, remedial. It focused on what was wrong with a person's performance, what needed to be corrected or improved upon. No matter how many praises were offered, the lasting memory was always of the criticism. I came to realize that if people were working in areas about which they were truly excited, they would excel, growing at an incredible rate. By trying to force them to improve in areas where they were weak, we often just discourage them and rarely get much improvement.

There is a caveat, of course. People do have areas of weakness or blind spots that they must recognize. But this shift in point of view allows you to move from remedial to constructive conversations about how to team each person with another who possesses complementary strengths. This means moving toward work assignments and teaming relationships that allow each individual to work with greater passion as well as fostering a higher level of respect for a teammate with different but complementary capabilities.

By changing your approach to annual reviews from "performance evaluation" to "professional development," reviewers enter the discussions without the anxiety they've previously had. Conversations become much more constructive with the reviewer's directive to identify assignments, continue education or be involved in a company-wide activity that focuses on an individual's passions and talents.

Like many processes in large organizations, a form is involved. But don't just relegate the design of this form to your human resources team. Make sure they involve representatives in your organization from among those conducting the reviews as well as those being reviewed. Forms don't shape careers, but this one and the process that you follow are your way of focusing attention on individual professional goals and what you and others in your organization can do to support them. The process should be heavily oriented toward a person's goals and passions, offering guidance on strategies to achieve them. It's an opportunity for an employee to find an advocate or two in your organization who can help them achieve their goals through the selection of work assignments and guidance in and support for continuing education.

Evaluating senior recruits

You may want to consider using an outside firm to profile potential senior recruits, helping you to determine the "fit" with your organization. We used a firm, Talent+, that employed in-depth evaluation of a rather lengthy telephone interview that became a valuable tool to help guide our hiring decision and to help us fit the new person better and more quickly into the firm. Talent+, brought us two distinct ideas that I find valuable to this day:

- A talent is a natural ability not acquired through effort. A person with talent for a particular job receives intrinsic satisfaction when his or her talents are being maximized. It results in spontaneous behavior on the part of the individual. Talent can be cultivated to achieve near-perfect performance.
- Be true to your strengths; have strategies for your weaknesses.

Remembering that each individual has different talents, it's important to use these tools to improve "fit" and cast people into roles in which they can succeed and grow, not as a "yes/no" filter or a template to obtain sameness. The only issue we watched closely for was integrity, our only "go/no-go" qualifier with a potential recruit.

At a point in time, since these profiles were kept very confidential, I heard concerns being voiced about whether an individual's career might be adversely affected by these interviews. Anything held in confidence creates a risk of speculation about its use. Nothing could have been further from the truth. They were and remain a highly valued tool to help the firm guide a person to perform to their highest level, but I felt it important enough to stress to the firm that the results were used as one piece of information in hiring, promotion and new assignments. We used these profiles as an ongoing career development tool to help in defining a job description and pairing with other team members with complementary talents that took best advantage of a person's natural talents and most enhanced that person's potential for growth.

Following this course leads to the development of a "strengths-based organization," a term used by The Gallup Organization in *Now, Discover Your Strengths* by Marcus Buckingham and Donald Clifton. The methodology they've developed also yields a profile, one which if shared in an organization fully versed in their vocabulary, can provide each individual and those with whom they work a tool to cast people into roles in which they excel and team them with people who complement their strengths.

Generalist vs. Specialist

Every professional worries at a point in time about the direction their career is taking. Am I being forced to become too specialized? Will this limit my horizons for growth or make me unemployable if the demand for my area of specialization dries up? In architecture and interior design particularly, professionals resist being "type-cast," seeking broad variety in project assignments. Law and medicine have made better progress in making a specialist career path desirable, but many organizations face the same dilemma of a population that wants to remain generalists, dabbling in whatever catches their fancy, in a market that demands highly skilled specialists.

Customers and clients have a strong desire to work with specialists—true world-class experts in the fields you pursue. It takes a deep passion and commitment to become a world-class expert; not many people in any profession have done so, and I've often wondered why. In architecture and design schools, we were all exposed to numerous opportunities through our design studios to experience a variety of project types. And, variety is fun—the spice of life, they say. So when young architects and designers enter the profession, they resist specialization, fight against being pigeonholed when they learn to do something well.

I've sat through many lengthy career counseling discussions with young professionals, listening to them complain about not being given an opportunity to do something different. I've been told, "I feel like I've got to quit and be rehired to get an opportunity to do something new."

For a young professional, I won't underrate the value of gaining broad experience, particularly in all phases of the work at hand. In the case of architecture, the AIA's Intern Development Program requires certification by employers prior to sitting for the licensing examination that the applicant has spent time in all phases of architecture, from design through construction documents and into the field. In fact, the most valuable experiences may be on the jobsite, talking to the subcontractors who build what we draw, learning from them how to communicate your design intent clearly.

This is an unvarnished prod to everyone in every type of business to get into your factories, your stores, your outside vendors' shops, in fact to immerse yourself in every component of what it takes to bring your product or service to your customer, no matter what your role in the organization. And don't just poke around, admire the work they're doing, and have a cup of coffee with the person in charge. Talk to the men and women who are a part of making your business happen for your customer. Ask them what is working and what isn't. Ask for their suggestions about how to improve what you, and your enterprise does.

But my topic is specialization, the pursuit of a subject or piece of your business with the energy, passion and commitment that leads to a reputation of being a world-class expert. There was a time in most businesses when an individual could actually know enough to do a credible job of most every aspect of the business in which the enterprise was engaged. The world changed. With the imposition of complex regulations, technologies and processes, every business has become a team sport, made up of specialists, just as with a basketball or soccer team. And just as in these sports, you wouldn't expect a completely competent soccer goalie to be much use as a guard on a basketball team even though they're fundamentally trying to do the same thing. The same is true in medicine where we've migrated from the country doctor who tended to every need in the community, including a little veterinary medicine on the side, to a world of specialists. Do you want a podiatrist doing heart surgery?

As an enterprise, your clients and customers will increasingly come to expect your people to be focused professionals, capable of delivering world-class expertise uniquely suited to their specific issue. In architecture, that means the team delivering an airport is going to have an entirely different set of skills and body of knowledge than a team delivering a hospital or a law office. It also means that, to be successful as a professional, sooner or later you'd better focus on a small number of topics in which you truly become an expert. With all due respect to the natural desire to proclaim the ability to do anything, let's face it, there just aren't a lot of Thomas Jeffersons around.

So, while it's important for each of us to respect and have a working knowledge of a broad number of building types and the processes involved in designing them, it is unreasonable to proclaim one's self an expert in all. Be a Renaissance person in your interests, but make sure you are an expert in something. Dedicate the time, passion and curiosity to one or two things that make you sought after as a professional.

Think about it. What are individuals in your enterprise known for? Who seeks their council, knowledge and wisdom, and for what, both inside the company and from outside? As people grow as professionals, encourage them to commit to one, maybe two subject areas. If they haven't developed a serious focus, it's time to help them get serious, to pursue their passions and let others know what they are. When the environment in your enterprise encourages people to do so, they embrace their relationship with your organization as a career. When they see others around them doing the same, the "employee" relationship is not enough, they want to be "owners."

Transparency

I can't overstate the importance of transparency in designing a business. Isolating people in an organization from the structural processes by which it operates leads to random questioning about why things get done. It creates a "we/they" atmosphere, relegating people to a utilitarian role as "employees" as opposed to "owners." While the time spent to make the working systems of an enterprise visible may seem excessive, it clearly makes people feel more positively disposed toward why actions are taken.

We spent a great deal of time openly explaining our financial systems and how money was spent to operate the firm; about human resources issues, hiring, benefits and all of the legal matters surrounding employment; about issues relating to contracts and insurance; and about marketing and public relations efforts. It reminded me of the concept of "Federalism" where each of our teams had a great deal of autonomy and authority over the resources they applied and the methods they used to deliver top-quality service to their clients. And yet they benefited through access to and support from a broad array of highly specialized, world-class services that even the smallest practitioner needs to operate a business today. The size of your enterprise provides the leverage to get the very best services at a very small incremental cost per transaction. But if the people in your organization can't see it, they won't appreciate it, and they won't use it well and wisely to support your customers.

Career orientation

We came to understand that the market drivers for our type of business benefited tremendously from long and deep relationships. If you find the same answer, want value to grow over time and want your people to migrate from "employees" to "owners," they must begin to think of their relationship with your enterprise as a "career." The continuity of their relationship with your organization benefits both you and them. You build embedded wisdom of great value to your customers through the leverage of their increased knowledge and relationships; they build deeper knowledge and skill and are able to leverage their network of relationships to increase their value and, therefore, their earning power.

I watched many mergers and acquisitions over the years. The primary focus always seemed to be financial terms, real estate issues and process consolidation to achieve increased efficiency, often accompanied by wild-eyed projections for market dominance. Most ignored the source of real value to their customers: the people in the enterprises being merged or acquired and the relationships they had with each other and the outside world.

Much of what you'll read in this book follows this theme. High-value enterprises have realized that their business strategies must look far past the next quarter to continuity of personnel for their knowledge, wisdom, and relationships, allowing them to do the work of your enterprise effectively and productively. That continuity only comes about if people feel that they have a career—not just a job, not just long-term guaranteed employment, but a commitment to the purpose that your company and the people in it represent.

On careers

During the 90s, most companies were hiring at a frantic pace. I had a significant concern that turnover might grow despite all the programs and the culture we had so carefully crafted to encourage a career orientation among our employees. Many of the people who were joining us, the brightest and most talented young professionals we'd ever seen, were expressing a restlessness after a year or two of employment. They carried so much knowledge that had high value to our clients. I began talking to people throughout the firm about what a career looks like.

On August 4, 1999, I reached my 30th anniversary with Gensler. I checked our employee roster at the time and discovered that one-third of the people in the firm were born after I started work in 1969. I guess you could, therefore, call my time at Gensler a "career." This caused me to reflect on what a career had meant to me at various stages along the way.

When I began there were a handful of people in the firm. We were doing a great deal of tenant planning, a large apartment complex in Newport Beach, a building for MasterCard and a few other wildly eclectic projects like Boom Trenchard's Flair Path Restaurant in San Diego (a bottle of wine to the first person who knows who Boom Trenchard was or what a Flair Path is without looking it up on the Internet).

It was a zesty time, I was 25, and thoughts about my career didn't take up a lot of my attention span, which was a lot more limited in those days anyway. I was hungry to learn and found lots of people around me who were more than generous with their time and knowledge. Somewhere, lurking in the back of my mind, however, was a nagging sense that I was supposed to either be with a larger, more prominent firm (read Skidmore Owings and Merrill in those days) or get out on my own as quickly as I could get my license. Incidentally my friends who were with SOM thought they should be with a smaller firm where they would have a broader opportunity to experience more facets of putting a project together or be on their own. And of course, those who were on their own envied the rest of us our steady, predictable income and our vacation time. Thus, my first observation about a career was that when you're young, the grass always looks greener somewhere else, and you're always in hurry to get somewhere other than where you are right now.

I guess I figured that out pretty quickly and decided since I was in a firm that, although of only moderate size in those days, had some pretty well informed "gray-hairs" who were willing to help a naïve kid who wasn't particularly shy about asking questions about things I knew nothing about. And when I asked, they didn't treat me like a fool (unlike many of my professors). Besides, I really liked the people with whom I worked. Since I asked a lot of questions and seemed to assimilate things fairly quickly, I kept being given increasing responsibility and more complex assignments. So, my second observation was: those that didn't ask didn't learn and didn't get very challenging assignments. If you let people around you know you'll always check before proceeding when you don't know something, you'll be perceived as responsible and be given more opportunity. If you try to fake it and stub your toe, you hurt your credibility and get relegated to more mundane tasks.

That didn't mean that I was relieved from detailing toilet rooms, pasting up presentation boards or coloring up a space plan many times along the way. In fact, to this day I still "wash windows" if that's what's required. My third career observation: you develop your personal "brand" through simple gestures, like picking up a paper in the hallway, cleaning up after your meeting or pitching in to help someone else trying to finish an assignment, just as much as you do by the work tasks you perform.

When I got my license, started a family, and bought a house with a rather substantial mortgage, the first signs of early career crisis began to haunt me: that sense of being trapped. Not that I particularly wanted to, but if I had wanted to, could I really go out on my own with the obligations I had taken on? Was I "stuck"? I really had no complaints. I was continuing to learn and grow. But that nagging sense that I had foreclosed an option kept cropping up. And then, every so often, I'd screw something up, have a fee overrun or miss a program function on a plan and have one of those embarrassing moments with a client. I would invariably have a nightmare a few days later that I had been fired and was out on the street looking for a job.

And then, every once in a while, something about the firm or someone in it would really annoy me. I would stew and steam and decide that it was time to explore other options (time to dust off and update the resume and go visit SOM again—after all, that was the pinnacle of desire for young architects in those days). Somehow, patience always prevailed, and I would conclude that the people I was working with were incredibly supportive. I could go somewhere else, but in the long run, it would only be different, not necessarily better. Besides I'd have to rebuild the wonderful support system I'd developed that helped me do what I did so well with clients.

My fourth observation is that you can usually accomplish whatever it is you want to do where you are. Moving will probably slow you down. You just have to change your outlook from one of dwelling on the obstacles (a really easy trap to fall into when you're frustrated) to looking for the opportunities.

It took about 20 years for me to realize the benefits of career continuity. As much as anyone (my father included) tried to tell me about the importance of long-term relationships, this sage counsel fell on deaf ears. But, a few years ago, the fact that I had spent a long time in one enterprise, with great continuity with the people in the organization and with a body of clients, consultants, contractors and vendors began to have a value beyond my wildest imagination. The leverage of my ability to get things done because I can call on someone I may not have seen for many years who will help me because of the relationship we've developed is remarkable. The value of continuity is extraordinary. Old-timers in many organizations will echo my experience. Then spend some time with someone who's moved around a great deal in his or her career. Compare the response.

My fifth observation should be clear. I'm a strong advocate of building a career in one place with people you trust and like. I advise people if you haven't found that yet, move on until you do. But once you find it, invest heavily, be patient and grow your career along with those around you. Do you feel comfortable giving that advice in your enterprise?

Keeping in touch with those that leave

I can't leave the subject of deeply engaging people in your enterprise without a mention of those who leave. And they do, from time to time, for good and valid reasons—their spouse was transferred to another location, they were unhappy with what they were doing, they had a conflict with the person under whose direction they were working. How do people leave? Are they gone and forgotten?

We were meticulous about conducting exit interviews. It's

imperative that the departing employee speak with someone with whom they'll be completely candid and that the leaders of your organization review the responses. You'll learn some fascinating things about what's going on in your organization. But, if it's a fundamentally sound place to be and the characteristics described at the beginning of this chapter are well embodied, there is a lingering bond that you will want to nurture.

Rather than turning our backs on prior employees as having been somehow disloyal by leaving, we kept in touch through newsletters or other communications. Over the years, we found that former employees often learned that the grass was not so much greener somewhere else; that the friendships and history were deep. Particularly, those who felt powerless to change what was bothering them discovered that the same complaint existed elsewhere, and it wasn't easy to change things there either.

We encouraged people to return, finding that those who did became the most loyal and committed members of the firm. If they had been reluctant to speak up before, they found their voice about things they wanted to improve and often became strong leaders in the areas that interested them the most. We created a recognition for them, a red boomerang emblazoned with the date of departure and the date of return (a few boomerangs had more than one set of dates). At any given time, about 10% of the firm had red boomerangs proudly displayed above their desks, a tribute to the connectivity with the deeper reasons why someone moves from being an "employee" to being an "owner."

Construct Compensation, Benefit and Advancement Programs to Encourage a Career Orientation

n Chapters 6 and 7, I discussed the soft side of why people want to be a part of an organization and how to make them feel like owners. The mechanics of compensation, reward, benefit and advancement programs may support or conflict with these objectives, working best when carefully designed with a common philosophy and alignment.

Long-cycle enterprises have learned that longevity, stability and continuity of the people and their networks are key value factors in accomplishing their objectives. High turnover means not only the loss of an individual and their unique skills and talents, but also the loss of their tacit knowledge of how to get things done and the network relationships inside and outside the organization that lets them do it.

It's also expensive, including the cost of recruiting, training and reduced productivity which, in high-knowledge work enterprises, can be as long as six months to a year. The costs had never been quite so clear to me until we worked with a call center operator who was experiencing high turnover. Their average longevity was just over seven months. We proposed a few management ideas with our design solution, suggesting that through design of both space and process we could improve longevity. The client was skeptical and had never considered their employees as much more than a commodity with the costs associated with recruiting and training just part of the cost of the business they were in. After a year in the new space incorporating the changes we proposed, longevity went up to 11 months. To us this seemed like an abysmal failure. To the client, recruiting and training costs were slashed by one-third, a value that exceeded the entire cost of the new facility.

So how do you use compensation, reward, benefit and advancement programs to augment the shift in attitude of people in your organization from "it's just a job" to "this is my career?" To engage people in a career path, each of these personnel programs must be carefully designed and integrated, with the philosophy, reasoning and mechanisms made openly visible. Nothing undermines the best of intentions in compensation, reward, benefit and advancement programs more than a veil of mystery and the speculation that follows.

Compensation

Compensation never motivates; it only satisfies or de-motivates. While it would be the rare individual who would say "no" to more money, people think of their salary primarily in terms of fairness. Am I being paid appropriately for the effort I'm making, the level of skill I have and the level of risk I'm taking? People are aware of the market for their qualifications and the effort expected. They seem to find out quickly what others in the organization are being paid no matter how confidential you try to keep this information. They will gauge their efforts and qualifications relative to their peers and expect to be compensated fairly. While I have certainly experienced plenty of greed and a good deal of delusional behavior, by and large I've found that most people are quite satisfied, at least at the direct salary level, if they feel that their base compensation is fair.

They will factor other issues into that gauge of fairness. The relative stature of the organization plays a big role. Larger companies and those that are deemed to be financially successful are expected to pay above the market whereas start ups and smaller organizations may still be considered fair at lower levels of compensation if employees feel that they have a stake in the future and will be rewarded if their efforts help the organization to become successful. They will also make allowances for enterprises that are engaged in work they consider to be extremely important to society or to their career.

Gender and ethnicity are core issues of fairness for long-cycle organizations. Since people do find out about each other's salary, tolerance for inequity is low, damaging both those being underpaid as well as those overpaid. People in long-cycle organizations are particularly responsive to equity relative to gender and ethnicity, responding well to merit and performance-based evaluation for compensation.

Practice varies greatly regarding compensation for hours worked versus a monthly salary. At one end of the spectrum are unionized organizations with strict rules about pay for hours, multiples of pay for overtime and other work rules. At the other end, professional firms may compensate on a monthly salary basis, expecting effort to be expended, appropriate to the work needing to be done, irrespective of hours actually spent on the job. The federal government has stepped in with rules governing "exempt" and "non-exempt" job descriptions, defining what type of work can be compensated on a salaried basis and what must be compensated at an hourly rate plus overtime beyond certain daily or weekly limits. But these are mechanical issues and allow a range of choices to be made to design a strategy that meets the employees' perception of fairness.

At Gensler, we employed a variation that seemed to work well for design professionals. Most design firm employees function at a professional level qualifying them as "exempt" from overtime at a multiple of their hourly rate past federal limits. Since much of the work involves careful accounting of time for billing purposes and performance measurement against fixed fees on assignments, we asked people to account for the hours they worked. This can also be a good strategy for organizations that aren't time driven relative to some mandate like client billings as it allows for measurement of work effort expended against budgets created. But be careful that people don't lose that "do whatever it takes to satisfy the customer" attitude, being driven instead to meet time budgets.

We found it important to recognize that at various points in a career, a person's ability or willingness to work more or less intensively varies a great deal. Early in the history of the firm and unusual for an architectural practice, we employed many women in senior professional roles and found that their family situations periodically demanded more time. We felt that a direct salary comparison based on experience and capability had to be tempered by the number of hours worked. We felt that paying the same amount on a monthly basis to someone who was willing and able to productively work 50 to 60 hours in a week versus someone whose personal situation limited their commitment to 40 hours or less was simply unfair. To expect the same commitment of long hours (when needed) of everyone uniformly would drive very capable and talented people away from the firm, so we made a decision to pay for hours worked. This was deemed a fair response to varying lifestyle situations, relieving pressure on those who felt they couldn't get ahead without committing long hours.

Today as we've moved through generations X and Y, this is no longer a women's issue, and this strategy allows an organization to accommodate a variety of lifestyle choices, retaining talent even if it means accommodating a part-time commitment, while meeting a test of fairness in compensation. Making this practice openly visible brings comments like "why am I working so hard while that person comes in at nine and goes home at five" to a complete stop.

When recruiting, compensation commitments are made in a competitive market. If times are good, salary demands are high, and to bring in key talent, salaries are often paid that are above current compensation at a peer level in the organization. Conversely, when times are tough, people are often hired well below peer levels. Neither is fair and, with the transparency that usually exists about salary, will cause dissent if not addressed over time. During the period of rapid inflation in the 70s and 80s, we adjusted salaries twice a year. Inflation allowed us to bring things to parity relatively quickly. From the 90s forward we've had low inflation. Annual salary reviews make these kinds of parity adjustments very difficult, especially since we've also all experienced both competitive and not-so-competitive hiring markets, creating some real inequities.

Few other issues can be as disruptive to an organization. To build a culture of trust and fairness, the leaders of the organization must respond, adjusting under-compensated people upward and over-compensated people downward or at least holding salary increases until alignment can be achieved. As tough as conversations about salary are, only an open discussion of the underlying need to maintain fairness and merit will build long-term satisfaction with your compensation program.

Blanket percentage salary increases, while seeming fair to some, particularly in inflationary times, ultimately are deemed unfair by most. People want to know that their compensation is a reflection of their merit and career growth. A general percentage salary increase will be discounted by everyone. As an employer, you receive no benefit. Each person will see only the increase above that amount as a true raise.

As rapidly as all businesses are changing, people must be adding new knowledge and skills to their repertoire every day just to stay even, so I favor, no matter what the rate of inflation, a zero-based approach to compensation adjustment forcing a candid conversation with each person in the organization concerning what they've accomplished to sustain their current value to themselves, their customers or clients and the enterprise they're a part of along with what they've done to increase that value.

Reward

People seek both financial and non-financial rewards. The "atta-boys," pats on the back and especially recognition in front of peers are enormously important in building an effective reward program. Non-financial rewards must be delivered consistently to build a sense of career orientation. It's simply another hygiene issue. You and the people in your organization must be constantly vigilant about saying "thank you," about taking a moment to stop what you're doing to look someone in the eye and tell them what a great job they've done and how important it is to the organization, the team or to what you're doing for your customers.

Reminding people to make this a habit is not just the job of the leadership. It can come laterally and from below. A peer complimenting a peer or a subordinate recognizing their superior is just as important as more traditional forms of recognition. Recognition forms a virtuous cycle. People love to know they've done something well and, if told often, will begin to look for opportunities to praise others. The more visible you make it, the more people will do to achieve recognition. Make it part of the culture of your enterprise. You'll be astounded at how quickly the attitudes about money change.

While formal recognition and reward programs are never as reinforcing as a direct comment at the moment of accomplishment (in fact big presentations embarrass some people), they are nevertheless important. They are best, and the potential for discomfort to those who are simply shy about public recognition is reduced, when they become traditions, almost formal ceremonies. Make them fun. Use enormous amounts of humor. Take the accomplishments, not yourself, seriously. And use them as teaching moments, always using the recognition being given to define the broader reasons why that accomplishment furthers the mission of the enterprise and your customers or clients. Describe why the thing that's been done is helping to make the world a better place.

But all the recognition in the world won't replace the desire for financial reward for performance. Nor, frankly, should it. If the recognition is based on reality, your organization is doing well financially, and people expect to share that success. So how do you structure financial rewards in the form of performance recognition? What behaviors do you want to encourage or discourage through the way financial rewards are arrived at and presented?

Some organizations focus on individual reward such as a commission on sales. Long-cycle enterprises are highly interdependent and less transactionally focused with people's combined accomplishments contributing to financial success. And long-cycle enterprises, by definition, can't measure results by the individual, by week, month or quarter, since so much of each person's activity over a long period of time is building the value that yields year-in/year-out positive financial contribution.

The secretary, receptionist and bookkeeper have deep tacit knowledge and network relationships that allow the company to profit, allowing the more visible members of the organization to perform effectively. Developing a deep career orientation for them is as important as the salesperson or, in the case of an architectural firm, the designer who can't function without the infrastructure others provide. A long-cycle enterprise celebrates the complementary character of each person's contribution in the structuring of financial rewards.

The Federal Government provides vehicles to defer taxes to individuals on certain types of income through defined profit-sharing, ESOP (Employee Stock Ownership Plan) and 401k programs. The commonly used 401k vehicle allows an individual to put an amount, limited to a percentage of their total annual income defined by the Federal Government, into a tax-deferred investment account. The employer is allowed to match a percentage or all of that investment out of the pre-tax profits of the company.

We formed a 401k plan to allow our employees to make such investments but did not offer any matching funds, choosing rather to provide a participation in the profits of the firm through profit sharing and ESOP plans. The reasoning was straightforward. The amount contributed by an employee to a 401k plan is discretionary by the individual with higher-income earners tending to contribute more, so matching amounts would tend to distribute funds from the profits of the firm disproportionately to those making higher contributions (higher-wage earners or those whose circumstances allowed them to save more). You also commit your company to make the matching grants no matter how high or low the profit is in a given year.

Instead, we opted to provide a share of our profits each year to all employees, based on a percentage of their total annual income. These funds were dispersed into a profit-sharing and an ESOP program, allowing us to recognize each person's contribution to the aggregate profitability of the firm proportionately with their total annual income. Profit-sharing and ESOP funds are treated similarly to a 401K by taxing authorities, deferring taxation on these investments until a future date. Our profit-sharing plan and the investments in it were managed by a third party and invested in high-grade securities and bonds. In the 35 years the plan consistently outperformed the benchmark markets we set for our investment advisor, a strong testimony to the care we took in guiding the investment strategy and far better than most people's 401K investments faired.

We formed an ESOP as a method to purchase a portion of the founding shareholders' interests and to provide true company ownership to everyone in the firm. We did this on a cash basis, purchasing shares in the firm only as cash from profits was available. It was not a leveraged liquidity event for the founders as many ESOPs have been, leaving the enterprise saddled with debt. Our strategy was to invest in the ESOP when prospects for the firm's shares were favorable and to invest in the profit-sharing plan when its prospects were better. Over the years, the increase in value of the firm's shares exceeded the value increase in our profit sharing plan. These are great statistics when they're positive. They can be a disaster when they don't perform. While they can instill a powerful sense of ownership, they should only be undertaken if you're willing to invest the time and care to manage them well—especially the value of your own stock!

Long-cycle enterprises give visibility to the process of where the profits of a company go, how much money is available for rewards, where it comes from and how it is allocated. We reported our financial results for the fiscal year, made contributions to the ESOP and profit-sharing plans and paid a performance bonus in mid-June of each year following the principles outlined above.

Our approach to performance bonuses deserves particular mention. While some minor adjustments to an office's bonus pool were made to reflect that office's performance, by and large we treated the bonus pool as a single fund for the entire firm rather than as separate pools for individual work groups, staying with our philosophy that interdependence and sustained action over a long period of time was what generated profits in any given year. Individual bonuses were then adjusted up or down for exceptional (or poor) performance that could be singled out in this context.

Highly profitable offices subsidized less-profitable work groups in any given year. While we had many discussions over the years as to the inherent fairness or lack thereof in this approach, the argument that over the long cycle a team may do well for a few years and poorly in other years was proven by the historical data, and any reward structure that pitted one group against another for a larger share of bonus funds would conflict with our objective of being a "one-firm firm," a single enterprise across multiple geographies and practice areas. It was most important that people understood the objectives for bonus award, and that care was given to how we assured that those objectives were assessed consistently across the firm.

In a presentation to the staff we always started with a discussion of how the retained earnings of the firm were going to be spent. After all, these were funds that were taken out of the bonus pool. On the investment side of the ledger in a particular year, we added substantially to the technology resources that supported the work of the firm and added cash reserves to cover the increases in our receivables. It was important that people understood that each new person we added got paid on the first and 16th day of each month. We sent bills to our clients during the following month and, on the average, received payments from our clients 45 to 50 days later. In order to avoid borrowing money to meet payroll or pay rent and other obligations, we operated in a very conservative fashion: we kept enough money in the firm to cover this time lag. So when I told people we were adding to our cash reserves, I made it clear that this didn't mean there is cash sitting in a bank somewhere. It was in our clients' banks (we hoped).

Covering this time delay between paying our bills and receiving payment from customers or clients is a cost of doing business. The people in your organization need to know this. Some companies borrow money to finance this lag (incurring "debt"), some raise capital in the way of ownership investment by outside third parties (selling "equity") to raise capital for this requirement. We elected to do it the old-fashioned way: we earned it and added it to our reserves to fund our growth. We made it clear that this was good news for our employees as stockholders: it built the value of each of the shares they held through their ESOP, and, because we didn't carry debt, the value of those shares was more secure. You need to create your own story, but you need to demystify where the money goes, particularly as a large organization. The numbers are just so big that they overwhelm most people.

For us, the stability and financial soundness told a story that the direction for the firm, the work it will do and investments it will make are determined by people in the firm, not by third-party investors concerned with the short-term return on their investment versus the long-term good of the enterprise.

In October of each year, Art Gensler and I delivered a more detailed financial review of the firm and a mid-year report of financial performance to the vice presidents followed by a circuit of the offices to deliver the same report to the entire staff. As participants in the ESOP, all members of the firm were shareholders, and this constituted an annual report. This level of discussion of the finances of a firm to every employee is highly unusual but delivered an incredible benefit, demystifying the workings of a very large organization and giving everyone in the firm a framework for the daily decisions that they made to positively affect the firm's performance, and by extension, their own financial reward.

How would a person in your organization describe your bonus or reward system and structure? This transparency relieved enormous pressure about money and, I later found, squelched the backroom chatter about what "they" were doing with the money the firm made.

During the 90s with the extraordinary and frequent publicity about individual compensation and reward programs during the dot. com boom, questions arose about individual versus team reward. As clearly as we thought we had made the case for the "one-firm firm," long-cycle revenue recognition and the contribution of many people over a long period of time to achieving success, the marketplace was telling our people otherwise. At the height of the dot. com boom, people were asking about performance measurement for individual and team reward. Having frequently referenced books like *High Performance Teams: How to Make Them Work* by Marc Hanlan and *The Wisdom of Teams: Creating the High-Performance Organization* by Jon R. Katzenbach and Douglas K. Smith, I had to address this concern following an open inquiry in our monthly newsletter from a young man who was both an architect and a business school graduate and whose peers in high-tech companies were rattling his cage.

I responded that we had several reward systems that recognized both individual and team performance. The most visible was our bonus program. Many individual high-performance teams in the firm saw direct and significant reward through direct bonus. The next was our profit-sharing and ESOP programs through which everyone in the firm participated in the larger construct of a great, big high-performance team by sharing in the profits of the firm at large. Finally, because of direct stock ownership, everyone benefited from the performance of the firm by realizing the appreciation of the value of their shares, reflecting the high performance of the firm.

We avoided more specific and focused reward programs for individuals and teams because we felt the nature of our business required broad collaboration across the enterprise to achieve success for our clients. Often, a serendipitous interaction with someone who is not involved directly with a project can lead to the innovation that sets the team on a true high-performance track. In other words, it's being part of the whole enterprise with the richness of its resources that allows teams to perform at peak levels.

A further consideration is the long duration of our relationships with clients. Projects and relationships don't have tidy finish points where performance can be neatly measured and rewarded. To recognize selling a job, making a brilliant design presentation or getting a set of construction documents into the contractor's hands within a tight deadline incrementalizes a profession in which the longer relationship with a client, the full engagement with their business enterprise and the ability to provide thoughtful leadership through many minefields over a long period of time are the performance qualities that have value to our clients. It's just not the same as getting a product to market or publishing a new computer game. So we kept our reward systems to components that placed a premium on broad participation, shared innovation and commitment to our clients' long-term goals.

I believe that as more companies develop deeper and longer engagements with their customers, they'll need to adopt a similar strategy.

Benefits

Beyond compensation and reward is a series of benefits that don't show up on people's W-2 form such as health, dental and vision care, vacation and sick leave, continuing education, support for licensing preparation and examination, participation in professional societies and policies about things like family leave and same-sex partner health care coverage. In all cases, to encourage a career orientation as a long-cycle organization, you need to set policies that treat people like a family. In a family, people support the family's common and individual mission and goals (things like educational objectives and career growth), care for each other, particularly in a time of crisis, with concern and consideration but still needing to meet the family budget. This requires that decisions be made in the open about what programs will be put in place, giving everyone in the organization an understanding of how and why the program was designed the way it was and what the budget constraints are that make your benefits program such a difficult balancing act.

Each of these kinds of decisions deserves your utmost care and consideration. The people in your organization are thinking about it. By involving an interested cross-section of your staff in the discussions and then letting them know why you've elected to follow the path you've chosen, you can relieve pressure spots before they become major causes. I'll make note only of health care as in today's explosive medical cost environment, the design of health, dental, prescription drug and vision care programs is an exceedingly tender subject. Decisions about HMO versus PPO type coverage, sharing of cost responsibility through co-payments for treatment, prescription drugs and what services are covered can have a major impact on an individual's cost of living. To the company, these costs are wildly variable by age group, family structure and other risk factors—way too much detail for the people in your organization to absorb. They're really interested in "how much is this going to cost me?"

Health care coverage, particularly, is renegotiated frequently and requires the most conversation and clarity within the enterprise to achieve a common understanding about why a particular approach was selected and why it should be accepted as "fair."

Advancement

Nothing is quite as important to a career orientation as visible progress along a path of professional growth. What does the future look like? What is my career path? Do I have to quit and be rehired to advance to a new level of responsibility or to diversify my skills? Am I being "type-cast?" These are all questions that people have on their minds.

Advancement can take many forms, the most common of which is a title. We constantly struggled with functional versus firm titles as most companies do. Is someone recognized on their business card and by their peers and clients or customers for their technical specialty (senior director of financial services) or for their stature and responsibility within the enterprise. Remember that titles can be risky, inside your enterprise and to the outside world. You need to carefully gauge the value or risk to your customer's perceptions in the titles you use, remembering, that once they proliferate, you'll have a line of individuals at your door wanting to negotiate theirs.

We limited our strategy to a few generic titles and it worked for us, given the flexibility we expected people to have, shifting roles constantly. The generic firm titles connoted a relative level of responsibility a person was able to undertake across a broad spectrum of assignments. It also leveled the playing field and brought parity of stature across functional boundaries. A given title in a technical field carried the same respect and stature as the same title for an administrative staff member. Your designations will be tailored to the specific needs of your organization, but these are the kinds of considerations that should guide your choices.

Design the advancement or promotion process to be visible, participatory and, above all, fair. A test of fairness would be whether a single individual with whom a person has a poor relationship can derail that person's career. It means thoughtful consideration of the person as an individual, not just part of a group. It means a good understanding of the criteria upon which promotion or advancement recommendations will be made. Our process was very visible and highly inclusive. This participatory structure made the promotion process highly peer driven. The people in your organization know who's performing. You just need to tap into this knowledge.

We reminded people that appointed positions in the firm were a recognition of performance, not a license for authority. They're made carefully and with great difficulty, and we wanted to curb behavior that would dilute the respect that accrued to them.

During periods of economic slowdown, lack of growth or even shrinkage, many organizations tend to put all career advancement decisions on hold. But people in your organization are still growing professionally. They're taking on new responsibility, they have matured in their relationships, they've learned new skills, and they expect their efforts and growth to be recognized. Nevertheless, it may seem inconsistent to be considering adding new appointees at a time when you've had to lay people off. But people assume new leadership roles that help the company to serve its clients better. It would be truly inconsistent with the values I've been describing not to recognize this personal growth through promotions no matter what the economy was doing.

Each year we made the criteria a little tougher—not to be more exclusive, but because our clients became ever more demanding. Every year our values remained constant and each candidate must live the values contained in our Vision, Mission and Values Statement. But the measures of performance evolve in response to an ever-changing marketplace for our services. These measures were used a couple of years ago as we considered candidates (they're the same measures that guided our judgment on layoffs):

- Does the candidate add value to our relationships with our clients? This is a tricky question as it demands a knowledge of what our clients really value. It's made more subjective by the fact that our clients often don't know something is going to have value until we've come up with a creative solution that they wouldn't have known how to ask for but that they now find incredibly valuable. An important measure is, do clients come back for more services and do they refer us to their friends?
- Does the candidate develop strategic relationships with those with whom they work? Since not all candidates for promotion work directly with clients, we looked at the relationships they created with their teams, consultants, contractors and vendors—everyone with whom they worked. A tactical relationship ends at doing the assignment given. A strategic relationship involves thinking broadly beyond the task at hand to understand the reasons behind what you're doing and acting as a true partner with everyone with whom you work.
The measures are: • Do the people with whom a candidate works go out of their way to be sure they can work together again and again? • Do design and implementation solutions stretch well beyond the obvious to align the places we make with the processes,

people and technologies of their organizations?

- Does the candidate continually redefine the way we do things to respond uniquely to our clients and to streamline the process by removing wasted effort? We're in an ever more competitive environment where cost pressures go well beyond the price of our services. Is the candidate looking beyond just the way we do our work to streamline the entire process of building things to achieve higher quality at lower overall cost for our clients? The measures include adherence to fee and project budgets while maintaining quality design and ecstatic clients.

- Does the candidate work daily to improve the quality of our work, helping us decrease errors and reduce our risk? Does the candidate respect the importance of checking and rechecking work, drawing on the expertise of knowledgeable people throughout the firm to help deliver the highest-quality work to our clients? We're in an increasingly litigious world. Doing work the same way we did it in the past actually increases our risk. There is less tolerance for error today even though time schedules are even tighter. We cannot afford not to check drawings and documents before they go out the door, no matter how tight the schedule or budget. This quality control time must be built into every project. The measures are the number of (legitimate) information requests we get during bidding and construction and, ultimately, the number of claims we experience after completion.

Are you making your promotion criteria visible in this fashion? I hope you'll use this as a template to design your own system of evaluation about what's valuable to your customers and your organization.

PART III

BUILDING STRONG AND LOYAL CLIENT/CUSTOMER RELATIONSHIPS

Let the Customer Drive Your Organization

Listening to young architectural graduates whine about clients being their only hindrance to doing great work used to really distress me. I began sharing my frustration with friends in other businesses and found that they were hearing the same complaint, "The customer just gets in the way of me doing my job." Who does everyone think pays the bills? Patrons supporting artists in lavish lifestyles to create as they pleased was mostly a myth even when a genius like Mozart was sought after by kings to create that special concerto or when Leonardo da Vinci was commissioned to paint the ceiling of the Sistine Chapel.

Customers and clients drove business then and drive it today. Not just customers and clients of the enterprise but internal customers for the services of an administrative or service department. No other more powerful factor should influence the activities of an organization and every individual in it. Much has been written about client- or customer-driven business, so I'll leave you to pursue the existing literature on the subject as you desire, lending only my personal experience and point of view.

Philosophizing about customer orientation makes good reading, but how do you bring it to ground in your organization in real time? How do you get your people to live and breathe a customer-driven attitude from their very core? How do you define who, specifically, the customer is and what they want and need (often two very different things)? How do you avoid becoming proscriptive about how serving a specific customer is done, nurturing an adaptive approach to a customer who changes on the fly?

I'll sample some of the things I passed along in our firm to show you how we approached it, hoping that they will stimulate you to pursue your own unique definitions and approach to inculcating the people in your organization with a customer-driven attitude that fits your culture, your market and unique circumstances. If you've defined the markets and customers you've chosen to serve along with the environment in which you and your customers are doing business as described in Chapters 2 and 3, the examples that follow can serve as templates to develop specific strategies and models for your organization.

It's important in any discussion of client focus to set the stage for the business you're in and how "what you do" and "the way you do it" becomes customer driven. It also defines the type of clients you're best suited to serve recognizing that not all customers will appreciate your point of view. Not all customers are alike, and some will be better satisfied working with or buying from someone else. Being a customer-driven enterprise doesn't mean you can or should try to be all things to all people. As you consider these examples, substitute the parameters of your own organization and the customers you have chosen to drive your business.

I was part of a design firm, one in which design permeated everything we did; where design is not a thing that gets added on to a project otherwise well managed to be on time and on budget, but rather one in which design is part of schedule, budget and every process that we employed in shaping the built environment. But think about your own enterprise through the same eyes. Think of the steps I go through as if they pertained to the processes you go through to design, develop and bring to market your product or service. What essential ingredients permeate those processes for you?

The clients' program was not just something to be tolerated but was the fundamental shaping force for our design work. Great design goes beyond "for the client." It's "from the client." We know that all design generates an emotional response of some kind, even if it's neutral. Like art, greatness is defined by your emotions, not a professional art critic telling you what is great. Architecture is the same way. Great design elicits a response from those who use the places we create that reinforces the purpose of the place itself. It's purposeful and demands that you be a student of your work and the work of others to gain the sure hand to bring forth emotion directed to purpose. That's the difference between art and architecture. What emotional response are you after from the customers for your product or service?

Start with an "attitude"

What if you stopped talking about the design of your product or service, your metrics, structure, committees and meetings and just focused on doing great work for your customers? It's time to stop gazing internally at your structure and process and focus 100 percent of our time on your customers and clients. Here are some background thoughts about how to set yourself up for a true customer focus.

- **Trust and Integrity:** Customers will only stretch with you, explore with you, seek innovation with you, if they trust you. They trust you if you constantly describe what you do or sell in the context of their business issues, their budget and their schedule. If you haven't schooled yourself in how to make these connections for your customer, start now. Your product or service is not about you, it's about the customer who will use it long after you've moved on. How have you given comfort to the fears of each of the people who have to say "yes" to the transaction at hand? This is about helping them to see your product or service from their point of view. And, frankly, it's about doing work that is responsible and responsive. That's when trust in you will be most richly deserved.

- **Research:** Every one of us carries the responsibility of research into the work that we do; not formal, structured, isolated research, but application research into the way people work, learn, shop and play, into how products, services, materials and systems can be applied in new and innovative ways and into the enduring improvement in your customer or client's business performance. Don't do this because you're given a research grant, do it because you have a passion for the subject, because you just want to know more for the sheer joy of learning and exploring. What are your passions? Are you giving them wings by taking some of your own time to just explore and share your learning with others?

- **Sustainability:** How do you shift your thinking about each mundane task you become involved in every day so that it has sufficient meaning that you'd be happy to tell your grandchildren about? The environmental quality of what you do today is shaping the world for generations into the future. The things we make and sell and the services we deliver will affect the culture of the institutions we make them for. Your leadership and behavior affects the entire community with which you're involved—employees, customers, vendors and suppliers, the entire outside world that supports what you're doing for your customer. Are you contributing through your actions to a community you're proud to be a part of?

By living these premises, you'll build the reputation that will attract the customers you want to be working with. This provides a template framing a mission and priorities for reaching it for which you know there is a body of customers. Defining it for the people in your organization whose charter it is "to become driven by the customer" helps them to stay focused on the right customer.

Engaging the customer on the customer's terms

Now let's get down to specifics about how to get deeply engaged with your customer on their terms. An often-repeated question is: "How do I get my customers to accept the great product or service I'm providing them?" It's a fascinating subject in that it has little to do with the process of doing great work or delivering a great product but everything to do with bringing that product or service relationship to reality. Do you ever experience frustration with customers who don't seem to appreciate the value of what you're doing or selling or who get cold feet when it comes time to "sign on the dotted line?"

Being a client-focused firm means immersing yourself in your customer's issues to thoroughly resolve all of the forces shaping the relationship at hand: the budget, schedule, program, user issues, the community at large, regulations, etc. A great product or service relationship with a customer reconciles all of these issues, enhances your customer's business performance and brings joy and inspiration to the people who use the product or service you create. When you're at your best, you've been able to balance these often conflicting mandates without a lot of either/or frustrations: either I can meet the budget or I can deliver a great product or service; either I can deliver the program or I can deliver the product that will truly enhance their business. At your best, you deal with each issue with a both/and attitude, delivering without compromise—in the customer's eyes!

But at the moment of truth, following the presentation to the customer or client, there is a hesitation. You receive the response, "I'm not sure if I'm going to like it. I'm not sure it will work for us. Maybe we should think about it some more." What's going on here? Usually, it's a subtle failure of customer confidence. Sure, the customer trusts you and likes you, but there's something missing. Let's explore how the highest levels of customer confidence are built; the relationship where the customer says, "Whatever you say is what I'm going to do because I know it's exactly what I need and want, even though I can't read it in the product solution design you're presenting."

Most of your customers aren't able to envision the outcome of the work you do or the product you sell. They have to use it to know for sure. But in today's world and for most products and services, that's not possible. They're making a leap of faith when they make a commitment along the way to buy a product or approve a step in the process of a service or complex product relationship.

I had a client once for whom we had built a very accurate (and beautiful) model of his building, and he was still expressing uncertainty. As I explored further with him how he visualized things, I realized he watched a lot of television and was better able to make a connection between a video image and reality than through a model which, to him, took on the character of a toy. We put the model in another room and scanned around it at pedestrian eye-level in real time with a video camera. He watched on the monitor and directed the action: "No, I'd like to see the building a little more from the left. I don't like the way the parking structure looks. It's too industrial." For him, an image on a television screen connected more easily to reality than a carefully and accurately constructed scale model. It was a revelation for him and for us, and resulted in "yes" to most of the design decisions that day. The more interesting aspect of the exercise was his confidence that we were listening to him and helping him to feel greater confidence in our ability to understand his objectives. Subsequent design discussions began to evolve into conversations of a different character. "You know what I like, just go ahead." How might you translate this experience to a customer of yours, allowing that customer to see what you're doing through his or her eyes?

So how does this kind of relationship develop? It doesn't happen overnight, and it's not based on a natural talent you happen to have been born with. Customers want to have a "peer" relationship with people whom they need to trust; "need" because they don't have the skills to understand the work you do in enough detail to make a judgment about that work for themselves, so they must rely on those who are advising them.

This sort of bond starts when the customer picks up on your sincere interest in their issues. It means being as involved in their enterprise, its challenges and opportunities, its personalities and politics, as they are. This means research on your part, some social time, lots of questions and the sense that you care. It means getting to know the people in the organization beyond your customer contact. And it only happens when the customer senses your genuine interest in them as a person and their business issues as if they were your own. When you convey: "I'm making recommendations based on complete empathy with you, your fears and reward systems, priorities and program," or "I have adopted your complete persona while thinking about and guiding work on your project," does your customer believe it? When the answer is "yes," you'll find you have a friend, a peer and better-quality work; work that is not only terrific by your measure but completely responsive to your customer's.

So, it's really not about "How do I get my customer to accept the great work I'm doing for them?" These are words that indicate a forced action, trying to get your customer to buy something that you want to sell. Great work is collaborative, borne of great relationships. You'll achieve your best work when you approach it with an attitude framed by the question: "How are we going to accomplish great work together?"

Defining your value proposition

In marketing, a value proposition is a statement summarizing the customer targets, competitor targets and the core strategy for how one intends to differentiate one's product from the offerings of competitors.

The value proposition should answer the question: "Why would I buy this product at all" for the consumer. It is a clear and specific statement about the tangible benefits a consumer receives by using a product or service.

Thus reads the definition for a "value proposition" in Wikipedia (www.wikipedia.org for those of you who aren't familiar with this excellent resource). To that, I'll add the following: it is your approach formed by combining your body of expert knowledge, tools and talent in a way which is uniquely and individually tailored to a specific client's needs at a particular moment in time. It is not a list of features; it is completely focused on benefits. And it is not generic, it is a unique, once only proposition.

To be able to describe a value proposition in these terms, you'll need to be able to see the client's circumstances from their personal point of view. What are their problems, their concerns and their constraints? What are their resources and what threatens them?

For each individual within the client organization with whom you interact, the value proposition must be defined differently. Who above or below the individual you're dealing with has to say "yes" for a program to go forward? Have you gained a base of knowledge of those influencers in order to help the person you're dealing with define the program appropriately for them?

And most importantly, have you presented the benefits of your unique packaging of resources in a way that helps the client to see how to solve their problem—in a way that no one else they've spoken with could possibly do?

What makes customers afraid?

Every industry or profession has its own unique jargon, often one the customer doesn't understand. Frequently words used innocently in the context of your business will frighten a customer. Architects and designers use a terminology that bothered me which I was worried would bother our clients: they speak of taking a risk with a design. In school architects and designers use the term "risk" to mean stretching an idea, experimenting with something that hasn't been done before. It's founded on the belief that doing the same thing you've done before is not worthy of you as a professional. Unless you're cutting new ground, you're not being successful. They believe that stretching to new limits is the only way you innovate and without innovation, your enterprise will be pushed aside by those who do.

But our clients are consistently risk averse. Their first questions following a design presentation are "Where has this been done before?" "Where can I see something similar?" "How can you prove to me that it will work?" Our clients spend large amounts of money on the things we do for them, and they expect the results to perform well for a long time. We are exposed to tremendous liability in the work we do, so the word risk was not exactly music to my ears. Yet the need to innovate is an imperative. This is consistent with any large and complex, uniquely tailored product or service offering from any business.

Fear is another piece of the problem. People in your organization have fears about what they're doing. Will it be good enough? Will everyone like it? Is my approach going to jeopardize my career? Do I have support for what I'm doing? They're often unwilling to admit these concerns, raising the level of risk to all involved. Let me show you how these issues are connected as I would describe it for a design practice.

I just can't help myself, it must be genetic or at least a strong predisposition to like the people I do business with or want to do business with the people I like. This can be a risky proposition in that you can sure louse up a great friendship by not performing beyond expectations when working for a friend. I think it's one of life's great myths that a friend will be more forgiving if you underperform when working for them. In fact, my stress and anxiety levels on assignments seem to be directly proportionate to the strength of the friendship I have with the client.

This brings me to the subject of fear and its role in a professional's life. The subject isn't too complicated and can be summed up as follows: not only is it okay to be scared most of the time, it's the only way to know if you're growing as a professional. In fact, cultivating a high tolerance for fear (my wife refers to me as an adrenaline junky) is closely connected to learning and innovation.

An aspiration to "raise the bar," which most of us want to do in our work and, frankly, have to do to stay ahead of our competition, connotes innovation. Innovation usually involves doing things that haven't been done before. Doing new things usually involves risk. Risk connotes potential for failure, and that always scares the daylights out of me. In fact, if you're not scared by the potential for failure, you're built differently than most folks. All customers and clients abhor failure and will get really angry if you put them at risk and then fail. They probably won't pay your bills, and they'll tell lots of other people what you did to them.

So, are you beginning to see the dichotomy here? If I play it safe (no risk), my potential for losing a great customer and perhaps a great friend is greatly reduced, as are my fear and anxiety. On the other hand, my potential for innovation, for "raising the bar," also goes out the window. If you're risk averse, you relegate yourself to a position as a technician. If you aspire to be a true professional and want to survive your competition, you've got to stretch until you're scared. And, in fact, it is that fear that keeps you alert, focused and so thoroughly engaged in the issue at hand that you won't let it fail. This reduces the risk to the client, saves the friendship and gives the friend what a true friend deserves: something that exceeds their expectations.

There's a footnote to this fear stuff that goes beyond risk on an assignment. Let's look in a broader context. I've always been concerned when I've lost an assignment I've competed for and try to get immediate and candid feedback from the client as to why they selected someone else. On several occasions, I've heard that I wasn't hungry enough; that my competition wanted the project more and the client felt that, on that basis, they would do a better job. You run the risk, particularly in a seller's market when things are going really well, of work coming too easily; of losing your hunger, your need to survive. I looked at our backlog frequently and was astounded at how quickly the pipeline cycled through and how much new work it took to keep our firm healthy and vital. It's one of the things that, when I make a presentation to a prospective new client, makes me energetic and passionate. I want and need the work. The fear keeps me focused. It helps me innovate. But then again, I'm an adrenaline junky.

Bringing the customer-driven philosophy to life

Now, I'll present some ideas about how to breathe life into the customer-driven approach for the people in your organization. Begin with a premise that you must add value to your customer that exceeds the cost of your product or service—but does it far exceed their expectations? This is a fundamental question because customers who have their expectations exceeded are customers that keep coming back and who create new ones for you through referrals. These are the customers you want to have.

- Great customers don't knock on the door very often. They are created and nurtured by the people in your organization.
- Always remember that your company is an image. But images never impress anyone. People impress people—the people in your organization are what clients value.
- Recruit people who are givers, not takers. There are two basic types of people in this world: those who give of themselves freely and those who take all they can get. Takers try to surround themselves with givers. Giving takes maturity, patience and faith. It is never easy. But it creates loyalty and trust, two essential elements in building great customer relationships.
- Spend some time every day making your customer look good. Most of the customer counterparts that your employees deal with are not at the top of their organizations. Many are responsible for multiple relationships. Most have to answer to someone else. If you spend time making them look good, they are much more likely to bring you into other aspects of their business. Time spent proving yourself right is more than time wasted; it is time spent burning bridges.
- Let others take credit. Everyone knows that nobody does it all by themselves. Successful people surround themselves with successful people. When you hear someone else receiving praise for your work, don't get upset, take it as a compliment. People know who actually does the work. The better they look, the better you look.
- Give your customers ideas they never considered. This is essential in exceeding your customer's expectations. Spending a customer's money more wisely than he could have imagined is only part of the solution (and an impossible task). Helping them think about

things they otherwise never would have should be part of the experience that comes with the relationship with your enterprise. They will then come back to you with ideas you never dreamed of. Be open to these ideas. Customers that believe they "own" a piece of what you're doing together are more likely to be ecstatic about the results.

- If you can't impress them with your knowledge, impress them with your questions. Customers love to talk about what they are doing. Ask good questions, and then be a good listener. "What is going to make this a successful relationship for you?" and "What can we do to help you accomplish this" are rarely asked. But the answers will give you an entirely different perspective of why you're doing business together.

- Be prepared. Do your homework. Customers are incredibly impressed when you've anticipated them and can respond to anything they throw at you. It's a great sign of respect.

- Don't tolerate finger pointing. Everyone loses. Propose solutions before blame. Everyone has an excuse, only the best people have solutions.

If someone in your organization wrote something like this would you feel like you'd gotten the message across? I adapted this from a letter I received from a young architect several years ago. He'd written it to be sure the many new people joining the office he was in understood what was expected in our culture. What a demonstration of how deeply instilled a customer-driven focus can become in your organization!

Building your reputation

Existing and prospective new customers are being aggressively sought by your competitors. Your reputation precedes you with both. It's built in many ways—through the word of previous clients, by your competitors and by the "partners" you depend on to do your business (in our case engineers, contractors, vendors and building officials). Your customer talks to all of them, so designing what you want your reputation to be then carefully building and maintaining it sets your customer relationship in motion.

I'll start with your relationship with vendors, contractors and consultants, the people engaged in delivering your product or service to your customer who are outside your organization. You all depend on these "partners" in the process of doing great work for your customers. Some people in your organization have a better reputation among this constituency than others. Let me be specific: phone calls don't get returned, meetings are blown off (the vendor showed up, and your person wasn't even in the office or walked out after five minutes). An occasional bit of arrogance coupled with a demanding attitude is observed.

My career and reputation have been built on consistent respect for the time, effort and professionalism that vendors, contractors and consultants commit to the work I do. Each of these "partners" faces the same tough environment that you do—there's never enough business, and price competition is brutal. Each of these professionals has their own marketing network, often including clients or key decision makers who influence customer selections. How they feel toward you in comparison with your competitors (whom they are also calling on) determines whom, when asked, they refer to as the best and most appropriate person or company to work with. Whether you like it or not, a big piece of your and your company's reputation is based on how these vendors, contractors and consultants feel about you. And, trust me; they do talk about you ...a lot!

My second observation comes from a book titled *Upside Down Marketing* by George R. Walther. One specific chapter caught my attention. The author proposed that it is cheaper by far to market your product or services to a customer you've lost than it is to secure a new one. Sounds counter intuitive, doesn't it? Walther points out several issues to support his premise. First, an unhappy customer will remember their dissatisfaction forever. It will haunt you for the rest of your career and, like that vendor whose phone call you didn't answer or whom you blew off for that presentation they'd prepared for late into the night, they'll tell many, many people about their experience with you. Not only do you not have that customer's business, but they're poisoning others' attitudes about you.

Walther's point is clear, whatever it costs and no matter how long it takes to recapture an unhappy customer, it's worth the investment. He further adds that once a customer has come back to you, the depth of their loyalty (as long as you keep the service level high) is much stronger than any other customer type.

Never forget the principle: your reputation is your most valuable asset, and, conversely, even a little bit of a bad reputation, no matter how insignificant you consider the transgression to be, will haunt you forever.

Continuously monitor your relationships

It's easy to get complacent about success with a customer or client of long standing. But their world continues to evolve requiring you to evolve with them. We were feeling pretty good about the depth, breadth and duration of our relationship with one of our long-term clients. We'd been doing work for them for nearly 30 years. We had recently completed a highly successful facility for them and had another under construction across the street. We were designing the interiors of their new headquarters in another location, and our total annual billings to them had increased every year. One of the facilities had won a prestigious design award, and the new building promised to be a winner as well. Not bad: design to be proud of, and an increasing amount of business for a number of our offices.

This is where the risk of smugness sets in. In a meeting with their facilities group, we asked what percentage of their work we did. We assumed we were their largest supplier of services by a wide margin. Not so. In fact, we found much to our chagrin that our "market share" of their work had been shrinking. They commission a lot of work every year, and there is no way we were going to get all or even most of it. But to learn that we were winning a diminishing percentage served as a strong wake up call leading to a wonderful discussion of how this client rates its consultants and which characteristics they look for when selecting a consultant for an assignment, or, more importantly, a series of assignments; in other words, a "relationship."

They do a regular evaluation of their service providers, reviewing the results to help guide that service provider's performance and priorities. In the case of architectural and interior design firms, they synopsized their evaluation criteria as follows (in their order):

- **Speed:** Not only how fast are design and construction documents completed (although this is certainly important), but how responsive is the architect. Do they return phone calls immediately; do they find answers to client and contractor questions quickly; do they convey by their demeanor a sense of urgency? The opening of a new facility is enormously time sensitive, and it takes more than just finishing the drawings on time to meet a schedule.
- **People:** The quality of the people assigned to a project and a relationship is critical. No assignment should be seen as a training ground for junior staff or filler work for someone who'd really rather be doing something else. They expect to have seasoned, committed, knowledgeable professionals assigned to their work. This was a very important issue for us to remember as we took on more and more extension or multi-assignment work with our global clients.
- **Business:** They expect their architects to know both how they do their business and why they do their business. Intimacy with a client's business issues, a theme we've talked about for a long time now, comes out loud and clear as a key issue in sustaining a long-term relationship.
- **Seamless:** They expect their architects to be a seamless extension of themselves. This does not mean rolling over and playing dead when we see something that could be improved or simply being a drafting service. It does, however, mean embodying a genuine empathy for the client's processes and internal issues and playing by their rules. It means learning how they do things, not telling them "this is the way we do it."

I suspect most of your customers, whether you're working with them on a single assignment or involved in a sustained global relationship, would concur. How might you gain similar insights into what your best customers really expect of you?

Using "Evidence Management" to achieve customer intimacy

Tough economic times can really distract an organization and require creative ways of talking about customer intimacy. Palomino, a restaurant across the courtyard from my former office in San Francisco, hands out little "sayings" with the bill, like a fortune cookie without the cookie. One I received awhile back seemed particularly appropriate at the moment. It read:

"I'm looking forward to looking back on all this."
– Sandra Knell

I looked up Sandra Knell on Google and found that she was the CFO of Coast Distribution Systems, a company that supplies porta-potties among other things. Isn't Google wonderful? Google said this had been the "quote-of-the-month" in some obscure venue. Sandra had achieved her 15 minutes of fame.

It got me thinking about the uncertainty of the market at that moment, the demands made by clients to deliver high-quality service at excruciatingly low fees, wondering when it would change. It reminded me of several past recessions and how, when I felt like it was just going to go on like this forever, things slowly began to pick up. At such times I wished for a crystal ball that would predict the date or a time when the market and our clients' attitudes would shift back to positive territory—if I could do this, I'd probably be a stock market investor instead of an architect.

But, there had been some interesting and hopeful signals. We'd been starting new assignments at a rate that was more than replacing work that was finishing up. Some offices had been borrowing help from other offices, and several had hired new people. We were seeing some pent-up demand for certain types of services from clients who, because of the economy, had stalled projects and actions and finally not been able to put them off any longer; leases do expire, requirements do change.

While the conventional office building market at the time was, for all practical purposes, dead with millions of vacant square feet to be absorbed before we'd see new commissions, we were evaluating some wonderful opportunities with existing, vacant facilities for clients whose leases were coming up. We were studying alternative use strategies for under-performing real estate assets. Although we were still seeing projects being competitively solicited at fee levels that bore no resemblance to the effort required, I was particularly excited by a number of new assignments that we'd been awarded that were much more strategic and less fee driven.

I began to focus on an article from Harvard Business Review entitled "Cluing in to Customers" that spoke of evidence management. The article, focusing on the Mayo Clinic, opened with the statement: "When a company's offerings are hard to judge, customers look for subtle indicators of quality." You may be asking yourselves, what does the practice of architecture and design have to do with running a research clinic and hospital? It analyzed the effect when "Employees at all levels take note of customer preferences and are empowered to solve problems on the spot, continually tailoring the experience to each person."

I was the fortunate recipient of frequent letters and calls from happy clients. Looking beneath the surface of every one of those communications, I found evidence of that exact characteristic—one or a team of our people had taken the time to do just that: continually tailor the experience to their client. What does evidence management, the analysis of the customer's take on the evidence left by seemingly small actions, look like? How can you become keenly aware of the "evidence" you leave behind in the work you do with your customers, colleagues, contractors and vendors—in fact, everyone with whom you come in contact? What message about the nature of your company is that body of evidence sending?

Stuff like this may seem pretty soft when you're faced with the hard job every day of doing great work with tight financial deals and customers who sometimes seem completely distracted by economic pressures. But it's the soft stuff that sets you up for the next wave of the economy. In fact, it's the stuff you do when you're at your best that brings you the work you want to be doing, now and in the future. Being consistently at your best is what evidence management is all about.

So, I went back to Palomino again a few days later and got another little card. It said:

I am always doing things I can't do—that's how I get to do them.
– Pablo Picasso

I liked that better.

"Owning" a customer's problem

Putting yourself in your customer's shoes, you can make no more significant impact than to "own" the customer's problem. The story starts with a hotel manager who has trained the entire staff to "own" a guest's problem, whether it's their department or not. And to stay with it until it's solved for the guest. In other words, if a bellman hears a complaint about room service, he doesn't ignore it or pass it off, saying, "You'll have to contact catering; that's not my department."

Apply this to your organization. Anyone, from time to time, may hear a comment from a customer (or an outside consultant, contractor or vendor) about something that is wrong with the way you're doing things. What's the action? Do the people in your organization ignore it; or do they pass it off to someone else; or do they dive in, staying with it until the situation is rectified?

Imagine what the reputation of your company would be if everyone were listening attentively for anything that is not being done to the complete satisfaction of a customer or any one of the consultants or vendors, suppliers or contractors upon whom you depend to satisfy your customers. Imagine how you would be known in the marketplace if each of your people personally embraced the responsibility to make the situation right. Every time. Imagine.

Do business with people you like

A caveat remains to letting the customer drive your organization. Not all prospective customers are nice people. Not all prospective customers should be driving your organization. But how do you select? It's so easy to get caught up in the chase, to convince yourself that the customer will be terrific to work with once you sign the deal. That is simply hubris. Having trodden this course for many years, I learned that I wasn't always a very good judge of which prospective client was going to be absolutely terrific, challenging and a joy to work with and which was going to emerge, both as an individual and as an organization, as an absolute jerk.

Bad customers, those that don't pay their bills, negotiate your relationship to a point where you cannot make money or place you at undue risk are problematic to any enterprise. I found that our involvement with bad clients followed the 80/20 principle pretty well—I spent 80% of my time trying to accommodate 20% of my clients, hoping they would somehow go away. But they didn't and, given the long-cycle nature of the work I did, they haunted me frequently and over a long duration.

I learned that being selective becomes an imperative. I also learned that withdrawing from a relationship, whether during the selling mode when things just weren't going well, during negotiations when in my zeal to conclude a deal and get on with the relationship or even after a project was underway, saved me enormous aggravation and expense. More importantly it saved me distraction from what I needed to be doing to build a great enterprise and great relationships with good clients. The cost of a bad client or customer goes well beyond monetary loss.

So, what are the filters to guide you in selecting your customer and client base? For short-cycle businesses, little selectivity is used. The transaction is completed quickly, and you move on the next customer. But even quick sales cycle organizations have aspects of their business with long cycles—relationships with suppliers and vendors, the employees of the organization itself and, most importantly, the company's brand reputation in the marketplace.

Short-cycle companies that think of customers as a commodity tend to treat their employees and others on whom they rely the same way. Long-cycle enterprises tend to build durable relationships with all stakeholders. The relationships look more like friendships, and they are most easily formed with people you like. How difficult is this? After all, not everyone is going to like you, and there are going to be customers who are a terrific fit to your strategic purpose that you may not like. But, if they pass the thresholds you set for integrity and fairness, your job is to align the people on that customer's team with individuals in your organization that they like and that like them. Many retailers do it, the best auto dealers do it, smart stock brokers do it, why shouldn't you? It's not just about chemistry between people, although that's a factor. There are proactive things that people in your organization can do to develop the depth of friendship that has durability for the long cycle, learning to weed out early those that you simply shouldn't be in business with.

Liking the people you do business with

So, how do you shape your organization to get this way? Our firm wasn't always big and filled with resources that helped us to realize our full potential as professionals; it wasn't always filled with enthusiastic, bright, curious people; it didn't always have such a rich mix of project and service types. There is a key and it's not so mysterious—a continuous focus on client service. The perpetuation and extension of this environment warrants summarizing in some detail what this "focus on client service" looked like for us.

When we thought about client service, our attention went to the long-duration nature of our relationships, not just with clients but those with whom we aligned to service those clients. Our focus went immediately to the individual to individual relationships that were built and sustained in the course of our business and how sacred the quality of these relationships was for us. We didn't make widgets or deliver services in an environment where the purchase decision was made quickly, the product or service was consumed quickly or the after effect minimal. Our clients took a long time before choosing to work with us; we spent an enormous amount of very personal time with them as they consumed our service and the after-effect of that service was long lasting and usually had a profound impact on their lives or businesses. This set some interesting parameters for us:

• It was important for our clients to like us and for us to like them. After all, we were going to spend a lot of time together. We've all experienced the converse at one time or another and know what prolonged agony that can be.
• The relationship had to be both fun and serious. The first because better work is done when everyone is enjoying what they're doing; the second because what we were doing was going to be around for a while, and a lot of people who weren't around for the fun stuff are going to have to live with the results.

So what does this look like day in and day out?

Our work was a team sport. That meant that doing what was asked (by the client or someone in the firm who was directing a person's work) without understanding "why" wasn't good enough. If you don't understand, ask; if you're asked, take the time to answer - in detail. This applied not just to the relationship with the client and each other, but to suppliers, vendors, consultants and contractors. How much more fulfilling is it when everyone senses a common commitment to an important mission?

It meant learning good facilitation, negotiation and team-building strategies and techniques. It's everyone's responsibility to foster an environment where everyone feels respected and contributory.

It meant being thorough and relentless in finding the best knowledge or expertise to apply to a particular problem; not working unilaterally but seeking expert knowledge inside or outside the firm. When a client sensed that each person embodied these attitudes (and they sense this stuff real fast), everything about the work we did improved. We did better work, we had more fun, the client told others about us and wanted to do more with us, other really bright and talented people wanted to join us, the quality of work for which we were considered went up, and the cycle continued.

All of this says that it's not about the specifics of what you do for or with your customer; it's about the enjoyment of a deep partnership with them, a sense of mutual interest and a commitment beyond the task at hand. That's what will get you there. It's both fragile and enormously strong. It's easy to mess up the minute you lose that personal commitment to the people for and with whom you're doing your work, but when the customer senses that commitment, it's virtually bullet proof in fostering an environment for great work, repeat and referral business and continued growth.

Building a Culture of Trust and Respect

10

Throughout this book I've emphasized the importance of trust. Integrity and respect are characteristics or behaviors by which one develops trust, and trust is the single-most important factor in the success of a long-cycle enterprise. Without trust, nothing gets done. Teams don't work, outside resources don't cooperate, and clients look elsewhere. Yet trust is a fragile and increasingly scarce relationship characteristic in business today.

Over the past few decades, the ability to depend on someone's promise or commitment has eroded. How or why that happened can be laid at the feet of many people and institutions, but the fact remains, people don't trust one another at the outset of their relationship. Despite this fact, as the speed of business increases, more and more companies must operate interdependently, frequently without enforceable contractual relationships binding them. They grow to depend more heavily on trust relationships as a lubricant to their business transactions. Yet trust must be earned an interaction at a time. It takes a long time to build but can be destroyed in an instant. So how does an organization build a culture of trust?

Integrity is the fundamental filter in the hiring process described in Chapter 6. Since long-cycle enterprises maintain long and durable relationships with employees, clients and outside resources, recruiting for the potential to build trust is key. Trust accrues to both individuals and the organization and must be built and maintained rigorously. For the individual, it's person to person in the enterprise as well as with individuals in the client's organization and each other person with whom the individual comes in contact, specifically those outside the organization upon whom one depends to accomplish one's work. Emphasizing the critical importance of trust to a new employee starts with that person's acculturation to your organization and continues with every interaction.

Mission, vision and values

At a fundamental level are your vision, mission and values. Has your enterprise defined these with specificity? Are they written down? Does everyone in the organization know what they are and why they exist? Is the behavior in your organization consistent with these statements? In other words, are they credible? Do you "walk the talk?" There are many ways to write a vision, mission and values statement. Those that involve a broad cross-section of your enterprise are best—they're participatory and have the potential to achieve buy-in, to be "owned" by the members of your organization. Those that are handed down from a group of senior executives, the human resources department or prepared by an outside consultant simply don't stick. They need to contain some "grass roots." Here's what I did.

In the early 90s, I was concerned that, as we cycled out of the recession and began hiring again, we would have difficulty communicating, let alone teaching our values. We were at a population of around 600, but it seemed like we were poised to grow much larger, and do it quickly. We had no written document. When I asked people in the firm what our values were, the answer I got was, "Everyone knows what they are." Nice response but difficult to pass on to new people joining what, at the time and for its size, seemed like a firm with a deep and consistent culture.

So I began asking more specifically for examples of what "everyone knew" and accumulated them into a list. At a point where

I was getting no new ideas, I circulated the list to a group of folks in the firm: the management committee, the board and a few selected people at various levels of the organization whom I felt would give me thoughtful feedback. My questions were straightforward: Does this sound like us? Are there things missing? Should we have something like this in writing? What format should it take? How should we use it in the firm?

The responses were interesting and thorough. I got a few "What, are you crazy?" responses, an occasional addition or modification and a lot of affirmation. I would then rewrite the document based on the feedback and re-circulate it to the same group until I stopped getting comments. Maybe I wore everyone down, but it began to feel like we had a consensus. A small folded card with a statement of our "Vision, Mission and Values" was issued to everyone in the firm. I used it as a vehicle to say, "This is the consensus of how we want to be. We aren't always this way but to the degree that we act this way consistently, we'll be able to achieve our vision and mission. It's also a way for each of you to challenge anyone in the firm for deviation from these values without fear of reprisal, without risk to your employment, compensation or potential for advancement." This sent a very strong message to the leaders of the firm particularly that "do as I say, not as I do" would no longer fly. Our value statement helped us to acculturate the wave of new people joining the firm. In recruiting, it was a marvelous pre-filter as we began to attract more and more people who said, "Yes, that's the type of firm I'd like to be a part of."

Sustaining your commitment

Revisiting your vision, mission and values statement from time to time is important. Not only do you calibrate how well you're living what you espouse, but you usually find some things that just don't sound exactly right any more. We found that the basic principles held but, particularly in the late 90s, we began to hear comments about the length of the piece. After all, we were in the New Economy of instant millionaires, companies that went from start up to their

IPO in a year and young people with decreasing attention spans. So we took a shot at being reductive. While we never got the document onto a wallet-sized card as many requested and several companies seemed to be doing, we definitely abbreviated the text, trying to adhere consistently to our message.

I was concerned about losing the spirit and richness of our value statement but, after being told almost daily during that period by the younger generation that I "just didn't get it," I relented and we re-issued the piece. By mid 2003 in the midst of the recession, the pendulum had swung back and several people began to comment that, with the pressures on the economy, we might be slipping a little in the rigor with which we were living our values. In fact, it was music to my ears when some of my younger partners asked if we could go back to the older version and republish it again for the firm. Reissuing the mission and values piece seemed like a great way to recommit ourselves to living that culture.

About the time I started to work on this, a quote from Gretchen Morgenstern, a New York Times financial columnist came to my attention: "When was the last time someone said 'Spend more time with your family' around here?" The New York Times was a client of ours so we'd followed closely the period of ethical and cultural turmoil they were going through. The plagiarism and deception of a young reporter resulted in public soul-searching, internal "town meetings," and ongoing upheaval in the newsroom. The atmosphere at the paper grew increasingly intense, almost like a battleground, ending finally in the resignation of The Times' executive editor and his deputy. In mid-July, Bill Keller was recalled from his year long assignment as an op-ed columnist to take the reins.

Keller's acceptance speech, given in The Times' newsroom, was published in full by the Wall Street Journal. It's a wonderful talk, and I was struck by the references he made to the paper's mission and values. In contrast to his famously hard-driving predecessor, Keller said, "We cannot operate a newsroom like an endless combat mission." I was feeling like we were running a bit under siege at the moment ourselves, so I paid close attention. "This is a better paper," Keller added, "if you bring to your jobs, along with energy and talent—some experience of life—family and reflection, art and adventure, a little fun. A little more savoring will enrich you and your work as much as a competitive pulse will."

Then Keller said something that really got my attention: "The great ambition of this paper has been to report the news 'without fear or favor.' I hope to run a newsroom that is, likewise, without fear or favor." Keller's point is that The Times' mission, its statement of purpose, is founded on its core values.

All of this made me think about our mission:

> We design great places. Places where people want to be. Places that enrich our communities. Places that contribute to our clients' success.

This was the great ambition of the firm, to which all of our work aspired. But we also aspired to have a firm that is a great place to work: "a place where people want to be; a place that enriches our community; a place that contributes to our collective and to each individual's success."

"When was the last time someone said 'Spend more time with your family' around here." This comment from a Times columnist, which The Times bravely quoted about itself, could be said in our organization at the time in reference to any number of values that we nominally espoused but sometimes failed to apply. Integrity, excellence and balance—these core values are especially prone to compromise when business conditions deteriorate.

The difficulties at that moment were tough. Some offices were short of work, and others were working their way out of "holes" on projects that were taken at fees below what we needed to deliver excellent service. This made for a lot of held time. Cash flow was tighter than ever. From those closest to the numbers, there was an understandable tendency to pressure others to pitch in with unpaid time to compensate.

To us, that was dangerous. Transparency and a sense of

shared mission were what we needed so that people understood the urgency and felt that the sacrifices they made were appropriate and appreciated. Everyone needed to feel they were part of a shared effort to move their enterprise to a firmer footing—to both renewed financial and emotional health.

I've alluded to Abraham Maslow's hierarchy of needs—his observation that when you're focused on survival, the question of self-actualization seems beside the point. When times are tough, issuing a new mission and values piece to some could seem pointless. Why bother? Yet those who focus on self-actualization, on becoming the best person and professional one can be even when times are tough, are much better positioned to overcome the obstacles life throws at them. It gives them the strength and focus to work through obstacles—problems that can seem insurmountable—to get where they're trying to go.

Missions and values should be what people aspire to, what they want to be, where they want to go. They make it easier for people to recognize and admit when they're not acting consistently with the proclaimed values, facing up to it and doing something about it. It's a safety net that allows anyone in the enterprise to challenge—"without fear or favor"—when they lose their way.

I liked what Keller had to say and watched The Times reorient toward values that would allow their people to live up to the best of who they wanted to be—taking seriously the values that had gotten them where they were, putting them broadly into practice so that they were not just platitudes.

How you work and what you produce must always be open to innovation and response to changing market and customer needs, but your culture should not. It should be both your wellspring and your conscience. When times get tough, it's all too human to set your core values aside. You do so at your peril. Cut corners, shave a little here and there, and before you know it, your best customers and your best people have gone elsewhere.

We reissued our Vision, Mission and Values, and it remains a vital conscience for everyone in the firm.

Storytelling and tribal lore

Storytelling, the allegorical tribal lore of your organization, delivers powerful messages about your culture. These stories seem to spring up, based loosely on an event that connects with a lesson about your values connected to behavior, action, success or achievement, and take on a life of their own, getting adopted into the oral history of your enterprise. In the biblical sense, they're parables. Monitor them closely because these stories make your vision, mission and values accessible. They tell about your people's relationships with each other and your customers and can reinforce or detract from the way you build trust. Are the stories in your organization self righteous or do they contain humility? Are they about winning and losing or accomplishing great stuff collaboratively? Are they humorous? Are the stories about heroes or losers?

You can shape stories, but they must feel and sound authentic, uniquely like you and your enterprise. They must be suited to the culture and nature of transactions that define your business. Here's a story I used to tell at new staff orientations and generally followed the same path I'd take talking to a new client with whom we'd not worked before and who was interested in what kind of a firm they were becoming involved with. Most clients are as fearful as new members of an enterprise are about getting lost in a large organization; they also want to know what you stand for and why they were going to get more value for their investment with you than the other firms they'd considered. Quite parallel concerns, aren't they?

I always began with a bit of history of the firm then used actual (well, maybe embellished a little) stories to make some simple points. If your enterprise has a consistent history, culture and value system, that's a very important message for both new members of your organization and new customers. You're reinforcing that they're becoming involved with a group of people whose roots are deep and strong and have been that way for a while. For us, those values started with a "one-firm firm"

This single characteristic of the firm had fostered a strong culture of collaboration and knowledge sharing across geographical and practice area boundaries. The benefit to the client and the staff member are similar: easy access to expert knowledge. The benefit to the client: smarter, faster solutions of higher value. The benefit to the professional: continuous learning, career growth and the ability to achieve higher-quality design results through support and collaboration.

Two other characteristics permeated the culture: a high level of interpersonal respect and high integrity. These aspects of are crucial in a society where trust has been lost in interactions between people and in a business relationship that revolves around interdependence between team members and clients.

The result is the assemblage of a friendly, relationship driven group of people. If there is a "relationship gene," a genetic predisposition to form strong, trusting relationships, it existed in higher proportion among our folks. From this, a "career culture" had evolved within the firm. People tended to find a supportive environment that helped them grow, they'd developed strong relationships with peers whom they trusted, learned from and liked, and they'd enjoyed the opportunity to work with clients on multiple projects where the design results improved as the relationship deepened. The reciprocal had been true for clients who had found that the beneficial impact of the work we did improved as the relationship developed. We got to know their businesses better, we offered design solutions that were more relevant to the unique characteristics of their organizations, and, as a result, the perceived value of our service increased.

These points helped a new employee or a new client to grasp the ground rules of our relationship. What are your ground rules?

Trust and respect extend to the outside world, and every organization has anecdotal stories that illustrate how behavior builds or destroys trust and respect. Here's a personal one that I passed along to make a specific point.

I moved to Los Angeles in 1976 to establish our presence in southern California. We were doing a tremendous amount of work for the Bank of America in San Francisco at the time and enjoyed an excellent relationship. They were then and still are the firm's banker. When I arrived in Los Angeles, I called the head of facilities at Bank of America to introduce myself. His secretary dutifully took my message about our relationship with the bank and told me he'd call back. He didn't. I called several more times, but he never had the courtesy to return my calls. Much later, I became acquainted with another person in facilities at Bank of America and, through him, finally met the head of the department who was cold, aloof and, generally, couldn't be bothered. As hard as we tried, we were never able to establish a relationship to do work with the bank in Southern California.

Years later, I got a call from this guy. He had left Bank of America and taken a lead position with a local general contractor. One of his primary new roles, it seems, was marketing, and he wanted to buy me lunch and solicit our business. I accepted, curious about whether he had any recollection about how he'd treated me. We had a delightful lunch, at the end of which I reminded him of my experience when I first moved to southern California, suggesting that I might not be the best person to approach for new business and watched the blood drain slowly from his face.

This delivered a story that said some days we're "selling" and other days we're "buying." It behooves us to remember how we like to be treated on both sides of a relationship. A relationship is profoundly affected by the speed with which we return phone calls to people who are selling ...even at times when you know all they're doing is trying to sell you something that you may not have time for today. I make it a personal point to return phone calls, all of them, within half a day (if my schedule or travel is particularly hectic, it may slip to, at worst, the next day). If it's something I'm not interested in or don't have time for, I'll direct the call elsewhere or tell the person the reason. I asked people to remember the old tale about satisfied customers telling four people about their happy experience and dissatisfied customers telling 10 people about their unhappiness, the same ratio seems to apply for sales reps and the experiences they have calling on you. Keep this in mind as you think about your personal marketing plan.

Making it happen

If the stage has been well set for an environment of integrity and trust, how do you actualize it with customers? Several key thoughts may help you talk to the people in your organization about building trust through the respect you have for the customer and the work you're doing together.

Let's start with a fundamental issue—dealing with an uncomfortable topic, a problem, a time when an error is made. Does the culture of your organization make it okay to address it squarely, to talk it through to find a solution or is it to sweep it under the carpet, look for a scapegoat or make an excuse? Turning a problem into an opportunity starts with admitting it's a problem and being forthright and open until a solution is found. Do you have a story in your organization that illustrates a successful conclusion of something that could have been a disaster? This is a great place to start down the road to trust.

Are your people presenting your product or service in the context of your customer's competitive business environment? What are their greatest opportunities and fears—recruitment and retention? Can you truly put yourself in your customer's shoes? Is your customer afraid he or she will be fired if there is a schedule or budget bust? In our case, we dealt with a lot of outside influencers like planning commissions and architectural review boards. We were always alert to a city council member coming up for re-election who might be afraid to support our project because it was unpopular in the community. This is the type of sensitivity that built trust with our clients.

Where are the preexisting trust relationships with your customer—are there those that will benefit you; are there any skeletons from previous relationships with you or others that will harm you? Are there things you can do as you proceed with the relationship to open those conversations to build and strengthen trust? What outside constituencies surround your business relationships—who are they, what are their issues, and how are you going to frame your approach to reconcile conflicts?

Benchmarking your customer's business environment builds respect and trust for you. Do you know what is going on in their industry and competitive environment? Do you know how they've solved the issue you're working on before and how others have solved it, and can you give them quantitative comparisons? What are the best ways the thing you're doing has been done before anywhere in the world, qualitatively, even if it's not your company's example?

Your customers want to know if their relationship with you will lead to innovation in their own business. Can you bring them opportunities that exist in their business and a program that would dramatically improve the performance of their organization? What things can be done to shorten schedule, reduce budget or enhance the value to the customer of the money being spent? Is your work together environmentally sustainable without additional cost and with dramatic life-cycle cost savings? In what unique ways can the work you're doing together yield a long-term benefit to the community? These are some starting points for beginning a relationship that demonstrates your commitment to your customer and builds trust and respect.

Dealing with crisis

Every organization must be concerned about crisis management. A sudden, unexpected event challenges the ethics of the people in any organization. With notable product failures in the pharmaceutical industry, financial reporting anomalies and other unexpected business issues making the headlines regularly, every company and its leaders must be prepared to respond instinctively since the immediacy of most situations means reporters on the phone or microphones and TV cameras in your face—right now. Pre-conditioning must go through the entire organization because to the news media, in a crisis, everyone in your enterprise becomes a prospective spokesperson. As part of that ongoing conditioning, I gained some insights from a business conference I attended.

The CEO of ValuJet spoke about how he dealt with the plane crash in Florida and presented some easy to follow advice. He said, take control of the crisis; don't let the press dominate the actions you take. Even if your plan of action is not yet fully formed, give the illusion of a plan. Don't stonewall the press, talk to them. In today's world, everyone gets the same information at the same time. We have instant media saturation which is visually impacting. Even the White House "Situation Room" tunes into CNN where news is often more immediate and current than government intelligence. Be consistent in what you tell the public. They will be most swayed by your expression of concern and the reasonableness of what's being said. Tell all the truth as soon as you can. The most important messages to deliver:

• We care what the truth is.
• We're going to find out what happened and are taking direct and urgent action.
• We're going to do the right thing.

As a firm, we were fortunate to have been free from crises. The preponderance of advice, however, was that it's not "if" you'll face a crisis but "when."

For us, should an event (which could be anything from an accident at a job site to an employment related claim against the firm) ever occur that will thrust us into the public eye, I asked that our people not speak with the press but contact me or Art Gensler immediately and directly. That's the level of priority we wanted people to know we placed on anything that might jeopardize our trust relationships. Of all the things I've learned, the need for personal involvement in such issues is of paramount importance to your enterprise.

While ValuJet as a brand didn't survive the crash of flight 592, the advice was sound. Other companies facing similar crises have saved untold dollars and reputation through following this course of action. Complete transparency about ethical issues of all types and open, ongoing conversation are critical elements in building a long-cycle enterprise.

Organizations can face a different kind of crisis, a moment where fear, personal loss and many other emotions may run particularly high. These are times when the nerve endings of everyone in your organization are most sensitive. They're also the times when the true personality and values of everyone in your organization show through most clearly. Your actions and responses at such times will have a long-term effect on the trust and respect relationships your organization enjoys. They're also catalytic moments and people's responses and reactions change things for a long time.

September 11, 2001, was such a moment for many companies throughout the country. Most responded with an outpouring of empathy for those involved, an embrace for the many affected and a bonding together unparalleled in this nation. I remember being in New York and Washington, DC, with our teams as soon as the airlines would take me there. The most important thing I did was to just listen to the stories that people couldn't wait to tell, of heroism, of loss, of fear, of sadness but most of all, of caring.

In the case of New York, the event changed trust relationships in a whole city. Reserve, ingrained fear and distrust on first encounter between people, so much the norm in New York, was being replaced by openness. Trust was once again being proffered among people as an opening position. I arose early the day I arrived in New York, before the restaurant in my hotel was open. I walked down the street to a local deli and was greeted by people who looked me in the eye and said "good morning," unheard of in New York pre-9/11. As I ordered breakfast at the counter, patrons in the deli did the same. I was fascinated by the conversations they were engaged in with each other. Seeming strangers were chatting about the day and themselves, not about the tragedy of the events of 9/11, but as neighbors who were part of a common community.

Our people were heroes, too. Our Wall Street office was just blocks from "ground zero" and a few of our people had just left a meeting in the World Trade Center as the first plane struck. We were very lucky that no one was harmed. After the initial shock, people pulled themselves together and helped out in the most amazing ways. People worked without rest to make sure everyone was okay, to find and reassure clients and then help them get into temporary space. Our IT group braved the cordons to retrieve back-up tapes and computers from Wall Street for the teams from that office who were temporarily located in our office in Rockefeller Center. They carried that equipment out on their backs.

Articles appeared in the papers about firms like Sidley Austin and Lehman brothers that were up and running by the end of the weekend, despite near total disruption. What they didn't mention were the teams, drawn from New York's architecture, design and construction community, who worked round-the-clock to make it happen. We were part of that massive effort, helping keep the heart of the world's economy beating.

All that Tuesday, the e-mails and phone calls streamed in. As the word spread, I heard from people in London and Amsterdam, Tokyo and Hong Kong. From every quarter, I heard grief and concern and the desire to help. This was not New York's, or Washington's, or even America's problem; it was a tragedy that befell our entire world.

As our New York office pulled together, managers and directors circulated through the office, urging people to take the time they needed to grieve and to heal. We set up a program management office, too, to handle the client requests relating to NYC space. And I kept getting calls and e-mails from the other offices: "Say the word. I'm ready to go." A whole new definition of trust and respect emerged.

Saying thank you

We can never say "thank you" often enough in our organizations. Appreciation is the ultimate indicator of respect for the efforts of another. 2001 evolved into a very tough year for many enterprises. Nerves were frayed, and pressures for financial performance were brutal with failure often hanging close in the balance. Too often I heard from people in client and competitor organizations about feelings of not being appreciated. I responded as follows:

As challenging as the year has been, it seems to have flown by. Speaking of flying, I asked my assistant last week if I was going to make 1K status with United Airlines again, this year thinking I had probably come close to flying the requisite 100,000 miles. She checked the Internet for my account and let me know that I'd clearly not been paying attention and had passed that threshold some time ago, logging significantly more than that this year. I knew it'd been pretty intense and was reminded of how focused we'd all been, wondering if I'd paused often enough to say something very important.

Thank you for the incredible effort each of you has put forth to support one another and to deepen our relationships with our clients. I receive phone calls and letters almost daily from the men and women in the organizations we serve thanking me for the terrific work you all are doing. I am humbled by these calls, knowing that they're coming to the wrong person. It's each of you who, through your commitment and dedication, have built the unparalleled reputation we carry in the marketplace. This is the greatest source of our strength and a magnificent tribute to each of you.

Throughout the year, challenged by restrictive fees and clients who have often seemed abusive as they are challenged by the circumstances confronting their businesses, you've remained professional, innovative and cheerful. You've done more with less. You've delivered terrific design when anything looking remotely "designed" (read expensive) was resisted by our clients. You've supported one another as professionals, sharing your knowledge and skills to deliver extraordinary work to our clients, and as human beings, lending a sympathetic ear and being supportive to one another when the going got particularly tough.

Take some time during the holidays for your self and your family. Charge up your batteries by enjoying the lightness of being away from the demands we've felt this year. And know, that if you haven't heard it often enough, you'll hear it again and again from me—Thank You!

Celebrating with humility

Occasionally, your enterprise has cause for great celebration. How do you handle it in a way that inspires further great work so the recognition is not an objective reached but a platform from which to grow? So often, when a goal is reached or a wonderful recognition is bestowed, the occasion becomes a plateau, something achieved with no motivation to stretch further. The chest thumping and back patting is fun. A glass of champagne or two is consumed, but how do the people in your organization feel when they return to work on Monday morning?

In the year 2000, Gensler was named the Firm of the Year by the AIA, a great honor for any firm. For us in particular with our breadth and scale of practice and focus on client-oriented design, it was an unusual recognition. Most previous "Firms of the Year" had been smaller, boutique design-focused practices. We were clearly a big business. We wanted this to be the launch point for further growth, not just in scale but in quality. Because of our size, we feared the onset of arrogance and the resulting resentment from our competitors, which would only hurt our business. How should a firm with a culture of trust and respect respond to deserve trust and respect, especially from our peers? Here's how I dealt with it:

> It's a very good idea to reflect on what this award is and what it's not. It is a fine honor to be recognized by our professional peers for what we've accomplished. Each of you can take personal pride in your own contribution to making our firm worthy of this award. It's fine to be proud of the firm, the

values that make us what we are, the collaborative spirit, the collegiality and the strong commitment to client service that has set us apart in the marketplace. It's a very good idea to be a visible role model for the profession, continuing to live by our values in every relationship we enjoy with clients, peers, contractors and vendors.

It's not a license to brag or make grand proclamations. In fact, it's a good time to remember that a little humility goes a long way. A great deal of attention will be focused on our firm this year, making us a very visible target for criticism from our competitors and others who, for reasons of jealousy or just plain competitive rivalry, might like to tarnish our image just a little; to knock us off our pedestal. The slightest error or arrogance has the potential to be amplified out of proportion. So accept this honor with grace and style, in other words, with a little humility. What we accomplished in the past may gain a bit of additional respect in the work we do, but it will be fragile and have a very short shelf life. Understand that we are in an incredibly dynamic and competitive environment and we're only going to be as good as the next thing we do for our clients.

Having now gotten the requisite warning statement out of the way, let's celebrate a little. For once, this honor wasn't just a beauty contest, not that we shouldn't be terribly proud of the quality of the design work we do. This was a real recognition that we've cleared a path for the profession in broadening services, managing well, enlarging the circle of ownership and focusing on our clients as the real source of design quality and innovation. Congratulations!

I'll bet you hadn't thought about why you would care about whether you have the trust and respect of your competitors. I found it most useful. Your competition has a lot harder time running you down to a customer if they truly respect you. My cynical side had always said this wouldn't matter but, as the years went by, I found it did. They, and customers I was after, would tell me so. A second distinct benefit is recruiting. You want your competitors' strongest people to be thinking of you as the best place there is to work.

11

Make Everything Transparent, Especially Your Ethics

I've talked a great deal about transparency in this book. It's a cornerstone of each of the strategies I've presented. Long-cycle companies are transparent about everything—their core mission and values, their compensation, reward, benefit and advancement processes, their customer and vendor relationships. That transparency is not a specific action that is taken but an attitude nurtured in everything they do, especially when it comes to ethical behavior. But ethics are a funny thing. When asked, people say they know what good ethical behavior is. If asked to describe specifics, they'll often shrug their shoulders and respond that everyone knows. It's a little like pornography—I'll know it when I see it.

Engaging in a conversation about ethics in your company can be risky business. No other subject exposes you more boldly to charges of moralizing. No other discussion puts you more quickly and clearly under a microscope—are you living up to the standards you're expecting of others? Or is this just another case of "do as I say, not as I do?" Many company leaders are honest enough with themselves to admit that they "shade" things from time to time, but that leads them to avoiding conversations about ethics because of feelings of guilt and, consciously or subconsciously, wanting to avoid confronting the issue. This is high-risk behavior for a long-cycle enterprise.

In many organizations, there is no clear, written document outlining ethical norms and expectations. The subject is especially difficult for people to deal with when there are things going on in the organization that could be construed as out of ethical bounds. If something is happening somewhere at a senior level in your organization and people are fearful for the security of their position if they mention it to anyone, they will avoid talking about it like the plague—except to their peers in the company ... and often to outsiders. This is the real risk to morale and reputation. If asked, the common response is, "Everyone knows what our ethics are," but when asked for specifics of what constitutes a breach of ethics, they lapse into silence.

A clear understanding of what constitutes moral and ethical behavior and appropriate norms of behavior is at the core of the integrity of your organization. It's part of your "brand." It's the moral compass that helps newcomers integrate effectively, giving them an early and clear sense of what's accepted as right and wrong in your enterprise.

`At a point in time, although I had no specific problems that I knew about, I decided it would be a good idea to document more specifically what constituted ethical behavior at Gensler. Consistent with a culture of transparency, I undertook this as an open discussion in the firm rather than an edict handed down. This way the resulting expectations for behavior would be shared, something everyone created together and accepted as the cultural norm for which we would all hold each other accountable.

About that time, I heard the following editorial on KNX 1070 radio in Los Angeles by Michael Josephson of the Josephson Institute in Southern California. I shared it with people in the firm to launch the discussion.

Russell Gough in *Character is Destiny* says most Americans agree on two points:

First, that our society is suffering from a poverty of ethics, that there has been a serious erosion in personal character and values. Second, we know who's responsible: he is, she is, they are.

His point is to highlight the tendency to finger point and blame throw when we are as much a part of the problem as the solution. Of course, none of us could possibly be bad enough to destroy the moral fiber the nation, but our behavior can and probably does contribute to the erosion of our moral ozone.

Are you ready to be really honest with yourself about your own ethics? Here's a small test. How often have you engaged in any of the following in the past year? More than once, only once or none.

1. Stealing. Have you taken anything from work, improperly charged phone calls or duplicated copyrighted products?
2. How about cheating? On exams, internal reports or time sheets, taxes, or taking sick days without being sick.
3. Lying. This includes deliberate deception to family, friends or employers and false statements on insurance claims, expense reports and the like.
4. Breaking promises.
5. Treating people badly, being unkind or abusive.
6. Have you demonstrated racial, ethnic or gender prejudice with words or acts?
7. Used physical force or threats in anger or to get something?
8. Used people for your own selfish ends— sexually or otherwise?
9. Borrowed more than you can pay back or otherwise neglected your debts?
10. Have you been drunk in front of kids or driven while drunk?

So no one's perfect you say? True enough. But on these

simple matters most of us could do a great deal better.

This had caused me to think about our business and the "opportunities" we may be exposed to. It's not terribly difficult to figure out that a contractor building a new deck on someone's house for free or at a greatly reduced cost in order to earn favored treatment on assignments is way out of bounds; or the carpet vendor offering to carpet someone's family room. There had been cases filed in New York against contractors and project management consultants who solicited and received substantial kick-backs and wound up in jail. So, when are such favors illegal and unethical, and when are they acceptable within the bounds of normal business practice?

Disney and agencies of the U.S. Government prohibit employees from accepting any entertainment, gifts or other gratuities whatsoever from vendors. How often are people in your organization treated to lunch or dinner by outside vendors? Is this appropriate? Or what about a golf game? Or a ski weekend? When do we incur an obligation? Is a business lunch okay? Where do you want to draw the line? We decided that it was important for us to have a consistent approach throughout the firm on such issues, particularly in light of the recent cases in New York. We were known throughout our profession as upholding high ethical standards. It was imperative that we continually reinforced that reputation. So, we solicited people's thoughts about ethics and where we should draw the line. Folks in our firm had many different points of view, and we wanted to hear from as many as were interested and willing to take a few moments to think about how we wanted to be known to each other and within our profession.

I received many responses and, in the end, assigned the matter to one of our task forces to assimilate and document. It turned out that the subject hit some tender chords in the firm. But the debates over what was right and what was wrong, where to draw the line, were ultimately resolved in an open forum leading to a much higher rate of acceptance with a great deal less cynicism than would have been the case had it been simply a dictum issued from management.

Each person in your enterprise is called upon to make judgment calls on a daily basis founded on their personal and professional values. And, for the most part, good calls are made. But the world is growing more complicated and competitive. More often lately I suspect the leaders in your organization are being asked for guidance on situations that involve ethical judgment. What information can I share with others about the work I'm doing with a customer? When can we work with two customers who compete with one another? Is it okay to go on an all-expense-paid ski weekend following an afternoon visit to a vendor's factory for a little "education?" Are a couple of tickets to a ball game going to affect my business judgment?

We developed an ethics guidelines document that went through many rounds of testing and discussion within the firm, and a workshop was held in each office to review these guidelines. We felt we had a responsibility to discuss our values with each other openly throughout the firm, to explore the application of these values to real-world situations and to provide examples of the integrity that had made us a respected firm. Our goals were simple: for our clients—to provide exceptional quality services that were unbiased and professional; for each other—to create a high-integrity environment where the brightest and most creative professionals could thrive.

While we didn't distribute these guidelines on a broad basis outside the firm, they were made available to anyone who was interested and as a reference point for a manufacturer, vendor or client when a situation arose in which they could be helpful. They did, indeed, find their way into the peripheral community with which we worked and were most helpful in easing the pressure from particularly aggressive salespeople who just loved using their perk budget on our designers. It helped our people to draw a line and was much appreciated by our clients.

No matter how well digested an ethics policy may be, no matter how much consensus there seems to be, some issue often remains unresolved. I always worried when I heard about backroom conversations about an ethical issue. Was it just the tip of the iceberg? I felt it important to get such things out into the open, if for no other reason than to find out if there were other things going on that I needed to know about. One of the more contentious issues among our designers was specifying furniture the firm had designed and from which we collected royalties. We had some passive aggressive behavior going on—designers who felt it was unethical to specify our products because we were collecting royalties, no matter how appropriate for the client, and would simply avoid even considering them for a project. This may seem like a small thing that could be handled by a simple directive saying, "Get over it." But when you do that, you run the risk of teaching your people that any concerns they raise will be treated similarly and that your company won't address ethical issues. So let me tell you how I dealt with this one.

Following Neocon, an annual furniture exposition held in Chicago each year, our presence was broadly felt through product design, showroom design and collateral marketing and graphic support provided to several manufacturers. We had become an important force in the interior furnishings industry with many of our products selling well and receiving positive comments from the design community.

Earlier product design efforts had not carried the firm's name. We and our clients feared that a connection to the firm and the fact that we receive royalties on the products we design might discourage other designers from specifying our products. The introduction of a specific product that year with our name prominently attached had proven that this was not the case. One of the case goods manufacturers with whom we had worked had specifically avoided connecting our name to his product and was surprised to find that customers discovering that we designed the line raised no objection at all. In fact, our connection to a product seemed to carry a very positive caché—not exactly the "Good Housekeeping Seal of Approval" but something like it.

But a few of our designers remained privately concerned about specifying our products on our own projects, referencing the

potential for a perception of conflict of interest. We had an explicit
policy available about full disclosure to our clients regarding our
relationship with any product from which we receive a royalty along
with a sample letter to the client explaining our relationship, but that
didn't seem to satisfy them

I opened up the conversation by reminding everyone to
remember that we had chosen to be in the business of product design.
Designers and firms employ different methods when working with
manufacturers. We used compensation to recover our costs, provide
a profit and to fund research and further development of new and
innovative products. As a firm, we were uniquely positioned to
deliver penetrating insights about the market for products to manufacturers. That's why we chose to enter this business. Clients came
to us for this knowledge, and it had a very real value to them. It was
one of our firm's assets and, as such, deserved to receive appropriate compensation. So we should have had no embarrassment about
charging and receiving a return on the investment we'd made over
many decades to develop the firm's intellectual capital that enabled
us to deliver this kind of value to manufacturers.

From the point of view of the client for whom we specified
products, the question remained about whether we were specifying
our own product in order to enrich ourselves rather than because
it was the best solution to that client's problem. We agreed that we
would never specify any product or system for any other reason
than its unique and appropriate ability to answer a client's needs.
Additionally, the royalties were quite small, and the revenue from
specifying one of our products on any individual project would
never be sufficient to motivate us to select one of our products over
another.

So, what should this mean for our designers as we worked
through the selection and specification process on our projects?
Clearly, we had to start with the question: "What's the best solution
for our clients?" And that must embrace all sources that provide
appropriate solutions, including products we'd designed. I was
extremely proud of the products we'd brought to the market. They

were well designed and produced by high-quality manufacturers. Avoiding products we'd designed as representing a conflict of interest was neither fair to the manufacturers who had put their faith and trust (and fees) in our firm and deserved consideration nor to our clients who deserved a look at all potential appropriate products, including the ones we'd designed.

It turned out that this was just an isolated concern and not a surrogate for something else that needed to be addressed. Through transparency and open discussion, the conversations moved out into the open, relieving a hot spot in the firm and teaching an important lesson—that when people in the firm were concerned about an ethical issue, it would see the light of day and get resolved.

Listen Carefully During Times of Economic Inflection

During my 38 years in business, I've experienced several boom and bust cycles. When I finished graduate school in 1968, the country, particularly the West Coast, was mired in a recession—at least in the architectural profession. I knocked on doors for nearly a year and a half before I found a job in an architectural office, biding my time working for a housing developer. The early 70s boom was followed in 1974 by an oil embargo that sent the country into a tailspin.

When I reached Los Angeles in 1976, things had perked up considerably and, frankly, finding new work was like shooting fish in a barrel. In 1981, things dried up again, and for a year and a half I wondered if we could keep the office doors open. The mid-80s were wonderful, stopped short by the Savings & Loan crisis. Construction stopped again, and business throughout the country seemed to be in a recession with no apparent end in sight. By 1993, there was a visceral energy emerging in the market, and by the late 90s, the country and our business were in a boom period the likes of which we'd never seen. Then, in a time frame so brief it seemed like it happened overnight, the dot.com correction sent the markets, the economy and our business into a tailspin.

The markets we all serve will continually fluctuate. It's the nature of a capitalistic economy to cycle down, learn from and correct for the cause, cycle up and then face a new crisis. Long-cycle organizations learn to creatively weather these cycles, behaving differently in each phase but staying consistent to their core purpose and mission.

During these times of economic inflection, the people in your organization have great difficulty seeing the forest for the trees, maintaining the confidence necessary to remain committed and acting with clarity of purpose. In down cycles, they're haunted by the often very real concern about whether they'll still have a job tomorrow; will they be able to feed their family and pay their mortgage? In boom times, they often find themselves working such long hours that they fear burnout, find their family lives deteriorating and wondering, what am I doing this all for, anyway?

These are real issues for the people in your organization. They're so present in people's focus that they affect work quality and the stability of the enterprise. As I reflect back on my career, I realize what a small percentage of the aggregated time was spent in an economic comfort zone and how much time I spent helping people deal with their concerns about how the economy was personally affecting them—right now.

Over the years I learned that I had to listen vigilantly for the fears nascent in people's minds. They were there, either they were repressed and made manifest through aberrant behavior on the job or at home, or they were being discussed at work or in the home without satisfactory resolution. Either way, I found it enormously helpful to give voice to these concerns, to open up conversation, to be honest and realistic about the state of the economy and the firm in order to remain focused on our long-cycle purposefulness.

When good times can be bad times
In 1998, when the dot.com boom cycle was reaching full strength, I received an e-mail following a "town hall" meeting in one of our offices that resonated with conversations I'd had with many of our folks over the previous year.

Ed,

I enjoyed your talk on Tuesday. I did not have time and didn't really want to talk about this in front of the whole group, but I do have a question regarding some of the things you were talking about. I spoke with our HR director about six weeks ago and have had several conversations with my studio director about some of these issues. I may not word them properly, but here's what I'm feeling:

How do you manage a client relationship to the quality expected from not only you, but the firm, and the client, when you have been stretched beyond the limit for more than 15 months? Cries of help to VPs and managing principals (which you stated are perfectly acceptable in this organization) have been heard and acknowledged but not addressed.

How do you balance constantly performing beyond 120% capacity (and I know I'm being rewarded financially and with a promotion!) with the fact that by working so hard, my personal life suffers due to stress and lack of personal time?

Obviously these are questions that are very broad in one sense, but to me right now they are extremely specific. I have actually for the first time in 13 years of professional life considered a two-month leave simply to get away from this ridiculous pace. I know we are trying to hire people and it is difficult - but where does it stop with bringing in new work and taxing the devoted and already overworked staff? I asked the question "what happens if I stop working 12- and 16-hour days and work a normal eight?" I got no response.

Any advice you have is welcome and appreciated!

Thanks.

I really empathized (because I'd been there myself many times over the years) and, unfortunately, had heard this story much too often around the firm over the years. This is one of the toughest questions any of us ever faces. We're all willing to take on a super stretch now and then to meet commitments, but when it becomes a way of life, it can create serious personal problems.

We all get caught up in the guilt connected with the "everyone else is doing it, so if I'm not working the same insane hours, I'm a shirker." This is very dangerous turf. It can screw up people's home life, make them sick and lead to errors in their work. But it seems to be a syndrome that people get caught up in.

Let me suggest some thoughts that I passed along to this young person. Why do you draw the line on the number of hours you work at 12, or 14 or 16? Or the number of days in a row you chose to do this at two, three, four, 30, 60? Or the number of Saturdays or Sundays you decide you've just got to come into the office to work? Is it really a choice or an obligation? When you do it once in a while to help out the team it makes you feel good; how far do you go before it starts to feel bad? The people in your organization need to feel that it's a personal choice, and at the time it starts to feel really bad, they have the right and, frankly, the obligation to choose to change it (or be prepared to face the consequences). In the end, there are still a finite number of hours that we, cumulatively, can apply to work that form a natural bound, both individually and as an organization, to the amount of work we can take on. When we exceed that limit, we have to say "no" in some fashion, as individuals and as an enterprise. Where we chose to set that limit is up to us. But it's always going to be better to set the limit by choice than by default.

What will happen if you say, "This is it. This is the limit of time I can effectively work before I jeopardize health, family and quality of work." I mean, after all, you're making that choice when, after 16 hours, you finally say, "Sorry, I've got to go home and get some sleep." Are you letting the team and the organization down because you're not working 24 hours a day, seven days a week?

There's no question that there will be extraordinary periods in your organization's life. New work seems to literally come in faster than you're able to accommodate it; times when you're certainly not growing for growth's sake and you're being selective about the work you take on. But sometimes the markets you serve are extremely busy, and you've done a great job for a lot of customers who keep expanding their relationship with you and recommending you to others. The result is tremendous pressure in your organization.

When you feel this in your organization, it's time to take a deep breath, slow down a bit and gear yourself to return to a little more balanced lifestyle before someone gets sick or you begin defaulting on work. It's an easy cliché to say, "We've got to make hay while the sun shines." Just be careful not to make it a way of life to the detriment of your clients and your people. Yes, you can hire as fast as you can and continue to do so. Yes, you can be increasingly selective about the work you take on and you must continue to do this. Yes, you can raise prices to discourage a marginal segment of work coming in to you. Yes, you can refer work that is not specifically suited to you to someone else or partner with another enterprise you trust to work as you do on behalf of your clients. But in the end, the risks to your organization and its long-term value and all that you've built are too great if you don't consciously start to move people's lives back into balance and make them aware that you're committed to doing so.

When you see bad times coming

You need to help your organization step back from localized issues and see the economy in a larger perspective. While we weren't economists, we could smell an end to the 90s boom cycle coming. We just didn't know when. But our people were as caught up as most organizations were (to say nothing of Alan Greenspan who, despite his "irrational exuberance" comment in 1997 continued to cheer an overheated economy along) with the "new economy" that seemed to have arrived. So I tried to provide a context for thought and some meaningful actions and responses that we could take.

I'm not an economist, but I can insert the thermometer and take the global economic temperature pretty well. In 1999, we were finally starting to feel the effects of the severe Asian recession, albeit less catastrophically than it was being felt in the rest of the world at the time. If you were in Russia at that time, you'd be very concerned about the impending winter, availability of food (and your ability to pay for it) and the very real possibility of anarchy. If you were in Germany, you'd be concerned about the potential of Russian refugees knocking on your door. Things had slowed dramatically in South America, Australia and New Zealand. If anything, we in America were blissfully insulated from the rest of the world.

It seemed so recent that the world viewed Japan as the new dominant economy with robust technology and streamlined, just-in-time production. Now, the second-largest economy had shown major structural and cultural problems in its governance and appeared to be like a deer frozen in the headlights as it continued to avoid dealing with over-valued assets and non-performing loans. Maybe we should have offered a new export service, the Resolution Trust Corporation. The whole RTC episode in America that forced our savings and loan industry to deal with the same set of problems may have seemed painful at the time, but it set this country on a solid foundation for the growth we'd enjoyed in the mid 90s. Or, remember the painful layoffs of the late 80s and early 90s (otherwise known as down-sizing or right-sizing)? As painful as it seemed at the time, it spawned a whole new generation of entrepreneurs in America who raised employment and improved efficiency tremendously. America became the model of high performance, high quality and low cost. Manufacturing jobs even returned from Asia and Mexico as America got to work.

The NASDAQ had collapsed, meaning that most of our technology clients who depend on borrowed funds or new stock issues to pay for the development of new product were pulling way back. The collapse was partially a result of the deterioration of Asian demand for their products but was probably more a response to the "psychology" of the market. Would investor confidence return bringing buyers back into the market or would the fear of continued deterioration further depress the market. And, of course, we had to think about financial institutions and law firms which comprised a large segment of our business. Would the banks continue their aggressive consolidation (good for our business) or would they hunker down as their lending activity slowed? At least law firms always seem to have something to do whether business was good or bad.

Since I certainly couldn't answer these questions, I proposed a couple of "one-size-fits-all" strategies. As hard as we were all working and as focused as we'd been on recruiting, it was time for caution. In other words, we could see that the market was definitely headed for a slowdown, and we didn't want to over hire and then lay off. We were cautious about further expansion of our office space. We asked people to be prepared for some displacement - being shifted from one assignment to another or being asked to pitch in and work in another office for a time in order to balance workloads around the firm without hiring in one city while folks in another city waited for a project to recycle. We'd worked very hard to find wonderfully talented colleagues to work with and needed flexibility to respond to this very volatile market.

I may not have been able to predict the future, but I knew that we were going to face a time of day-to-day uncertainty. This meant our clients would be fearful (their project might be stopped; they might find themselves out of a job), they'd be in a hurry (quick, let's get it done before someone changes their mind) and they'd be "people" (meaning that they'd remember how we dealt with them when they were experiencing high anxiety). We asked that people pay special attention to their clients listening with a "third ear," that intuition that tells you when to spend a little extra time empathizing or probing a little deeper to search out the real issue you're solving for right now.

Value was going to take an entirely different form for a while, and it wouldn't be the same from client to client. Design would be the intrinsic value we'd be remembered for long after the project was in place, but wasn't a topic of great interest to our clients at that time. So we said, "do" design but "talk about" value in terms that were important to each individual client at that very moment and keep asking that question because it kept changing during the course of the project. We asked people not to get caught in the trap of saying, "But that's what you said was your priority; now you've changed your mind on me." Our clients would value highly our ability to be anticipatory with them as they navigated the economic minefield driving their businesses.

Remember, things weren't that bad yet. Not many projects had been stopped, our revenues were marvelous, but we had to prepare people for what was almost certainly coming. There is always a fear that this sort of dialogue will scare people; have them updating their resume. I believe it has a positive effect, demonstrating a clear sense of realism coupled with a commitment to keep the enterprise vital, no matter what the economy brings.

The inflection point

From that gnawing intuition that the economy was going down, it took us nearly a year and a half to reach the real inflection point. People's mindset was still one of disbelief and non-acceptance. In late 2000, I began thinking about the coming year and felt it was going to be a disaster. A phrase from a book my wife had given me for Christmas came to mind. It's a great book titled *Prince Borghese's Trail* by Genevieve Obert, one of two women who piloted a 1968 Hillman Hunter from Beijing to Paris in 1997 as part of a rerun of the classic 1907 Peking to Paris car rally. Since I've met Genny and know her partner in the race, Linda Dodwell, along with a few others who participated, the book had particular relevance for me. I followed the daily web postings when the race was run (43 days to traverse over 10,000 miles in September and early October of 1997) and was thrilled by this great adventure. Each chapter of the book is headed by a quote from the journals of the original race held 90 years before. The one that caught my attention was:

On certain journeys it is better never to settle things. Any settling of plans is a deplorable act of presumption; it is an attempt to limit and direct Fate. Fate would avenge herself and humble our pride.

And so I began speculating on the journey of the new year knowing that, come January 2002, we'd have had our eyes opened wide again by an ever-changing world and, no matter how carefully we planned, it would all turn out differently. So what was the context for the coming year around which we should shape our actions? Once again, the pundits were projecting an economic slowdown, perhaps a recession. Circumstances were certainly aiming in that direction more clearly than the previous year. Venture capital had dried up for the dot.coms, and the market value for most technology firms had collapsed. There was less money available to invest although most argued that the inflated values in the market were synthetic anyway and present market values were a more realistic representation of the underlying value of companies.

Energy prices were up dramatically in this country, most significantly in the West, seriously effecting many companies that were energy dependent (and there are more of them than you think, from obvious ones like hotels to less apparent ones like diaper services and flower growers). It's always interesting how extensive the effects of reduced available capital and increased energy costs are on all businesses. In Silicon Valley, companies who used to deliver fresh fruits to dot.coms were going out of business as the demand for their service dried up and ad agencies were laying off large numbers of people as advertising budgets disappeared. I suspected the ads on the Super Bowl that year would finally return to companies that did or made something we could actually understand and those 30-second slots would sell for somewhat lower prices.

So what was our strategy? Many in the firm had never "participated" in a downturn of the economy and needed to be reminded why we did so well in the last one. To use an old fashioned phrase, some truths remain self-evident. Simply put, we took great care of our clients. We'd gone through a period where everyone had been extraordinarily busy, not just in our firm or our profession, but throughout the country and much of the world (not dissimilar to the late 80s although this time business volume growth had been much more intense). We'd had more work made available to us than we'd had time or talent to serve thoroughly and completely. Notice that I said "made available" as opposed to "we'd sold more work." Most of our assignments had come to us with very little marketing, selling or competition.

We knew that, during an economic slowdown, the continuity of our work would come from clients who were "fiercely loyal" to us, as they had been in the early 90s. What causes a client to be "fiercely loyal" to you? If you'd gotten terribly busy on a fascinating new assignment and forgotten to follow up on something a client asked you to do the odds are against you. In fact, "fiercely loyal" only results from going way beyond just following up. It comes from anticipating and showing passionate concern about a client's matters.

We focused our strategy on this attitude. The fact that most of our clients had grown accustomed to poor service with very little true caring in most everything they consumed in the 90s (airlines, taxis, restaurants), because everyone was selling more than they could produce, won't help when the market turns competitive. And dialing up the marketing efforts wasn't going to keep us busy when there was less demand for our services. Only "fierce loyalty" would preserve and extend our client relationships and, therefore, our workload. So, we asked people to make a New Year's resolution, to nurture "fiercely loyal" clients. We asked people to take a client to lunch each week. Find out what was going on in their world and what could be done to make it better; to anticipate what they needed before they asked; to protect their budgets and schedules with great care; to dream up a wonderfully creative way to make their business work better; to make their job more than just "getting the pants out the door" (the watch word of the 90s) by caring about whether the proverbial pants fit and make the client look beautiful.

The market hadn't stopped being competitive during the 90s when there was more business around than any of us could handle (I never understood why—fees should have gone up). I knew it would be even more competitive in a slowdown. Streamlining what we did needed to be a constant mission. But it wasn't enough. We needed to invent whole new ways of accomplishing our work, eliminating processes for which clients did not ascribe value. I suggested another lunch date with a client, one that knew us and our processes well. I suggested asking that client to be open and frank about the way we were doing our work. What steps, processes or documents seemed to make no sense to him or her at all? What things that we were doing had no value and just shouldn't be done?

There was greater potential, though, in creating higher value than in reducing costs. What things that we weren't doing would have great value to our clients? What is of the greatest value of all as an outcome of our relationship? Speed? Budget adherence? A design award? Higher retention, lower absenteeism? How could we learn to interact and deliver in a way where everything we did had high value to our clients? If everything we did had high value, the perceived relative cost in a competitive market may be very low. We weren't going to learn about this by talking to each other.

I asked people to take the engineers on their projects to lunch, one at a time. I suggested starting out individually so they knew we were sincere and then getting them all together to stimulate ways to get the most out of our work together. It had always interested me that we negotiated so hard with our engineers for lower fees but then made their work more difficult by not using them on multiple assignments, learning together how to work more efficiently, effectively and creatively. In the same way that we work better with a client when we work with them over a broader range of assignments, our engineers blossom and become more cost-effective when they work with us again and again. We're selling this advantage to our customers; we needed to start buying it and nurturing it from our suppliers. There could be a residual benefit as well. Engineers were out in the marketplace just as we were. Often, they knew of a project before we did and would alert us to it if we happened to be the design firm they enjoyed working with the most.

Maybe there wouldn't be an economic slowdown or a recession after all. But who cared if you had clients who became "fiercely loyal" to you and the firm no matter what happens in the economy. That's simply a better way to conduct your business in a time of economic slowdown, and a pretty good way to conduct your business in an era of hyper competitiveness in a global economy.

When you hit the wall

Empathizing with the concerns people have about their colleagues being laid off is critical. In a long-cycle enterprise where much of the recruiting is done through referrals from people in your organization, someone who has brought a friend or colleague to the company has real heartburn if that person is laid off. So taking stock of what's going on, assessing change and, most particularly, assuring people that as an enterprise, you're planning to weather the downturn by taking definitive actions to assure you'll be stronger than ever when the economy turns is imperative.

We launched a campaign to keep our focus on the fundamental values of the enterprise, citing examples of projects and client relationships that fit our core mission to be a collegial and collaborative enterprise that shared resources across the firm in our clients' interests. When work tightens up, it amazes me how quickly business units want to return to incremental financial statements to find a way to protect individual interests, losing sight of the broader value of the enterprise as a whole. It becomes a time to reinforce the reasons for staying the course to assure people that there is a conscious direction to the enterprise and that the leadership is not going to adopt an expedient reactionary approach.

You also need to remind people of why you lay people off and trim costs aggressively in certain areas. There will always be hand wringing about the special circumstances of someone who just has to be kept on but the mandate of a long-cycle enterprise is to free up the capital to invest in core programs in order to be well positioned to capitalize on the upturn in the economy when it comes—things like continuing education and infrastructure.

The challenge remains to communicate what you're doing

and why, responding directly to voiced as well as unsaid fears and concerns in a straightforward fashion. For many companies in the 90s, it was the first time younger people had experienced the impacts of a recession. For some, it was impacting them, their families or friends in very personal ways. It's not fun. When you're old enough to have experienced more than one economic downturn, you learn some lessons: keep your business financially sound, continue to adapt your products, services and systems to your clients' needs, and don't stop investing for the future.

And yet, the recession dragged on. But our constant focus on core issues had begun to yield results, both in business revitalization and, more importantly, in innovation. This is an interesting long-term strategic outcome. Following this approach of listening to the people in your organization, being honest and open about what's happening and continuing to invest in the future keeps people engaged. Rather than the most talented and entrepreneurial leaving to find greener pastures, they become more deeply committed to your and their future. Whining dries up when the leadership of an organization stays focused beyond the current state of affairs.

Stay with the program and breakthroughs occur

For us, September 2002 was a breakthrough in many ways as innovative ideas started to flow. We continued to invest in and support the research taking place in our practice area groups. Their leaders began to present the innovations that had come out of their work, disseminating that knowledge, helping others to take advantage of the very best work being done in the firm and establishing their priorities for continued research and expansion of knowledge. These presentations gave everyone in the firm a renewed sense of the breadth and quality of thinking going on, suppressing speculation that the recession had put innovation on hold.

One particular innovation, shifting the firm's focus to "performance consulting" was truly a breakthrough concept. Rather than thinking of the firm as an enterprise that did architecture, interior design, graphics or planning, we began to recast ourselves as being in the performance-consulting business. We began to describe our mission to our clients in different terms. An organization's performance is a result of alignment among their people, process, place and technology, working in concert to serve their customers. Architecture, interior design and planning were simply tools to affect positive change in the performance metrics of a client firm, and we set out to become experts in measuring those results and presenting from a new point of view: how would our design solutions specifically impact measurable elements of performance.

This change of thinking would simply not have taken place without a constant focus on our clients, what they wanted, where we wanted to be in that value proposition and how we wanted to be thought of as their business partner. And it bubbled up from within the firm. The environment in the organization must also be open to venturing into uncharted waters, dealing with radical change in its vocabulary. But there is nothing like a time of economic crisis to nurture that environment. Finally, the enterprise must be willing to cannibalize its existing lines of business with new approaches and methodologies. Turf battles and protection of existing lines of business have no place in a long-cycle enterprise.

The result of these efforts—our good people stayed, and the best from other firms wanted to join us. Clients came back because they saw stability, commitment to purpose and innovation. Remember these lessons when you think you're scraping the bottom of the barrel.

PART IV

NURTURING
NETWORKS

Build "Real Time" Connectedness

As organizations grow, sharing knowledge and resources across broad boundaries requires a culture of real-time connectedness throughout the organization. Real-time means right now. How many great plans and strategies have gone awry as a result of a crucial piece of information delivered late? But how do you build such a culture of urgency into your company?

Growing an enterprise beyond those magic numbers discussed in Chapter 4—beyond a group of 35 or a business unit of 150, beyond multiples of what can be communicated to a group of people in a single room—requires new patterns and systems. When the entire organization can fit into a single room to discuss what's going on and what needs to be done, an individual's physical absence from the conversation is apparent and peer pressure can be a strong motivator to participate. Once these limits are exceeded these new constructs, to be effective, must take on the form of "rituals." They must be thought of as sacred by those expected to participate; so important that no one would think of missing out. I'll describe a number of communication elements with that depth of importance. The vital characteristic of each, though, is its real-time urgency and sense of criticality to your business process.

Regularly scheduled real-time communication: In an enterprise that spans broad geography, you need a frequently held interactive forum that gets at the vital right now issues that drive your organization. This element must be sacred. I chaired Gensler's equivalent for many years and participated from places as diverse as a phone booth on a motorcycle vacation in western Michigan, poolside on another holiday in the south of France and a hotel room in Shanghai. I never missed the call, nor, for the most part, did anyone else. This is where the "action" is. This is where opportunities and needs, business unit by business unit, client by client were shared. This is a place to make the resources of your enterprise openly available in real-time.

Office leaders meetings: develop a standing meeting to deal with real-time issues locally, following up on regional, national or global needs. I recommend weekly.

Subject-specific task forces: Develop task forces dealing with short to medium term issues of finite duration as well as long term. These may deal with technical issues such as design or the unique requirements of an industry segment and should have a common purpose of identifying and making available the most current knowledge on a wide variety of subjects. Each should sponsor research and foster innovation to expand your enterprise's knowledge base, meeting or conversing frequently across geographic boundaries. More importantly, they will evolve over time as a robust series of real-time networks to bring expert knowledge to bear as needed by tapping members of each for access to the latest knowledge on a project specific basis. Best practices and research can be made available on an intranet knowledge network, always with a reference to a specific individual to contact for more detailed information.

Cross referencing

Develop a vehicle to bring these groups together, not only as subject specific task forces, but across interest boundaries. Individuals from different geographic locations within a task force need to meet face to face, to develop the social bonds that foster trust, responsiveness, collegiality and a sense of common mission when one is asked for help without which, sharing never really happens.

Individual groups can spend time working with others in their group on issues of shared interest, but the most important work that will happen will be across interest groups where a sense of common mission can be instilled, reinforcing the vital nature of all pieces acting together in the client's interest.

Intranet

Your resource and knowledge base forms the backbone of connectivity for your task Forces, and should be structured to provide the most current information which comes out of the work of these groups. In years past, it has been exceptionally difficult to populate an Intranet site, requiring trained staff to format and input data. Today, internet protocols make this effort easier, allowing the work done by task forces to be immediately repurposed for such a site.

The real value of any site is not realized through the data stored there but through an individual's ability to access a person who has specific or extended knowledge relating to the subject being researched. Data contained on the site, no matter how current, will always be subject to update. But even more important, it will never be an exact match for the project or purpose for which you need it. The only way to understand the information in the context it was presented or to make it relevant to your particular needs is to talk to the expert. As you develop your own knowledge network, be sure that every citation has a person's name attached and, preferably, a hot link to their e-mail address and their phone number.

Board

A Board of Directors is mandated by laws governing corporations, both public and private. Since Sarbanes-Oxley, the regulations governing the operation of a public Board have become much more onerous and cumbersome. A discussion of public Boards is well beyond the scope of this book so I'll limit my comments to the Board of privately held corporations or the governance committee of a partnership. For convenience, I'll simply refer to these as the Board.

While a Board is certainly accountable as a fiduciary to the stock holders of a corporation (in our case, the stock was held by the Chairman, President, Vice-Presidents and the ESOP) its real value in the context of this book is to provide guidance to the leadership team on strategic direction. Outside directors or board advisors add a certain discipline to the board forum and, with the continuity of a long involvement with the management team and history of the enterprise, can provide unique points of view removed from the day to day turmoil of operating the company. It's a bit like that old adage, "When you're up to your ass in alligators, it's sometimes hard to remember that your mission here is to drain the swamp."

During my tenure at Gensler, the Board consisted of four of us, all working members of the firm, plus an outside advisor or two from time to time. We were able to guide growth on a macro level, making final judgments about businesses and markets we should be in, actively recruiting senior level staff, making recommendations regarding under-performing senior staff and acting as a review committee with responsibility for major capital decisions. Without outside shareholders and committed to a long-term strategy, we were able to focus our attention on much more interesting governance issues than a public Board responsible to shareholders for quarterly performance.

Understanding and shaping the nature, structure and priorities of your Board is essential in orienting your enterprise toward long-cycle strategies.

Operating Committee

Every organization requires an operating committee to provide day to day governance. To be effective, this group must also be full participants in your regularly scheduled real-time communication forum and should meet formally at least qurterly. This level of connectedness sets a model for in-depth knowledge about the operation and issues of your enterprise, allowing a long-cycle strategy to evolve effectively across its breadth. In each meeting you should review the activities of each business unit, particularly noting problems and opportunities with clients and people, reinforcing an environment of sharing: of knowledge, talent, client relationships, best practices and innovation. You may receive reports and act on corporate related issues such as personnel policies, public relations and communications opportunities, legal issues and, of course, finances.

Each meeting may take on a different subject such as long range planning, professional growth, compensation and promotion or subjects relating to growing professional excellence.

Vice Presidents

In a corporation, Vice Presidents are officers, carrying the responsibility and authority to make commitments contractually and to commit the resources of the enterprise in the conduct of its business. With the liabilities inherent in an architectural practice, selection, grooming and acculturation of Vice Presidents are particularly crucial. Their grooming must begin long before being appointed through coaching by Vice Presidents under whose direction they work. An orientation at appointment can bring them into more formal and specific contact with administrative resource information in areas of finance, legal, and human resources for which we expected them to be responsible.

As important as any other factor, however, is their role as a knowledge resource to the people with whom they work. Their ability to take a broader view of your enterprise's activities is usually a key factor in their initial selection and their deeper leadership participation in some subject specific area of importance to your mission continues to build their network of relationships beyond their own specific job structure.

Bringing the officers in your organization together outside the work environment builds social networks that reinforce your ability to accomplish the work of your clients and customers. I encourage spouse participation as well, after all, without their support, the deep commitment you want of the people within your organization will never come about. Do this at least once a year.

Telephone and E-mail

Every organization has its own culture about telephone and e-mail usage and etiquette. Gensler was no exception. Because of the deep reliance on rich networks throughout the firm and because of its geographic and time zone spread, immediate response to inquiries was a constant challenge. We made it an ongoing cultural priority to be highly responsive. It's how people get their work done. They depend on just-in-time expert knowledge in developing high quality solutions for their clients.

Add to this the fact that most teams communicated with a broad variety of sources outside the firm, contractors, sub-contractors, engineering and other specialty consultants, product vendors and building officials. Maintaining a consistently high level of responsiveness is an imperative. While response time to an inquiry within the firm was always pretty good (we expected a response within a day, maximum, to an internal inquiry reminding people frequently that to put off a call or e-mail from a colleague was simply unacceptable), nurturing the same responsive relationships outside requires constant hygiene.

Our work continued to come to us through referrals from the many friends that each person had made among our clients. But it was also wonderful to see how often we received referrals from consultants, contractors or vendors; or even a building or planning official. But it was much more difficult to get people to be as responsive to outside sources. I heard regularly, "Easy for you to say but have you seen the 50 e-mails I got in the last half hour," or "I'm never going to be able to clear my voice mailbox at the office to say nothing of my cell phone and my home answer machine." I reminded people that this may be telling them something about that balance factor. Their reputation, their "brand" as a professional (as well as the firm's) is built one e-mail or promptly returned phone call at a time. We were in a highly collaborative profession and the responsiveness we needed from others to help us do our job was the result of our own responsiveness.

Finding balance, being able to take the time to be this thoroughly responsive, may be the most important goal people in any enterprise can set for themselves. It's what customers and colleagues need and expect. It sets the stage for each person's professional future as well as that of your organization.

Spreading tribal lore

Every organization has its share of tribal lore, those war stories about how the enterprise came into being. These are great stories of heroism and villainy, good and evil, stories about the people and events that made the enterprise what it is. Stories about the history of a company and the people in it are really small morality tales. They're used to illustrate values and deeply held beliefs. These stories are usually embellished over time and finally settle in to a tale that many people in the organization come to know and are able to repeat to others to illustrate a point.

New staff orientations are great places to tell these tales but it helps if they are delivered by tribal elders, someone who participated in the making of the event or knew those who did. As a firm grows larger and reaches its next generations, try not to lose these tales. They take on a mystic quality, helping new people integrate into the culture. And, they'll be added to over time as new stories about people and events more current to the organization's business add to the anthology of experiences to illustrate particular values or ethics.

We told and retold these old stories in many places: new staff orientations, certainly, but also at many of the meetings described above, usually in the evening after several glasses of wine. People new to the particular meeting loved them and people who'd been around for awhile joined in the fun or began to add embellishments or tales of their own. Through such events, a rich tribal lore about a company, its history, values and heroes is passed along.

Risks

Each of these components of communication constitutes a strong, interdependent network. Those who participate think of themselves as members of a "tribe," bound to it by the information they share, feeling that they can not do their work without the support that their particular networks provide. Beyond simply being a part of the enterprise, participants also feel they are a part of making the enterprise better. These networks should also be highly visible, encouraging those who are not direct participants to access their rich store of knowledge through individual members.

In fact, in any long-cycle organization where an individual's work is highly leveraged, it's done through a team that sources knowledge from beyond the immediate team members to complete its work. The work gains its most important value from real-time, world-class expert knowledge. These networks are the intrinsic value of the enterprise.

One of the tragedies of mergers and acquisitions is that so often rich networks and tribal lore are lost and with them the shared sense of values that guide people's judgment as they conduct the business of the enterprise. The combined organization is rarely able to incorporate the stories of one entity or the other and embrace them as part of the new whole. People tend to leave, voluntarily or by request as the new entity is "streamlined" or "rationalized," breaking the connective fiber that allows people to get their work done. Long-cycle enterprises build value by planning more diligently for the integration of people, their talents and their networks than for the mechanics of financial, reporting or physical structure, building on the value of the communication systems, networks and cultures of the predecessor companies.

Nurture "Two Degrees of Separation"

n 1993, I saw a rather oblique little film that really got me thinking. *Six Degrees of Separation* was loosely based on a science that has since developed into a robust study of "small world networks," best described in *Nexus: Small Worlds and the Groundbreaking Science of Networks* by Mark Buchanan. The film was based on a corollary of the study of small world networks, the theory that every human being on the face of the earth is separated by a maximum of six degrees. In other words, I know some one who knows someone who knows someone ...times six until I can reach anyone in the world. We're all connected that closely.

As I wrestled with trying to understand this idea I realized that in a world of accelerating knowledge proliferation, none of us could possibly be refreshed at all times with definitive expert knowledge on any subject about which our customers may seek advice. Architecture, particularly, is a broad ranging field, demanding a synthesis of disparate bits of knowledge to arrive at a solution. The world of design, construction, facility management and operations have become so complex that no single individual can possibly be current in all areas about which they're likely to need and be expected to have the latest knowledge. In addition, clients occasionally have a unique inquiry about an oblique technical issue that comes out of the blue.

We insisted on absolute integrity, meaning that if you were asked a question or working on an assignment for which you were expected to be incorporating the most current expert knowledge and you weren't confident that you had it, guessing or faking it was simply not acceptable. The ethos was, "if you're not sure, ask." This is a difficult cultural characteristic to instill in a society where admitting you don't know something is, somehow, a diminution of your stature among your peers or in the organization. But in an enterprise where risk and the attendant liability is as high as it is in architecture (and this is true in more and more industries every day), any other behavior is simply unacceptable.

The film led me to an idea that real-time, just-in-time access to definitive expert knowledge is not about an electronic database. As rich a research resource as the Internet has become, it's still much slower and more cumbersome than talking to a real, live expert. Only a human being with experience and knowledge can interpret the context of a question to provide meaningful information. The Internet won't do that for you.

As I searched for an application for this notion, it occurred to me that everyone is passionate about a thing or two. Many of an individual's passions may not be connected to work, but it always amazes me how often they are. After all, a person wouldn't have entered their chosen field if they didn't have some passion for something about it. "Passions" are interesting, quite different from mere "interests." I'm interested in a lot of things but subjects I'm passionate about receive an inordinate amount of my attention. I read about them, talk about them, think about them and, while I may not be the definitive, world-class expert, I know who is.

Thus was born the idea of "two degrees of separation." If a question came up for which I didn't have immediate expert knowledge, all I had to do was to know someone who was passionate about that subject, ask them for their thoughts, and invariably I could get to the true expert in the field. It was simply a matter of making everyone's passions visible and nurturing the network of relationships within the organization to give each person access to expert knowledge. The corollary is, of course, that this is a reciprocal process. If I'm going to be leaning on others frequently in their area of expertise, I better have some areas of expert knowledge to offer in return.

So, I began a campaign to encourage people to make their passions visible. At new staff orientations in which a group of recent hires would get together for dinner and a little wine and beer while we passed along some history and lore about the firm, introductions were made and the question was asked, "What are you passionate about?" This always led to interesting knowledge about a new individual and, more importantly connected them and their passions to others with similar interests. In all staff meetings, presentations by subject matter experts made their knowledge visible. In professional development discussions, areas of personal passion were explored and encouraged. We worked hard on building and sustaining this behavior.

We had spent years developing as a "one-firm firm," a single enterprise with many disciplines in multiple geographic locations acting in collaboration. This characteristic supported the needs of our clients' increasingly diverse requirements in a seamless fashion. Over time, this notion became embedded in the corporate culture. One of the most frequent comments from people joining the firm concerned the remarkable connectedness they felt, how easy it was to get answers to questions, how often they would be referred by the person they asked to another person who had greater expert knowledge and how fully forthcoming and cooperative people were. They simply never felt put off if they asked for help. This is another of those self-fulfilling ideas. If the person I ask stops what they're doing to give me direction, I'm likely to adopt that behavior myself.

Over time, and of course distance, with the increasing scale and complexity of the organization, several concerns about this strategy became apparent. Not every office had individuals with personal passions on every subject. Some offices were considerably smaller than others. How could we be sure that everyone in the firm had a good shot at accessing the expert knowledge they needed in real time?

Since people moved from office to office for a project on occasion, the network relationships through which people accessed each other's expertise certainly crossed geographic boundaries. I might overhear a question about a subject for which there was no expertise in my office, but I had worked in another office and knew there was an expert there. The culture of sharing and collaboration was strong enough that a total stranger calling from another office would always receive an immediate and thorough response.

In fact, an historic anecdote is indicative of how strong that culture was. In the early days of high-speed connectivity, our information technology manager in Los Angeles recommended a high-speed data line between Los Angeles and San Francisco. At the time, T-1 lines were extremely costly and, despite the number of clients and projects shared between the offices, I couldn't see how this expense could be justified. This ever-resourceful manager had done a spread sheet showing how adding direct dial phone connectivity between the two offices over the T-1 line would offset a rather high long-distance phone cost each month. The amount just happened to equal the cost of the line. Surprise!

I was shocked. What were people talking about between the offices to rack up this kind of a phone bill? I mean, how many inter-office romances can there be? The diligent manager had already done his homework, sampling some of the longer conversations. All of them were technically related, usually between a person who had worked with another person in the corresponding office, tapping into their specialized knowledge.

It was time to carry the idea further with the advent of the development of an Intranet, a repository of frequently accessed information available to everyone in the firm. We developed this tool following the underlying precept of "two degrees of separation." That is, it's not about the information itself, it's about the person who owns it. Citations in a database will always be a little out of date and are frequently based on a different context than the problem I may have at hand. So, the Intranet was structured to connect to the person, not just facts. Today, with the combination of the Internet, a specialized Intranet knowledge base, e-mail and plain old telephone, access to real-time knowledge can be quite robust. But it will only work if the culture of "two degrees of separation" is well embedded.

Since Intranet knowledge bases are not yet prevalent and often simply assemblages of data, I offer some advice for an underlying theme. As your organization has grown, the richness and diversity of skills, knowledge and interests in your company has exploded. Connect your Intranet to people, not just data.

- Feature passionate experts on a regular basis with articles that are not just about the unique knowledge they have, but the story of how and why they got it. These kinds of stories fascinate people and form a memorable link when someone is scanning their own cerebral cortex for that unique knowledge they need right now.

- Connect every expert knowledge citation with a person or two through a hot link to their e-mail address or a phone number giving someone making an inquiry a first contact that can help them find the true expert they need for the context of their unique problem. Be sure that the person listed is willing to act as this kind of gatekeeper and to take the time to deal with inquiries. Rotate and/ or update these contacts frequently. There's nothing worse than to receive a response that the person is no longer with the company.

- Create on-line discussion forums to encourage networks of people and their passions to form around unique subject areas. Support these discussions—they're going on anyway in your enterprise, why not harness them to everyone's advantage?

- Be diligent about removing old or outdated material. The medium here is the message. If you encounter dead or irrelevant material once or twice, you've discredited your entire Intranet.

- Teach everyone in your enterprise a few web logging skills to make this a grass roots effort. Nothing slows the development of a knowledge network more than requiring every citation to go through and be posted by a staff group. It costs too much and defeats the purpose of directly connecting person to person. But make your support staff liberally available to help individuals to do this work themselves.

• And don't worry about whether the material has been finely checked and edited. Self policing works extremely well when information is tied to a person. They have their name and pride attached and if someone gets a faulty piece of advice, the author will hear about it real fast.

"Two degrees of separation" is a simple idea, very difficult to accomplish, but incredibly powerful in today's fast moving knowledge society.

Commit to Continual Learning

L earning can be tacit or explicit. It can take place through experience working on something with a proficient expert or through content delivery in a formal classroom setting. Curricula can be developed in house or, through tuition reimbursement, employees can be encouraged to expand their knowledge and skills utilizing outside resources.

No matter what form, long-cycle enterprises have an enduring commitment to continual learning. It's what keeps employees engaged and growing as professionals. If, as described in Chapter 5, you've created an environment that provides access to and support for continual learning and, as in Chapter 6, you've recruited curious people, your employees will demand it. Why is it so important?

When I finished graduate school many years ago, I walked away with the impression that the education I'd received had prepared me for a lifetime in my profession, that my very expensive diploma certified that my mind was fully prepared for my career. Shortly after I joined the firm, Art Gensler decided that we needed some business education. We were all graduates of architectural schools that are notoriously short on business classes. He brought in Glen Strasbourg, a professor from the business school at California

State University in Hayward, across the bay from San Francisco. Glen had wanted us all to attend his class there, but we were far too busy to be driving back and forth to the East Bay once a week so he was good enough to come into the office one evening a week for eight weeks of business basics.

At the end of the first class, Glen assigned homework. Wait a minute; I thought I was through with homework when I finished college. Those of us participating in the class were brought to attention quickly. Heaven help the poor soul who hadn't completed the homework assignment. Glen's scorn, always delivered quite theatrically in front of the entire class was pointed and relentless. But something he said during our second evening together left a deep impression on me. He asked us to consider the half-life of our knowledge—the time period after which half of it would be replaced through new research and discovery or simply a change in the way something is done. At the time, he proclaimed that it was 10 years and went on to say that after 10 years half of everything you know will be useless. The problem is you don't know which half! His point was made and my attitude appropriately adjusted. The real problem is that the half-life of knowledge has shrunk continuously since that date (I estimate it's running at about three years today), making the case for continual learning an imperative. If you aren't replacing the correct half of your application knowledge every three years, you're not only not moving ahead, you're falling behind.

Business cycles tend to govern an organization's commitment to continual learning. When things are good, you're too busy; when things are slow, you can't afford it. So, sustaining such an effort requires real commitment. During the 90s when things were truly chaotic—new people were being hired in unprecedented numbers, people were working extensive overtime often to the detriment of their family lives—the need for and our commitment to continual learning never abated.

Most were working harder than they'd ever worked to keep up with client demands as we continued to recruit aggressively in a market that was as busy as we were. In that context and with technology exploding, the rate of change continued to accelerate. Of course, continual learning is not just about classroom time. Each of us learns daily through the work we do. Small details of change in products or systems, new issues of software and an increasing dependency on the Internet makes each of us smarter (or at least more knowledgeable) every day. But we never postponed an ongoing investment in building people's skills, through classes we taught, through tuition reimbursement for outside courses or through relationships with mentors or coaches, within or outside the firm. And we never stopped encouraging people to stay the course in making time available for new learning.

The risks in architecture are extraordinary and require a deep level of proficiency in documentation to avoid problems during construction and ongoing liability after occupancy. But this is becoming true in all enterprises today. A large organization with multiple offices sharing clients or customers across broad geographic boundaries requires maintenance of uniform standards and protocols across all work teams. Bringing new employees to a threshold of proficiency within those standards quickly mandates training courses specifically structured for the various types of people in your organization.

Because we were deeply committed to thoroughly training interns, we had some mechanisms in place based on programs we'd designed for summer interns. When recruiting was high, these were ramped up to full-fledged teaching systems developed in conjunction with an outside resource that had done a good deal of work on adult learning processes. We designed a full practice curriculum, the content of which everyone in the firm was held responsible to know.

We found teaching this sort of program with in-house experts to be much more effective and relevant than subcontracting to an outside resource. People know the instructors as fellow professionals, their examples are more relevant, and they're available for follow-through. But in-house sources don't necessarily know how to construct a curriculum or teach. Adult professionals digest information much differently than students in a university setting. I recommend engaging an outside resource to develop "train-the-trainer" programs to teach your in-house experts how to tailor course content to be relevant and easily absorbed by adult practitioners.

Let's take a look at a case study. Over time, a concept called "Gensler University" evolved to include:

- Intern orientation classes held to give student summer interns a broad overview of a design practice
- Gensler 101, the basic knowledge courses covering a broad spectrum of elements of practice with commonly used protocols to allow people to work interactively across the firm
- A senior-level seminar for a group of future firm leaders who spent a series of long weekends over the course of a year to do research and develop recommendations in a subject area representing the practice of the future
- Tuition reimbursement to support individual areas of study relating to professional development
- Lunchtime seminars in each office provided by outside resources on new products, materials and systems
- Gensler Online, an Intranet knowledge base

Reaching outside your enterprise

Ideally, the commitment to continual learning starts for people during their university years becoming an embedded attitude with which graduates enter the workforce. Unfortunately, many young people are leaving their university experience with the attitude I had: "I'm glad that's over; I don't have to study anymore." Universities continue to search for ways to remain relevant to their graduates—if for fund-raising efforts if nothing else—yet have done little to instill this value in their graduates or to reach out to their constituents or related professional communities to offer continuing education or extension programs. Because of the shift from practitioner/professors to full-time academic faculties, many university curricula have lost relevance to the professions they're charged with preparing students for.

Recognizing this gap, I mentioned in an earlier chapter the Large Firm Roundtable of the AIA's Dean's Forums, pairing deans from major architectural schools with CEOs of large architectural firms to explore the misalignment between academia, practice and client expectations. One result was a closer connection between schools and practitioners to encourage this sort of continual learning.

In interior design, I led a three of fundraisers to develop a similar series of forums leading to action plans through the IIDA (International Interior Design Association). Being an ardent motorcyclist, there was only one logical approach. This particular adventure started in an amusing fashion. A group of us were sitting at a black-tie opening party for the annual interior design and furniture exposition watching a giant check being presented on the stage in support of interior design education. I think the amount was about $6,000 dollars. I suggested that the dresses worn by the women at our table had been purchased for the evening and cost more than that. Surely, as an industry and a profession, we could do better. Thus began the great motorcycle adventure in support of interior design education.

In 1999 the third and final year of our fund-raising efforts for interior design education we rode from New York to Chicago via Canada. The year before, I led a group of motorcyclists across the country from Atlanta to Chicago. We presented a check for $100,000, which we raised from sponsors in our industry to the IIDA Foundation at Neocon. The funds sponsored a study of interior design education by E-lab in Chicago. The results, recommending changes in curriculum and other aspects of the profession to bring education into closer alignment with professional practice, was presented at Neocon at the Midnight Affair. Practice had changed a great deal faster than teaching and there's a dramatic need for updating.

Our final ride started in Manhattan in front of our office in Rockefeller Center (which also happens to be in front of the *Today Show*—did you see us on Friday, May 28, 1999?). We rode to Chicago again, and raised another $100,000 to take the results of the study to the universities for implementation. This was an exciting endeavor that made a dramatic impact on the profession. We began to feel it within a few years, but, since the participating firms would be around for quite a while, I figure it was in our best interest to invest this way in the future.

And I suggest that every long-cycle enterprise must invest similarly so you might as well make it fun!

PART V

LEADERSHIP AND DESIGN

16

Make Design and Sustainability Key Drivers in Your Enterprise

Well-planned strategies for both design and sustainability are critical to long-cycle enterprises. I'll talk about each separately, but, in the end, they're integrally linked. Sure, an architecture firm is in the design business. But so are a graphics or product design enterprise, and maybe I can persuade you about an automobile manufacturer and a clothing retailer. I guess you could say that a magazine publisher and a toy-maker are in the design business, but what about a hospital or a school, governmental agencies or the local laundromat?

Every business is in the design business. Every business makes decisions about things that customers and employees see, touch and feel that are design decisions—products, brochures, employment manuals, advertising, the space the organization occupies, along with its service offerings and the way they're presented. These design decisions are instrumental in shaping the company's brand—the public's, their employees' and their customers' perceptions about the enterprise, its products and its services.

As consumers, we're very aware of companies that take a well-designed approach to everything they do, to the way they do it, to their products and services, to their facilities, to the clothes the people in their organization wear. Think about Apple or Porsche and how your perception of them differs from Dell or Toyota. The former consider themselves to be design-driven enterprises. The look and feel of everything associated with them is considered and, taken together, builds a strong and cohesive image and attitude. The latter companies design products but spend little time considering how the design of their entire organization impacts their image in the marketplace.

I'll be forever grateful to Tom Peters who, in his latest books and on stages around the country, has proselytized for design as the critical business driver and differentiator of this era. My clients always questioned whether my rather strong views on the subject were a bit self serving. After all, I was in the design business. But I've watched companies with whom I've worked begin to live and breathe a designed approach to everything, profoundly impacting their brand image, their employees' commitment and their business success.

I like to think about design, not as something I'm selling or something to be added on, but as the essence of the way one thinks about a problem. You don't have to be in a business with a recognized design purpose to be purposeful about design. Everyone makes choices every day that are, by their very nature, design choices. You choose what to wear when you get dressed in the morning. You chose the flatware and china from which you eat. You chose your furniture and the car you drive. When you get to work, you choose among alternatives in everything you do, in selections of products you use, in the way your services are presented and in the facilities you occupy or in which you sell to your customers. What message are you sending? What atmosphere are you creating? What story are you telling to your employees, your customers and others about who you are, what you stand for and what you represent? Are you telling a story of confidence and calm or frenzied chaos? Stable and predictable or innovative? Conservative or *avant garde*?

Every corporation, whether it thinks about it consciously or not, is making a design statement. The problem is, most don't think about it allowing things and processes to come into being through serendipity, through choices made by individuals making random decisions without any strategy for how they knit together to form the brand and image of the enterprise.

Because design is so important to your business, I'm including a number of models for thought that I hope will be helpful to you in considering how to make yours a design-driven business. While some of the discussion may seem a bit biased toward the built environment, I hope you'll find that they provoke some thinking about how to infuse design throughout your decision making process.

Architecture and interior design are truly both art and craft. The artistic side, "Design" with a capital "D," is not an additive feature. Clients who say, "I can't afford Design," are missing the point. Our emotions about every place we experience are affected by color, texture, shape, lighting, shade and shadow, temperature, acoustics, every nuance of the physical elements that make up the built environment combined with the ways in which it interacts with the natural environment. Big "D" Design is the part of the process where decisions about these things are made; it's not about adding frills that one thinks they can't afford. But the same is true about the design of your product, your stationary and business cards and your marketing material.

Designers who say they're unable to achieve great results because the budget is not adequate are not designing, they're decorating. This principle applies to any product or service offering in any business. Think about your own enterprise and the time/cost constraint arguments that compromise the quality of the offering to the customer. Are these arguments about additive elements that are perceived as "what the customer wants but is unwilling to pay for" or is it about aligning the fundamental Design of your product or service with the customer's needs?

The craft side is what separates the design professions from art. Designers are held accountable for their work through laws and court precedents that look very much like product liability laws. A building, for all practical purposes, is just a large, one-off, highly complex custom product that takes a long time to manufacture.

So let's say you decide to move your organization toward a design-driven future. How do you even start to think about design? In America, we suffer from design illiteracy. We don't know how to talk about it, let alone to define specifically what the characteristics of good design are. I hope this helps you to build a design vocabulary, to move toward design literacy through strengthening your focus on design. As you read the following, substitute the references to the design of a "place" with the design of your product or service.

For us, design was the element of our work that delivered the highest value to our clients, although they rarely thought of it that way and only occasionally bought it that way. Anyone can compete on adherence to schedule and budget (although much of our competition didn't do this very well, which was bad for our whole profession), and quality project management and world-class technical skills are pretty much expected in the work we did. These are no longer points of differentiation for clients.

Design basics

Tom Peters says that in today's world, quality is assumed and expected. If he's right, and design is today's most important differentiator, it's a good time to step back and take a look at what makes really great design. So I'll start with some basic ideas about designing:

• **Great design is surprise:** When you turn a corner and see something you've never seen before, hold a product that gives you a visceral thrill, that puts a smile on your face or gives you a feeling that reinforces why you're there and how to use it, you've given people a start on great design.

• **Great design is appropriate:** A place or product should feel like the purpose for which it's made. The elements from which it is constructed are consistent with and supportive of the use for which it's intended.

• **Great design is never neutral:** It's the thing to which people have passionate attachment. The principle difference between love and hate is design. It impacts people's emotions.

• **Great design makes places and things that people want but never knew they wanted:** When a client tells you that the result of your effort did something for their organization or life that they would never have even known how to ask for, or your customer buys something that no amount of market analysis could have predicted they'd find joy in, you've achieved another element of great design.

• **Great design is dynamic:** It wears in, not out. It adapts continually to changing use, organizational and lifestyle needs. It gets better as people use it and change it.

• **Great design transforms the perception of what's possible:** When a client says "I never knew that could even be done, and yet it's completely consistent with what I set out to accomplish," you've brought another element of great design to your client. When a customer never even thought about what they can do now that they have your product, you've delivered great design.

• **Great design is simple:** It looks to the past to find the future, employing the intuitive in new and creative ways.

• **Great design is respectful of people, community and environment:** Sustainability in great design goes well beyond material use and recyclability, altering the way people live their lives in a more sustainable way.

Making everyone a designer

How do you shift the way you think about design and make everyone in your organization "design aware?" Shape these thoughts to your organization, to the design of the products or services you offer and to the processes that allow you to deliver them to your customers. Are your product and service offerings "raising the bar" in the marketplace in which you compete?

How might you set the stage to "raise the bar" in your organization? What if you challenged people from each of your business units and administrative support functions to present what they're working on, using the discussion to explore each thing in various ways, searching for processes which would encourage a stretch of ideas and an energetic exploration of each element's opportunities for great design.

To truly "raise the bar" in your organization, you should start with the question: "How can we all be designers?" After all, design doesn't truly raise the bar because of style, shape or color. The greatest design work innovates and has lasting value because it is exactly right in its context; because of the impact it has on your emotions; because it is extraordinarily well executed; because it continues to adapt to its users' changing needs; because it was executed within its budget and schedule mandates; because every system functionally supports the uses intended with grace and style, without undue consumption of energy and with low maintenance.

To "raise the bar," you must be innovative in the way each area of knowledge, and creativity supports the making of your products and services, solving for all of these issues. You need to start thinking of the people in your organization as interdependent and collaborative teams comprised exclusively of "designers," which means that each team member, whether technical expert, project manager or administrative support team member must have a complete vision of what you're trying to accomplish and must have the vocabulary and respect from other team members for them to participate fully in the "design" of each project.

So, here are some thoughts about how to make this happen more fully in everything you do (and, in the process, help everyone in your organization to share in the thrill of doing things which are truly innovative):

1. **Internal process:** Every project or process has a customer, whether it be internal or external. Create a graphic storyboard for each project or task, illustrating the program and derivation of your design solution using words and pictures to illustrate your objectives. Make them easily read at a glance so that it's easy for others in your organization to quickly grasp important issues about what you're doing. Summarize each project's "big ideas:" the reason

you're undertaking the project, your greatest aspirations, the design opportunities (including technical systems) that the program offers, any problems or obstacles to be solved for, the budget and schedule, outside issues and concerns and, of course, how the design response, if achieved, will profoundly and positively impact the people who will use the product or service when it's complete. How about posting this storyboard in a public area so anyone, at a glance, is reminded of why you're doing the project; so that someone asked to participate in the project for a brief period of time is able to understand the importance of what they're doing to the overall aspirations of the team and the customer. How about leaving some white space on the storyboard so that thoughts can be added over time that are important for the entire team to be alert to as the project progresses? How about bringing the storyboard to customer (whether internal or external) meetings to allow you to continually revalidate the reasoning driving the project and to remind you every time you're with your customer that your mission is to exceed their goals and "raise the bar?"

2. **Customer interaction:** People who formally study design seem to think they have a corner on the market for visual literacy. It often drives customers nuts when you communicate in words that you are comfortable using with other designers but your customer may think of as psycho-babble. It's important if you're going to "raise the bar," to be able to communicate effectively about design issues which are visual and often esoteric. While the things you do may be composed of mundane elements, their purpose, when used in combination, is to elicit an emotional response. For your projects to "raise the bar," several people have to get excited about the potential to achieve this beneficial emotional response and behave in a supportive manner. Customers, financial types, often regulatory entities or the client's legal department have to say "yes." Others that may be brought in such as outside suppliers have to perform in a supportive manner and not poke fun behind the team's back because they haven't bought in as partners in achieving the greater aspirations of your project. This requires the ability to inspire by communicating the

benefits of the outcome of what you're doing in language that each of these constituencies can understand. How about using your entire team including administrative staff to conduct mock presentations using visual elements at intervals during the process with the stated purpose of learning to communicate product, element or system design ideas effectively. This delivers a side benefit of teaching visual literacy to a lot of people who otherwise don't think of themselves as designers.

3. **Research opportunities:** For years, I've been a fan of Chris Alexander's *A Pattern Language* as a method of thinking about how various characteristics of physical design affect each of us physiologically and emotionally. How about making this a major theme of study in your organization, looking at each element and process that your people and your customers touch, see or feel. Whether we like it or not, the mere fact of what you do, create a product, deliver a service, house your employees or customers, send a mailing, publish a manual, elicits such responses from those who come in contact with it. Isn't it greatly to your advantage if you're going to "raise the bar" to be extremely well equipped to predict with some accuracy and scientific grounding the physiological and emotional responses your products, services, materials and places are going to bring about?

The time dynamic of design

Design must be pragmatic, focusing on the specific benefits of your design strategy as it applies to your customers. Design choices have a time dynamic. They're not a snapshot. They have a life cycle, and the cost and quality implications of material and system selections can be dramatic. When you are convincing your customer to make the "buy" decision, whether it is a product or service purchase, or an incremental decision along the way in your customer relationship, the "sale" is usually done based on that momentary excitement about what's before them. Here are some thoughts about consciously adding the time dynamic and its value implications to the conversation about that design decision.

I'll elaborate on the concept of designing buildings and

interiors that "wear in, not out," places that adapt and evolve as the occupancy program changes over time. You can do this for any product or service relationship but think about it for your own facilities. You're confronted today with the most uncertain business environment anyone has ever known. Spaces and buildings often change in their use several times in the course of a year. In the design and facility management professions, we have very few case studies to show how well or poorly our buildings and interiors are holding up to this reality, no tools to teach young designers, communicate with clients or help us to evaluate our design work for its potential to perform in this environment. With an ever-strengthening emphasis on sustainability, what could make your work more valuable than their ability to adapt to new or changing uses with a minimum expenditure of money, energy and waste? The logical place for such a design task to reside is in your facilities or real estate group and is exactly the kind of design process challenge I refer to above that would allow everyone involved in a new or renovated facility to be a "designer."

But the value of the place comes from an alignment of people, process, technology and place. This is the true "design" challenge in making facilities that wear in, not out and cannot be solved by your architect alone. This is where the potential for performance enhancement resides in the "design" problem and underscores why everyone should be a "designer." If architects and interior designers (or product designers, engineers and marketing or application people) are working in isolation, you'll get disconnects in the way your facilities or products work. Highest value occurs when everyone treats these as integrated design problems.

So you've assembled the team for your next facility. You're beginning the storyboard for the project as described above. Start with the questions about people—who are they, what are they like, what will it take to attract and retain them, what motivates them? Lawyers are different than computer programmers, customers for a computer are different from customers for a car and the spaces you'll design for each must be in alignment with their styles, needs and wants.

Next comes processes—what is the nature of the work or activity being done and how is it likely to change over time, how do the people who will use the place collaborate, when do they need to be private, how do they interact with customers/clients of the organization?

Finally, technology—how is work process changing, how is it likely to evolve over time, should it be visible or completely concealed? I'm sure you can think of dozens of other questions to ask which develop the criteria for the place you're making and will be meticulous about pursuing these issues when developing a program. But how many of you work the design problem by describing how well aligned the place that you're making is with the people, process and technology issues of your enterprise?

For those of you who think this is not what design is about, think again. What if your internal discussions focused on improvement in recruitment and retention rates, or reduction in absenteeism, or enhanced communication leading to better solutions from your work teams? What difference would it make to the performance of your organization if the design team for your new facility was part of that conversation rather than being isolated with your facility staff to shape the place around a fixed program? The people, process and technology considerations are the design palate that your architects and designers should be using. Better design is better because it has meaning and importance to the people who will use it, and that's a consequence of the process you employ.

But this is not just isolated to facilities; it is a characteristic of the range of choices that are made in every aspect of your business. This is what design is really about. Design just happens also to include how something looks.

Developing a design attitude

Your attitude about design acts as a filter for your decision making. Building consistent tenets of that attitude takes time and thought, followed by plenty of reinforcement. The results, however, can be quite astounding, contributing greatly to the way decisions get made in your organization and, ultimately, by building the market's brand consciousness of your company. Most importantly, it requires a process on every project you undertake in your organization.

- **Design to the "big idea":** Starting everything you do in your organization right means understanding all the issues and key drivers before developing the "big idea." The "big idea" is a high concept for the project you're undertaking that will be innovative because it is based on a balance of people, process, place and technology, not just a narrow band response to one or two of these drivers. Have a "big idea" before starting design, making sure you have buy-in from all parties and then track progress for consistency with, fulfillment of and even stretch from the "big idea." If the "big idea" needs modification (the team has learned something new, identified a new opportunity for innovation) be sure to get buy-in from everyone involved.

- **Design with "strategic intent":** Don't start a project, no matter how simple or seemingly mundane, until you've identified and communicated to the team the strategic opportunity to enhance your business performance through the work you're going to do and the way you're going to do it. In other words, we're not just solving a problem here, we're changing our company and its potential for high performance. Remind the team regularly of this "strategic intent" so their enthusiasm and sense of fulfillment remains alive throughout the project. Working with a "strategic intent" means there's opportunity for innovation on every project you undertake.

- **Design to performance metrics:** Understand measurable performance metrics (reduced absenteeism, improved recruiting and retention, return on invested capital, improved process efficiency) before beginning design. Take before measurements so you can evaluate after measurements. Present design solutions in the context of how they are going to improve these performance metrics even if they aren't very sexy. In future economic climates, simple measurements like cost/person, reducing space requirements, speed to delivery, in other words, "better, faster, cheaper" will hold the highest priority in a competitive market.

- **Design sustainably:** Apply sustainable practices every day on every project, in processes as well as specifications. In buildings, seek at least LEED™ certification on every project. Become knowledgeable about costs and benefits (or engage someone who is) whenever discussing working on the sustainable design aspects of your project. In all instances seek opportunities to innovate, particularly in finding a sustainable approach in which first cost is lower than a more conventional approach. Look for solutions that yield long term cost savings. Always be aware of the life-cycle impacts of the project at hand. Add solutions you find to your company's body of knowledge for future use by everyone.

- **Design using best practices, skills and knowledge:** Stand on the shoulders of giants! Never start a project without exploring the best applicable practices, skills and knowledge that have been employed in the past, whether in your organization or outside. Tap into your broadest resources and share your successes and lessons learned with others in your company.

Giving metrics to design performance

Everyone's customers today are driven by their own pressures to perform. They look for proof statements about the products and services they buy to assure them that they're receiving a quantifiable performance value that exceeds the cost. And this is as true for your outside customers as it is for "customers" of projects inside your organization. Structuring products and services to deliver this kind of value and creating the tools that will communicate this to customers is a design problem and one that every enterprise faces.

You can do this by starting with some fundamental business drivers at the core of your model, such as financial management, customer satisfaction, employee effectiveness and organizational capabilities. As you begin a project, enumerate the goals you have for improvement in each of these areas that will be affected by your project. Be as specific and quantitative as you can. Add a next layer of people, process, place and technology strategies to achieve these goals, and then identify the metrics you'll use to monitor your success. Document the metrics before you start and at some appropriate points after, like three months following completion and a year later.

The risk in such a program is that it becomes an isolated number crunching exercise. To be successful, it has to be an integrated design tool, understood and embraced by everyone and used in their vocabulary with clients and customers. This means that you need to get comfortable with the idea that "soft side" metrics like employee or customer satisfaction data have real economic value to your organization.

While our clients appreciated us for the processes we employed such as budget and schedule control or expediting plans through a planning department, the highest value we provided was how the completed places we were part of making impacted organizational performance. It was our deepest responsibility. Our work style needed to respond to our clients' needs, especially those that were financial and performance driven. We'd lived in a world where the normal financial measurements related to the operation of the physical building were easy to quantify. We felt it every day through competitive fee pressures and budget scrutiny but it's short sighted to design strictly from a cost-reductive point of view. In fact, we found that the performance drivers that came from the other parts of an organization could be just as compelling for our clients.

Normally we weren't able to gain access to broader organizational performance metrics that were going to be affected by our work. We started with low hanging fruit like personnel issues of absenteeism, recruitment and retention. Every organization kept them and our clients were forthcoming with the data. These were also interesting touch points for softer issues of employee satisfaction and often affected by non-financial design decisions. Through before and after measurements, it was possible to discern whether an indirect lighting system that reduces eyestrain or cleaner air from an under-floor air conditioning system in a call center will result in reduced absenteeism. Over time, we stretched well beyond these simple measures and you can too if you take the time to think through the broader impacts of each project you undertake and not just building cost and operations-related ones.

Many designers whose perspective on whether their work is successful or not are more narrowly focused on the visual and physical aspects of their end product and fear that this is simply another left-brain activity destined to sap their creative design juices. This is no different than getting so trapped in the numbers that you forget that a very important reason for doing a project is the physiological and emotional responses that the people using it will have. Those affect important performance metrics as well. In other words, understanding and balancing all impacts of each thing you do in your organization may well be the greatest "design" tool you'll ever embrace.

As architects beginning a design, our concepts and ideas are informed by a vast array of input, some from the client, some from the community or context, some from our own experience and knowledge. Most designers go through their careers responding intuitively through their design work with only the most rudimentary documentation of the client's objectives and the outcomes and responses that are expected as a result of their efforts. And when it comes time to present the design concept, talk about what it "is" rather than what it is expected to "do." But, of course, this is true of most product presentations and, certainly true when you're simply solving for an internal issue.

Just like your customers (whether external or internal), an architect's clients make a judgment—do they trust the designer? Do they believe that the designer empathizes with and understands their business drivers? Is the design going to have value? And what does value mean to them? Is the client merely buying the cheapest first cost solution or is there recognition of a causal benefit through changed behavior of the people using the place being made that enhances their organization's performance? This is the difference, in architecture, of selecting the cheapest route, producing some drawings and getting the enterprise housed—in other words, creating adequate shelter—and creating a place that not only emotionally effects those who use it in a positive way consistent with its purpose but also profoundly improving the performance of the enterprise.

Every project you undertake in your organization, not just construction, has this sort of multi-dimensional impact. Design is simply solving for an optimum outcome across all factors of people, process, place and technology. By now I hope you understand why I say that design is not just about style and ornamentation and that you're beginning to think of yourself as a "designer" in your organization.

Finding a philosophy for design

Great design is founded on theory. It's not just an imitation or extension of what someone else is doing. It's not easy to engage your entire organization in the theory of why you do what you do. But when you can infect people with an idea, get them thinking about the theory on which your work is founded, really interesting things begin to pop out of the woodwork.

Every piece of your enterprise should have a philosophy that grounds it, the "why" behind your actions. You may think that this quest is a fruitless intellectual exercise. I certainly had my doubts from time to time but my innate curiosity kept me asking the "why" question. When you know why you're doing things, you accomplish them more simply, more quickly and with fewer false starts. When the people in your organization have even a subconscious awareness of "why," their work and their effectiveness improve dramatically.

Let me liken this to our retail, entertainment and hospitality work, an area where imitation is rife and the body of work coming out of many organizations working in this area tends to look alike. Much of the other work we were doing like airports and schools was benefiting from ideas spawned in the retail, entertainment and hospitality area so I kept working toward posing the right "why" questions for us. A trigger point for me was a conversation I had with a reporter for Time magazine who was doing an article on David Rockwell and retail trends in general. We chatted for a while about what Rockwell was doing and what we were doing (our work on the Apple Stores and the Toys-R-Us store on Times Square was to be mentioned in the article). I described Rockwell's work as being based in the theater (stage set design and lighting are a big part of Rockwell's past) where a successful set can deliver powerfully emotional sensations in support of the story line of the play and likened that to the experiential trends in retail design where great and successful environments help the customer to become emotionally connected to the product and brand.

The reporter challenged me, asking whether, with increasing amounts of merchandise being purchased through other channels such as "big-box" stores like Walmart and Target or through catalog sales, this was just a passing fad. In other words, is the investment in elaborate, experiential and immersive retail environments a flash in the pan that will soon disappear, giving way to the next fashion of the moment or is it a trend, indicative of broader movement in the retail industry?

This got me thinking once again about Abraham Maslow's *Toward a Psychology of Being* and his pyramid of human needs. I began telling her of this notion, where I felt we were along Maslow's pyramid and how it was impacting design of retail space, products and organizations. Briefly, Maslow described a "needs" pyramid, the base of which is formed of basic human needs, like security and food, rising to things like self esteem and achievement and reaching the pinnacle of self-actualization. Thinking about the U.S., European and many Asian societies today, most of our places and products are solving for issues well beyond Maslow's lower level need systems. This means that many people are living lives where most of their base needs are being accommodated and they're able to spend a proportion of their existence in experiences that help them self-actualize, that state where becoming your true self or the self you aspire to become (you've got to read some Maslow to really understand this). We're comfortable that our buildings are going to keep us warm and keep the rain and most intruders out. Judging from the general level of body fat around these days, most people aren't exactly going hungry.

In fact, restaurants are a good way to look at this "progress." We're a long way from going to a restaurant merely to sustain our bodies. Today, it's even gone beyond going for good food. Today, we want the "experience" and, further I will argue, for self-actualization. This is an interesting departure from eating and socialization at a restaurant; now you actually become a different person in the setting and within the experience. That is self actualization.

Let me take another aspect of design—automobiles—to illustrate the point. We no longer use a car to get us safely from point A to point B. We've come to expect comfort and reliability, style that our neighbors admire or even envy. Today we actually feel as if we've become James Bond if we're able to afford to drive an Aston Martin or Arnold Schwartzenegger if we drive a Hummer—self actualization again.

I believe this is where retailing and entertainment are going and why I believe that it's important that we understand Maslow at this time. And further, why I think the kind of fantasy, immersion design that David Rockwell is so well known for is not just a passing fad. This may seem a bit "out there," but I think it applies to all aspects of design today as a response to many of our other product or service needs. Being generally satisfied at all fundamental levels, our minds are looking for that opportunity for a more immersive, self-actualizing experience. This is where design opportunities will be.

I urge you to define the "why" issues that surround the business you're in, the service you provide or the product you make. It will help the people in your organization to focus and direct their work with a strong sense of common mission.

I'll end this discussion of design with a little poem by the architect Moshe Safdie from his 1982 book *Form & Purpose* that fits well with what I've been saying:

He who seeks truth shall find beauty.
He who seeks beauty shall find vanity.
He who seeks order shall find gratification.
He who seeks gratification shall be disappointed.
He who considers himself the servant of his fellow beings shall find the joy of self-expression.
He who seeks self-expression shall fall into the pit of arrogance.
Arrogance is incompatible with nature.
Through nature, the nature of the universe and the nature of man, we shall seek truth.
If we seek truth, we shall find beauty.

Sustainability

I have described design as consciousness and purpose in the choices you make about things you see, touch and feel as well as the processes by which you accomplish what you do. You make these choices anyway. Design is simply a matter of making them in a fashion that yields a better quality result—true to your purpose, more supportive of your mission, consistent and reinforcing of your brand and in a way that elicits a physiological and an emotional response from your customers and employees that reinforces your objectives.

Sustainability is an added filter on those choices, tying the two integrally. Every choice you make about material or process has an environmental effect. Sustainability, another part of design, is not an additive thing you do like recycling your waste or buying organic products. It's embedded in your every decision. All design decisions have environmental consequences and, as a society, we are for the most part, as environmentally illiterate as we are design illiterate. The steps required to become a sustainable enterprise are part of becoming a design-driven enterprise. It's a matter of becoming conscious of the choices you're making, their relationship to other choices and the outcome, response and impact each has.

I find much of the sensationalism and fear mongering associated with environmental degradation, global warming, rapid climate change and other favorite subjects of media and enviro-terrorist hype a sad distraction from the real need and opportunity to build environmental awareness in individuals and corporations. The style of media coverage in the last decade has been a real threat to and distraction from learning to be discerning in our design choices. While each of us as individuals make choices each day that impact the environment, corporations are making wholesale choices that offer far greater leverage to enhancing sustainability. The irrational behavior by both the media and our government discourages and fosters resistance from corporations. Methodical learning and change can enhance the environment and corporate performance. My frustration level with the scrutiny applied to whether we're properly sorting our trash for recycling while we're ignoring the processes that generate that trash in the first place is at an all-time high.

So I'll return again to one of my favorite reference points, Janine Benyus' book *Biomimicry* where I learned so much about how nature achieves a sustainable balance. It's a wonderful starting point for gaining sensitivity to the decisions you're making in your own organization about material and process. Janine describes our penchant as a society to try to conquer nature, to forcibly change materials forging them to our objectives, a process she refers to as "heat, beat and treat." Yet we find a material in nature, a spider's web, that is dramatically stronger than the strongest material man has yet made—Kevlar, which requires considerable heat, pressure and toxic substances in its manufacture. By contrast, a spider manufactures its web at ambient temperatures from fly parts with no pressure exerted and no toxic by-products, a classic example of one of Janine's themes about nature: one plant or animal's food is another's waste.

How do you begin to build your knowledge about how nature might achieve things that you're doing, both in the manufacture of your products, the specification of materials you use and the processes you employ throughout your organization? These, again, are simply design choices. But they have profound implications to you and your business. The concern I hear most often expressed from corporations about being environmentally conscious is that it costs more. That's because we think of it as something additive, something we do to correct something we did wrong in the first place. Thinking about sustainability as a design possibility shifts the paradigm from remedial action to doing it right the first time. In the simplest terms, it's the difference between a concern for the recyclability and disposal of the packing materials in which you ship your product to a focus on reducing or eliminating those materials in the first place. One costs more, the other costs less. They're simply the attitude and knowledge you bring to the design problem you're solving.

I've taken a sustainable approach to design for many years. My first real opportunity came with a project for Pacific Gas & Electric, the utility company in the San Francisco Bay Area, who hired us to renovate an old Blue Cross/Blue Shield building in Oakland for their use. Their primary concern was, "Make it look cheap. When it's done, we'll be under scrutiny from the regulatory authorities for a rate increase, and if it looks too expensive, they'll question the way we're spending the rate payers' money." While PG&E didn't resist my efforts to reduce energy consumption by 2/3 through the use of indirect lighting and an advanced (for 1972) mechanical system redesign, it wasn't of great concern to them. After all, they were in the business of selling more energy. They didn't appreciate the value of what we had done until 1974 when the oil crisis hit and the building was given an award for its innovative energy reduction strategies.

I've spent my career tuning my design decisions this way. It wasn't a "tree-hugger" approach, I've never been a radical in my environmental views, I've merely thought that sustainable design made sense and was really just a fine tuning of the design choices I was making day in and day out anyway. It's only in that last decade since it's been such a highly visible concern that I've spoken openly of it with my clients if it seemed important to them. A decade ago, many clients simply weren't interested or, worse, took it to mean that I was going to spend more of their money to achieve an inferior result. That's not the case today and, in most cases, the net cost in initial dollars is lower, evidenced by a building we did for Dell computers that included a full complement of energy reducing sustainable design features that had a lower first cost than one they had completed just before without them.

One of the most interesting exercises I ever did was to send out a questionnaire over 20 years ago to various materials and systems manufacturers whose products we specified—paint, wall board, ceiling tile, floor coverings and the like—asking them some simple questions: what toxins were used in the manufacture of their product, how much energy was used, how much waste was generated and how was it disposed of, how much and what type of packaging was used and how was it disposed of; and so forth. At that time, we were already a fairly large specifier of such products but certainly didn't represent a large market share for any one of them. Nevertheless, the results were astounding. Most said they hadn't even thought about it but were glad we asked as our inquiry had stimulated them to put an environmental program in place. Several asked if we were using such information as a basis for specification (even though we'd made no such indication) or were going to do so in the future. And we subsequently heard back from quite a few of them on a frequent basis as they made progress with their programs. It's interesting how often a simple inquiry can represent a tipping point—not by forcing or demanding an action, but simply getting people to start to think

We continued to use sustainable specifications in the design of our projects, some were given great fanfare because our clients wanted it; others just got built that way. Sustainability is not an either/or proposition.

In several forums on sustainability that I've attended, issues ranging far beyond design and construction practices have been presented. The dominant theme has been: "sustainable practices are good business!" It's enormously gratifying to hear case studies from companies like Texas Instruments, Clorox, AT&T, Interface Carpet, Patagonia and many, many others filled with example after example of improved profitability and quality with reduced cost through the incorporation of sustainable practices.

The entire conversation surrounding the Kyoto Agreement on reducing hydrocarbon emissions has sadly become heavily politicized. We see once again why government intervention and regulation are not the answer to environmental improvement. It's really up to the private sector to take a leadership role in protecting and restoring the environment. This will only happen to the degree that private enterprise sees sustainability as good for the bottom line. Attending conferences and reading case examples provide wonderful models to stimulate thinking about opportunities in your own organization. Each company needs to find its way toward positive change driven by competitive dynamics, not by regulation.

Environmental, Health and Safety (EHS) departments, where most sustainability efforts reside in organizations, are generally not well integrated into an enterprise's business strategy. Because of government intervention, most EHS groups are structured for "compliance," meeting minimum standards rather than optimizing processes. EHS units respond to risk avoidance and regulatory compliance instead of developing creative responses to market based incentives. They're structured to respond to a "command and control" prescriptive environment. This may be the most difficult hurdle to overcome since it means a change of skills and mindset in EHS departments. They need to be strategic and technically integrated into the business, connected to increasing profit rather than merely containing the cost of compliance.

Patagonia makes a particularly compelling case for inserting emotion into the process, describing the benefits of integrating suppliers into their process, having transformed their relationships by demanding quality, but for a cause; with a purpose. By sharing a focus on a purpose that is outside yourself, you enlist a whole new dimension to your and your business partners' commitment to a quality outcome. Patagonia has significantly enhanced their brand (and gotten lots of free advertising) as a result of their commitment to sustainability. Their advice: "Announce your commitment early and get the credit." There are rewards for those who have a long term vision. Patagonia's is that all products will be recycled or recyclable, grown or created organically, fueled by solar power within 75 years. Their mission is to foreshorten that time frame to 25 years by leadership that they demonstrate or inspire. Not bad, huh?

A further Patagonia piece of advice: be honest with your customer. Patagonia admits that all of their practices are not sustainable. In fact, to achieve the quality of product their customers have come to expect from them such as dyes that don't fade and fabrics that are abrasion resistant, they use copper and chromium in their manufacturing processes. Copper comes from open-pit mines which create serious environmental problems. They have polled their customers, asking: "are you aware of the trade-offs?" The response from their customers has been consistently, "Yes, we are, but we want products that don't fade; but thank you for your honesty." This ongoing dialogue and display of concern has developed one of the most loyal customer bases in the clothing business.

Interfacē Carpet has a deep commitment to sustainability in all of their products and processes. I encourage you to read their "Sustainability Report." They were the first ever to publish such a report. They deal with their progress with great integrity, being very open about what they have and have not accomplished. But they've made tremendous strides in waste and emissions reduction, energy conservation and "cradle-to-cradle" product responsibility, moving toward leasing of carpet which they will reclaim at the end of its useful life and recycle as new carpet. They've been able to pay for their program through cost savings that have resulted from their initiatives.

Has this commitment to sustainability cost more? Ray Anderson will tell you that Interface's environmental approach has helped them to reduce costs and be more competitive. Their competitive position in the marketplace and the growth of their business internationally is a compelling testimony to sustainability as good for the bottom line. Like other companies I've spoken with, I've learned that it's the quality of your products that sell, not the sustainability program. Interface is a design-driven company but it also acts sustainably because it's the right thing to do and it reduces costs, a most important shift in attitude.

This is a theme to remember: "green products" don't sell; quality sells. The "green" quality of a product or manufacturing process is an outcome of today's definition of quality which focuses on manufacturing efficiency, cost reduction and the lifecycle of the use of materials and systems. Successful companies today are focusing on the same "cradle-to-cradle" relationship with customers and products that Ray Anderson described.

The subject of design always makes me feel poetic so I'll end this chapter with another poem which was written by one of Interface's employees after a talk Ray Anderson delivered in San Diego:

Tomorrow's Child

Without a name; an unseen face
    and knowing not your time nor place
Tomorrow's Child, though yet unborn,
    I saw you first last Tuesday morn.

A wise friend introduced us two,
    and through his shining point of view
I saw a day which you would see;
    A day for you, and not for me

Knowing you has changed my thinking,
    for I never had an inkling
That perhaps the things I do
    might someday, somehow threaten you.

Tomorrow's child, my daughter-son,
    I'm afraid we've just begun
To think of you and of your good,
    Though always having known I should.

Begin I will to weigh the cost
    of what I squander; what is lost
If ever I forget that you
    will someday come to live here too.

Glenn Thomas © 1996

I offer a final note on design. Many years ago I was given a small book by Betty Cornfield and Owen Edwards titled *Quintessence*. The Merriam Webster dictionary defines quintessence as the essence of a thing in its purest and most concentrated form. In other words, something that can be nothing else, something which exists solely as it is and perfect for the purpose intended. I became fascinated by the concept. So far, I've talked about design as making informed choices. But there's another step. An object, and this can as easily by applied to a process, achieves the quality of quintessence through continual refinement. So as you move along the path of design and sustainability to conscious choice-making informed by your knowledge, know that as your competence increases, you can begin through refinement to search in everything you and your organization makes and does for the ultimate standard of design quality: quintessence.

Leadership Exists Everywhere in Your Enterprise—Use It

Leadership has many faces—from the brazen style of a George Patton to the quiet assurance of a Mother Theresa. Successful leaders range everywhere along that spectrum but seem to share some common characteristics. They have learned that they don't always have to be in control. In long-cycle, networked and collaborative environments, each person must learn when to lead and when to follow, emulating a jazz ensemble where the lead shifts from musician to musician as the piece evolves rather than a symphony orchestra where the conductor takes a command and control role to execute a preordained work.

But some characteristic behaviors are prerequisite without regard to personal style or the needs of the enterprise.

Great leaders

Great leaders have impeccable integrity. Through the history of their actions and responses, they've built a reputation of complete trust. They are dedicated to what they commit to and when they make a commitment, no one has to check back to see if they're following through. I refer to this characteristic as "set it and forget it." If I agree to undertake it, you can depend that I will it follow through to completion.

Great leaders have determination. They'll pursue something to which they've committed to its conclusion, but they won't do it blindly. If the path they're on is no longer tenable, they will take the initiative to redirect their efforts. But not before touching base with those who are depending on their dedication and determination to complete what they've undertaken. They respect those they work with, letting them know the circumstances that warrant the change and what the new direction entails.

Great leaders know where they're going and make sure those working with them understand their direction as well. All the integrity, dedication and determination in the world are useless without a sense of the direction in which the efforts are being applied in the context of the greater mission of the organization. They and those working with them understand why what they're doing is important.

Great leaders leave their egos behind, celebrating the individual and collective efforts and accomplishments of everyone who is part of the mission they're on. They're careful to gain consensus. They help each person to see the contribution they're making and to be celebrated for it. They're generous of spirit.

These are the characteristics I watched for in others and encouraged in my career.

Leaders and managers

Let's take a look at some differentiating elements of focus in people's personalities. Generally, people fall along a spectrum of characteristics between leaders and managers. These are personality characteristics and both are important to every organization.

Leaders stand out for the direction they provide, the following they have and the respect they engender. They tend to be conceptual, they often create chaos and they are concerned with the "why" of an issue. Their theme is "are we doing the right things?" Managers want to bring order. They are negotiators and peace makers. They're concerned with the "how" of an issue. They ask, "are we doing things right?"

Neither set of characteristics is good or bad. Both are necessary in every business to find balance and thrive. To be successful, both leaders and managers must embody the elements of "great leaders" described above. In any organization, it's important to understand each individual's predisposition and help them to be true to their strengths and have strategies for their weaknesses. The most successful long-cycle organizations structure teams throughout the organization, from the most basic business unit to the most senior governing body, with a balance of these personality types. But each embodies the leadership elements I've described as prerequisites.

People are natural leaders

Despite much opinion to the contrary, most people have a natural capacity to lead. Their inhibitions come from conditioning in authoritarian work models or from parents or peers who caused them to question their abilities, diminishing their self confidence. In a work setting that fosters an expectation of taking action and accepting the responsibility for it, leadership flourishes. As I sat through numerous meetings in our firm over the years, the most significant impression I came away with was that in an organization with broadly distributed creativity and empowerment, many people asserted elements of leadership as each meeting wore on. We were certainly not a "command and control" organization with a centralized authority directing new initiatives but it always intrigued me how often the process looked just like that jazz ensemble mentioned above where the process and solution evolved as the leadership of the meeting shifted from person to person.

Once empowered, people's hunger for learning about leadership seems insatiable. Over the years I was continually asked for books to read about becoming a better leader. A few of the best are included in the resource list at the end of this book. We often speak of leadership in our organizations. In fact, the word appears so often that it can lose definition for us. Long-cycle companies depend on grassroots leadership—an organization where everyone has the capacity to lead when it's appropriate. I'm always looking for something that resonates with this philosophy. A past issue of *Fast Company* contained an insert titled "Make Yourself a Leader—State of the Art Leadership Kit," which I found superb. When asked: "What does leadership entail; where can I read about it?," I'd pass along these twelve instructions. In fact, the article so parallels my own philosophy that if I'd put forth my own list, I'd probably be accused of plagiarizing this one.

1. LEADERS ARE BOTH CONFIDENT AND MODEST.
Sure, you need a healthy ego to lead—but you also need to be strong enough to check your ego at the door. Being a leader is not about making yourself more powerful. It's about making the people around you more powerful.

2. LEADERS ARE AUTHENTIC.
You earn the trust and respect of the people you work with when you know who you are—and when you walk your talk. Who believes in leaders who don't believe in themselves?

3. LEADERS ARE LISTENERS.
And great listening is fueled by curiosity. It's hard to be a great listener if you're not curious about other people. What's the enemy of curiosity? Grandiosity—the belief that you have all the answers.

4. LEADERS ARE GOOD AT GIVING ENCOURAGEMENT AND THEY ARE NEVER SATISFIED.
Leaders are always raising the stakes of the game for themselves and for their people. That means they're always testing and building both courage and stamina throughout the organization.

5. LEADERS MAKE UNEXPECTED CONNECTIONS.
They organize and lead conversations among people who don't normally interact with each other, and they see the kinds of patterns that allow for small innovations and breakthrough ideas.

6. LEADERS PROVIDE DIRECTION.
But that's different from providing answers. No single leader

is smart enough to know everything about where markets are going, how technology is changing, what competitors are plotting. But smart leaders do know how to pose revealing questions. Important reminder: You're not in control, and you're not really in charge—but you are in touch, and you are out front.

7. LEADERS PROTECT THEIR PEOPLE FROM DANGER—AND EXPOSE THEM TO REALITY.

The dirty little secret of life in organizations: Most people want leaders to insulate them from change, rather than mobilize them to face it. That's why leadership is so dangerous.

8. LEADERS MAKE CHANGE—AND STAND FOR VALUES THAT DON'T CHANGE.

One job of a leader is to help people identify which habits and assumptions must be changed for the company to prosper—and to ask, "Which values and operations are so central to our core that if we lose them, we lose ourselves?"

9. LEADERS LEAD BY EXAMPLE.

They use small gesture to send big messages. Leaders have a fundamental obligation to live their lives according to the principles they espouse. Remember: You are always under a microscope.

10. LEADERS DON'T BLAME—THEY LEARN.

Even the smartest businesspeople around make mistakes. Remember when Bill Gates decided that the Internet wouldn't have a big impact on Microsoft's business? These days, the right mind set is an experimental mindset: Try, fail, learn, and try again.

11. LEADERS LOOK FOR AND NETWORK WITH OTHER LEADERS.

Want to make yourself even more effective as a leader? Want to heighten your influence and deepen your impact? Stop playing the role of the Lone Ranger! Look for allies, network with like-minded colleagues—and help those people to become better leaders. Remember: It's lonely at the top only if you place yourself on a pedestal.

IMPORTANT!

12. THE JOB OF A LEADER: MAKE MORE LEADERS.

After you use this kit to make yourself a leader, look around your organization. Do you see enough leaders at all levels to keep your company changing and charging into the future? Remember: The team with the most and best leaders wins! Your ultimate task is not just to be a leader—it's to make more leaders.

I'll add a couple of extra points of my own. Leaders need to see beyond the obvious. I'll use a couple of motorcycling examples. By now you've seen at least a couple of passing references to my passion for motorcycling, so this should come as no surprise. Besides, who needs another golf or football analogy? The other day when I was riding with some friends, a fairly new rider said: "I'm always afraid entering a blind corner. How do you figure out where the road is going?" I gave some advice: the center line disappears rapidly around the corner, but the white line painted on the far outside edge of the road gives you a longer view into the shape of the corner as it will unfold. His riding improved markedly as the day wore on. Leaders have to figure out where the "white line on the far outside edge of the road" is to get a sense of the direction we're heading— the not so obvious signals that help us to anticipate how a situation is unfolding.

In motorcycling, you're taught when following others to "ride your own ride." Following another rider and fixing your attention on his or her motions has resulted in many a rider following another right off the road. Great riders focus on the road ahead, not on how other riders are riding it. Pretty sound leadership advice as well. Don't slavishly imitate what others have done; do what's uniquely appropriate to your business.

Finally, a leader stays focused on the path they're on. Trying to lead in too many different directions at once is distracting for the leader and the team. The temptation to have a finger in too many games has been the downfall of many a capable leader.

These ideas are simple, down-to-earth, and easy to understand. But that doesn't mean they're easy to implement. If leadership were easy, it would be easy to find lots of great leaders. But leadership potential is embedded in everyone in your organization, and these types of ideas help people to develop their natural talent.

Nurturing empowerment

The strongest long-cycle organizations are visibly supportive of people's actions, particularly when they make mistakes, asking only that they share what they learn with others to help them to avoid making the same error. But a bias toward action requires guidance. The framework must be static at its core, in its values and ethics but elastic and adaptable in its application, subject to changes in the marketplace.

Leadership comes in many forms and certainly crosses an entire organization, from entry level professionals and administrative staff to the most senior officers of the company. When someone is deeply engaged in the organization as described in Chapter 7, they truly act as "owners" of the company. Their leadership becomes manifest as they initiate action on issues that affect company performance. I've seen it over and over as an office assistant makes a decision about how to purchase supplies more effectively to a receptionist caring enough to learn clients' and consultants' names, following through on an issue for outsiders that builds bonds between them and the firm.

It's far simpler to build a command and control organization, but long-cycle companies thrive on networked, interdependent relationships that have empowered each individual in the organization to act on behalf of the greater good of the enterprise. Think of Nordstrom's empowerment of its sales staff to do whatever it takes to make a customer happy. It's so easy to slip into an older thought pattern that only ascribes the term "leader" to someone who gives orders, someone who is directive.

Teaching creativity

Many of the strategies described in this book are designed to nurture and empower leaders, guided by a culture (the way we do things), a value system (are they the right things to do?) and a code of ethics (do they fit the laws and expectations of a just society?). But this type of leadership throughout the organization cannot be mechanical or formulaic. In fact, it only blossoms when seasoned with creativity. Not creativity in bending culture, values and ethics, but creativity in applying those elements in an inspirational way. I believe that creativity in this sense is teachable. I have told the following stories for years because I believe they help people gain a greater consciousness that what they are doing and how their interactions with others nurtures creativity in leadership.

Everyone who is part of an enterprise has an equally important role in the work it does. Some people deal with customers or clients directly; others' impact is indirect through supporting the organization's ability to do great work and deserve appreciation every day. In that context, it's sometimes difficult to understand the role that each person has in the larger purpose of the organization and to remember that it takes every person working together to accomplish great results. These thoughts are as important to the office assistant or stock room clerk as they are for the CEO.

I attended a seminar in January 1975. I remember the date because my daughter was one year old, and we were in the middle of an oil embargo. The economy was in the tank. Spending money to attend a fairly expensive three day seminar seemed a questionable investment at the time, not to mention the fact that I would be away from my young family for a weekend. But a couple of lessons I learned that weekend have stayed with me ever since.

The instructor was Mike Vance, a creative thinking "guru" on the speaking circuit at the time. Vance had been a congregational minister for 10 years, left the clergy and joined Walt Disney to lead idea and people development for the 10 years preceding Walt's death—an interesting career path. The weekend was filled with enlightening insights about opening your mind to creativity, but two stories stood out.

The first connects to the film industry and talks about "dailies." A "daily" is the film footage shot during the day, which gets developed at night and is viewed by the director and producer before the next day's shooting begins. Movies and television are shot in disconnected scenes that get stitched together to tell a continuous story so it's sometimes difficult to step away from a scene you're shooting to see if it is going to fit seamlessly into the broader story you're telling. Dailies help the movie's creator get a sense of how things are going, to step back from the previous day's work and ask how am I doing?

Vance asked us to think about the story we want our lives to tell, to understand that each day is a scene, often only a small paragraph of a chapter that will fill the book of our life and often as disconnected as that movie scene shot out of sequence. He asked us to think about what we wanted that story to be. His proposition was simple—our lives are not written in a day but if we think about each day and how it's added to the story, it's likely that the story we'd like to tell will be told. He proposed a simple exercise: run a "daily" on your life. Before you fall asleep, in the shower in the morning, jogging, wherever; take a few minutes to consider how the previous day went. Run a "daily" on yourself. Did your actions support the story you want your life to tell? If not, how are you going to adjust the next day's "shoot" to bring the story back into focus? This is blame free. Whatever you did yesterday is an opportunity to learn how to do better tomorrow.

I like to think of it as doing what you do every day in a way that you'd be proud to tell to your grandchildren. This could mean the way you interacted with the people around you in your work and in your personal life as well as the actual product of your work. Having only completed mundane tasks during a day doesn't mean that when you run your "daily" you can't be proud of the chapter you've added to the story of your life. It's not just what you do; it's how you do it.

The second story has to do with a young boy who lived near the Disney studio. He was intensely curious about what went on behind the perimeter fence and managed to find his way into the studio uninvited, nosing around among the creative types who made animated films and the like. He became a mascot of sorts because he was so very bright. The creative artists began using him as one-person focus group, asking him what he thought of their work. In fact, one of the enduring processes used at the Disney Studio, "five sensing," came from this young man's observations. It was a simple concept, really, which he passed along as a throw-away line while talking to a group of animators: "Why not think of how you can affect all five senses, taste, touch, sound, sight and smell, in the way your story is portrayed? How do you get the audience to think of how something "tastes" by what you show them on the screen? Is it consistent and supportive of the story line?" This approach to optimizing impact and recall in the cerebral cortex through affecting all five senses was later validated through advanced brain research.

After a while, the studio started paying the young boy real money for just hanging around. Walt happened to notice the expenditures and asked to whom these vast sums were being paid (Walt was very tight with the buck, watching studio expenditures very closely). When he was told about the profound insights that had come from the boy, Walt sent Vance out to find out how such a young man had become so astute.

In his story, he went to the boy's house, a modest bungalow just outside the studio and introduced himself to the boy's parents. They described him as a normal young man who went to school everyday, participated in sports and led a generally unremarkable life. Vance continued to probe but came up with nothing that could explain his wisdom at such a young age. On the front porch as he was leaving, he finally said to the boy's father, "You must have done something different in raising your son." The father thought about it for a while and finally said, "Well, I always answered all his questions."

He probed a little further, asking for an example. The father related this story: "My son once asked where the water went when it went down the sink drain. Now most parents are too busy to answer that kind of question. But, I had some time so I opened the doors under the sink and explained to him how the curved pipe below the sink held some of the water to keep sewer gases from coming back into the kitchen. Then we crawled under the house to see where the sink drain connected to the waste line from the rest of the house. We went out to the street, I pried open the manhole cover, had his mother flush a toilet and showed him how our waste joined the rest of the community's. We then drove down to the sewage treatment plant and asked the superintendent to explain to us how our waste was treated and returned to nature. I just answered his question." Profound.

How often are we asked a question, only to give a perfunctory answer? How often has someone asked you a question, you gave them an expedient answer but you knew they really wanted to know why that was the right answer? How much could the creativity of those around us be stimulated if we just took the time to "answer" each other's questions? These are the great teaching moments in any organization. Just answer the questions—as fully and richly as the asker has the patience for. It's the highest-value time you can invest in your enterprise.

Large enterprise leadership

The most senior leaders in any organization bear an awesome responsibility for creating an environment in which this predisposition for leadership can flourish. As the organization we led passed 2,000 people, we were often asked what we did to control the firm's direction. Interesting question. I found an analogy one day in an article about supertankers, an unlikely place to study leadership. The article discussed how they initiate a turn. The hydraulic pressure on the rudder of a supertanker, a flat slab as tall as a multistory building, makes it impossible to simply steer the rudder as you might do on a sailboat, so a small pilot rudder is installed in the lower-leading edge of the main rudder. Moving this pilot rudder causes a water current to press against the main rudder, moving it with only the small expenditure of energy necessary to move the pilot rudder.

Shifting the direction of a large organization is similar. If you try to press against the entire organization, it won't budge, but setting a small but well-placed force current can move it where you want to go quite easily. I began to think of myself as a pilot rudder. It helped me to choose my paths and my energy expenditure much more wisely.

Plan Leadership Transitions Long in Advance—Have More Than One Option

The very essence of long-cycle enterprises is their ability to transcend the tenure of any single leader or group of leaders. Their sense of mission is deeply embedded throughout the organization with leaders who are the exemplars of their culture. In fact, for a long-cycle enterprise to be too dependent on the presence of any single leader places the organization in great jeopardy. We referred to it as being "bus-sensitive." In other words, what happens to your organization if that key person is run over by a bus?

All positions in a long-cycle enterprise require an understudy, a person who can take over the role of a key individual if they're incapacitated, and a successor, a person in training for the transition of that role in the future. This is simply good business practice, safeguarding your ability to deliver to your customers who depend on you over a long period of time, no matter what. And these are long term processes. Most senior leadership roles in a long-cycle organization aren't easily assumed by outsiders. For most leadership roles, it takes several years at minimum to groom a successor. But the understudy role is just as important. As in a theater production, no one should be the holder of a unique body of knowledge or set of skills that cannot be covered in an emergency. The show must go on.

Conceptually, this begs a couple of questions. Does this mean that a new leader cannot be brought in from outside? Must all leaders be homegrown? Can a leader from a merged or acquired organization be effective in the newly combined enterprise? Long-cycle organizations have generally followed the strategies I've outlined in this book so their leaders are deeply immersed in the organization's culture and richly networked to the people in it. This applies to leaders at all levels, not just at the top. So, while leaders can and will be brought in from outside the organization or assimilated through an acquisition or merger, it will take much longer to achieve optimum effectiveness than it would in a command and control enterprise.

In our organization, we followed several principles in guiding leadership transition. We were by and large homegrown. We never acquired or merged with another company. We did, however, have a few smaller architectural firms close their doors with their staff joining us en masse. With these large blocks of hiring, leaders came with the group and we found that it required enormous care and patience along with a conscious and focused effort to guide their assimilation before they could truly be effective, usually on the order of a year or more.

During periods of rapid growth, we couldn't grow leaders fast enough and hired a number of senior people who had been leaders in other organizations. Similarly, they only became fully effective following a consciously followed immersion into our culture and networks. Strong people will create a following. That's part of what defines them as leaders. They're able to quickly build relationships of trust and respect and can pull together an effective team in rapid order. But if they're doing it based on the culture they bring with them, without the value systems and protocols that make a "one-firm firm," an understanding of the philosophies, beliefs and strategies that bind the enterprise, making it work for its customers, they take on the independent characteristics of a franchisee.

We understood this well, holding to a policy that no newly hired person, no matter how senior and capable as a leader, would be appointed as an officer of the corporation for a full year. This allowed a period of time to assimilate, for many people around the new person to evaluate the fit. It sent a clear message that the person was not a lone ranger able to set their own rules and expectations different from the firm's culture and values and that they were not expected to build an independent business. As difficult as this often was for someone who had carried a title and authority in their previous position (and we lost a few candidates over this issue), over the years this proved a valid motivator both for us and for the individual joining the firm to invest in becoming part of the larger construct of our long-cycle strategy.

Planning for transitions in this context takes time and investment. Future leaders need to be identified, groomed and monitored, usually for a period of years. Referring to Chapters 7 and 15, which describe the many programs for coaching, mentoring and continuous learning, will give you a sense of the breadth of opportunity we had to evaluate future leaders and the array of teaching opportunities we kept constantly in motion.

No matter how carefully you've structured your transition-planning activities, there are always surprises. Someone moves or leaves the firm, has a health problem, changes their leadership style in inappropriate ways or is simply not interested in the new position of greater responsibility when the time comes. Any number of things can throw a monkey wrench into the most carefully planned scenario, making it imperative that you have more than one option at all times. But if you've invested continuously, your options will be there.

Investing in future leaders outside your organization

Despite my comments about the difficulties of bringing in an outsider, not all of your options need be in your organization. As a successful and effective alternative to employing a headhunter when a surprise need was suddenly upon us, we invested in relationships with leaders we had come to know in other organizations through our participation in industry forums. Leadership on an AIA committee, a chamber of commerce or other organization connected to our business brought many of us into contact with potential recruits, allowing us to observe their skills, values and leadership style. It also allowed us to expose these potential recruits to the culture and ideas behind our firm, a little pre-grooming. It always fascinated me how often someone we had spent this kind of time with would call up one day and ask to join us and how often when we were actively recruiting, we would review the people we knew well through these kinds of relationships, make an approach and receive a positive response when we made an offer.

The first experience I had to test my ideas with this sort of transition, to see if I'd done the homework I asked of others, was when I stepped out of my role leading our Los Angeles and Irvine offices. It was time in the firm for me to undertake the role of president of the broader enterprise. Nothing is more difficult than stepping out of a position of deep friendship and the support of a large group of people both inside and outside the firm, into a new role which, at the time, wasn't completely defined or resolved. Art Gensler was the firm's founder and maintained his role as CEO and chairman, so I stepped into an entirely new adventure as we were beginning to explode in size and to take on the assignment to be Art's understudy.

In Los Angeles, Andy Cohen had been my understudy for several years, he was ready to step into the leadership role I had held, and he knew several years in advance that he was being groomed for the position, but then comes the day of reckoning. I learned my first key lesson: when you hand over the reins, do so completely. Be available as a coach and mentor, but never second guess your successor. It's all too easy, particularly when you're still in the same office (as I was), for people who have always come to you with their tough problems to keep looking to you for answers and advice. In fact, it disappoints them when you refer them to your successor. But it's even more difficult for your successor to do the job if you don't support him or her fully.

Andy was at my doorstep more than once with the perfect question, "What do I do now?" I tried to follow Mike Vance's advice from Chapter 17: I answered his questions, not with specifics, but with background and how I'd grappled with similar situations. I never told him what to do. I always drove him to find the approach that was uniquely suited to his leadership style. Within a few years, it was time for me to step into the CEO role. Andy was flying on his own wings, and I was able to leave the Los Angeles office in great hands.

Every so often, a moment of truth arrives, that moment when someone in an important leadership role with a long and respected history with the organization, decides it's time to move on, to retire, testing the effectiveness of all the programs you've so carefully put in place to safeguard your long-cycle enterprise. The first of the firm's founders, Tony Harbour, left in 2002 after 33 years of terrific leadership. We had followed our own advice and had young and talented understudies ready to begin filling some very large shoes, and the first transition from our founding partners to the next generation was underway. We had a young architect whom Tony had recruited years before take on his leadership role in the London office and another partner who had spent a good deal of time with Tony as he led our Design Steering Committee efforts ready to step into that role.

The following year, I made a decision to follow Tony. After 34 years and an incredibly rich experience, I was nearing my 60th birthday. I had a number of things I wanted to do outside the firm (including writing this book) and concluded that it would be a lot easier to transition into them at 60 than at 65. Since I'd assumed the role of president eight years before, the firm had tripled in size, and the structure of my role as I was living it was unsustainable. We'd put a fine leadership team in place and had begun a strategy for the leadership roles in the firm to evolve, allowing me to step aside.

In reflection, it's a thrill to see the firm continue to grow, to do incredible work for its clients and to be a place that people want to be part of. There can be no finer testimonial to long-cycle strategies and no better sense of accomplishment for me than to have helped make the type of place that my father had envisioned and worked so hard to embody in his business.

Although I knew I couldn't "rule from the grave" (when I left, I handed over the reins completely as I had done with Andy), I couldn't resist a few parting thoughts about the client experience that I wanted my successors and the people in the firm to be mindful of. While it's written in the context of a design firm, try substituting the parameters of your own enterprise. The concepts are completely universal:

> Reciprocity is a beautiful thing and a lesson I hope all of you are learning: if you send out things that you think will be of interest to people, they send interesting things back. Not long ago, John Bricker sent me an article by David W. Norton, PhD, titled "Toward Meaningful Brand Experiences" from the Winter 2003 Design Management Journal (Norton is vice president, experience strategy and research for Yamamoto Moss).

> The article explores the evolution of customers' relationships with "Brand" over the last 20 years. I found Norton's observations profound and connected in an important way to our practice of architecture, design and planning. In the 80s, brand image connected to products and services. The physical product or service was something the customer used. Think of mass produced units like Nike shoes, Guess jeans and DeLorean cars. Things were sold as commodities with a brand name attached. The objects created the cache for the company brand and in turn, the brand name gave cache to new products.

> For our profession, that equated to "drawings as instruments of service." Our clients bought drawings from us from which to build things, but conceptually it was the drawings they were buying. We used to price our services by the cost per sheet to produce the drawings or at a charge per square foot

of area planned. The Gensler name became a pretty fair trust mark. By and large, we did good drawings, and when we did so consistently, it brought respect from contractors and building officials, helping our clients to receive better value or faster processing time.

In the 90s, customers began to look for an experience along with their product. "Accumulation" (we are an acquisitive society) had to do with experiences, not just things. Think of the Hard Rock Café T-shirt from Paris or Rome or the logo merchandise from the exotic locale you stayed in. These symbols provided a recall for you or a statement to others of an experience you'd had.

The design professions struggled against commoditization (the "buy it by the pound" marketplace) in the 90s, unable to create a unique and desirable experience that clients wanted to tell their friends about. The manifestation of this market trend found its application through working with a "star" architect. Frank Gehry or Richard Meier provided bragging rights for their clients at cocktail parties. Unfortunately, the actual experiences of getting the thing built weren't always so great.

Gensler was different. We've focused since our inception on providing a great client experience:

1. Consciousness of and respect for budget and schedule (not very creative but very important—relieves anxiety)
2. Designing for the client, not for ourselves (quite the opposite of the "stars" who were really throwbacks to the 80s world of brand image—in other words, they produced "collectibles" as in "I've got a Gehry or a Meier in my town.")
3. Explaining to a client what we're doing and why we're doing it (pretty comforting compared to much of our competition

that simply presented their glorious design as a *fait accompli* and became insulted if the client had the audacity to suggest a change. Perpetrators will remain nameless, but each of you has one or more in your community. You may even have worked for one).

4. Making places designed to reinforce their purpose to enhance organizational performance and create lasting value (I haven't seen that listed as an objective on too many "star" websites although I heard Phillip Johnson use similar words on occasion as he pitched a design to Jerry Hines).

The consequence was, we were well positioned for this very important societal trend, creating a brand experience, as we entered the 90s and we positively exploded as the decade played out. Generally speaking, we delivered a good experience to most of our clients. We weren't as good at it as we could have been. We were just a whole lot better than our competitors. Think what we could have done if we'd really worked on being rigorous about the experience our clients were having.

So, what is in store for us as consumers evolve into the new millennium? In Norton's words, "Today, seeking to renew cultural capital, the challenge is to go one step further, to create experiences that add value and meaning to life." Gensler has a unique opportunity to respond to this trend. Already positioned as a design firm that listens to and bases its solutions on each client's unique needs, this is a time to refocus attention on the client experience protocols that we set for ourselves so long ago, adding cultural meaning and value to both the experience and outcome of our clients' relationships with each of you, the professionals that serve them.

So, what does that mean, and how do you do it? I present you today with this design problem because it is your opportunity to recapture our profession and its value to our world.

The steps start with the charter above. Have you thought through each of the four protocols above before you begin working with a client? These are fundamentally hygiene issues, simply the price of admission to being a design professional at Gensler in the coming decade.

Now, let's talk about how to bring meaning and purpose to the work we do with our clients. Before you push back with a cop-out (all our clients are interested in today is the bottom line, they aren't thinking about "meaning and purpose") reflect on how many of your friends are asking the question of themselves, "What have I done with my life? What am I doing that has meaning?" Do you really think that the individuals who represent our clients are so very different at their core despite the surface bravado of "cheaper, faster?"

Norton in his article suggests five requirements for building meaningful brand experiences. I'll interpolate for our profession from his points:

1. Learn how to get customers to want to spend time with you. What have you done to make the experience of working with you satisfying, fun and rewarding? This is your first design challenge. Think back to a time when you and a client were having a great time working together on a project. What made it that way? What did you do that contributed to that experience? What are you doing with your client right now that is detracting from that experience?

2. Identify your brand truth. What matters at Gensler? We speak of our commitment to sustainable design and planning. What have you done to make yourself part of that commitment? Have you become LEED™ certified? Are you doing anything outside the firm that is an extension of your commitment making our planet a more livable place for future generations? Are these commitments visible to your

client? Study biomimicry. The finest lessons for sustainability
are to be learned from nature and natural processes.

3. Design to allow customers to produce their own meaningful experiences. Have you found a way to help your client
feel good about the work you're doing together? Do your
clients feel like they're participants or are they just being
presented to? And do they feel like, together, they and you
are creating something meaningful?

4. Measure the cultural capital created. We've made tremendous headway with our Performance Mapping initiative.
We've even included "soft" measurements but we can do so
much more to help clients see the tangible benefits of cultural
capital in their organizations. Take some time to learn what
"cultural capital" is and how it benefits an organization.

5. Care deeply. As Norton says, "You can't fake it." When
the passion for what you do is visible and from the heart, the
experiences you have with and give to your clients will have
found resonance with this decade.

It occurred to me that the people in an organization are its
brand—how you behave and the experiences you and your
clients have is what makes Gensler. It's not the number
of offices, the gross billings, the computing power or the
website, it's the people and how you do what you do. As I
was writing this, John sent me another reference point, the
Interbrand website. I pulled the following quote from the
lead article:

"Companies may say they understand the power of branding
and they may even translate brands into dollars on a balance sheet, but many are clueless about a large part of brand
management. It seems obvious, but unless employees act consistently with the brands they represent, any other branding
activity can suffer."

"I reckon about 20% of a brand is its physical attributes, like a logo, color, letterheads. The rest is all about behavior," says Ian Buckingham, head of Interbrand Inside. "Employees bring a brand to life; they are its ultimate custodians."

You are Gensler.

I will miss greatly being as close to each of you as frequently as I've been privileged to be. But I won't be far away. Don't be strangers.

InsideGensler September 2003

And you are your organization. Every enterprise is the people in it. Each of you is playing a role in shaping your organization, whether you're aware of it or not. I hope this book will help you bring consciousness and direction to your actions. They're shaping your company's future. Be a part of making it what you want it to be.

Further Reading

Developing a body of thought and building an organization requires constant learning and mental stimulation. Throughout my career I've read extensively and, in some cases, had the wonderful opportunity to explore the ideas contained in a book or an article in greater detail with the author. I am extremely grateful to the many thoughtful people who, through their research and insights, have helped shape my thinking.

During my tenure as president of Gensler, I shared a book or resource that I found particularly compelling with the firm each month. While I was reminded regularly by my colleagues that my voracious appetite for new ideas could be a bit overwhelming, I also know that many of them read much of what I recommended, creating some common vocabulary elements that got woven into the behavior, strategies and philosophies of the firm.

Books such as this often contain a bibliography referencing citations and sources but I never have a sense about whether I'd enjoy reading further in some area that really interested me. So rather than just passing along citations, I thought I'd provide an impression of several of the books and authors I've found compelling in case you'd like to explore some of the ideas I've shared with you in greater depth. While several of the sources are now a bit dated, many of them are classics offering ideas that are as current today as when they were written.

Leadership and Business

Stephen Ambrose

I came across a quote from Stephen Ambrose, who wrote *Undaunted Courage: Meriweather Lewis, Thomas Jefferson, and the Opening of the American West*, which, by the way, is a fabulous book about one of the great adventures of all time. Any of you who have traveled through the west have seen trail markers commemorating the Lewis and Clark expedition along with numerous high schools, streets and parks named in their honor. There may even be more Lewis and Clark than Martin Luther King commemoratives. But most of us never knew much more about the importance and difficulties of this venture than the brief notes in our history books in primary school. It is historically accurate, based entirely on letters and journals still in existence (it's remarkable that this much material from the early nineteenth century is still around).

I had an opportunity to meet and spend time with Ambrose just after he returned from a tour with Stephen Spielberg and Tom Hanks to promote the film Saving Private Ryan which is based on an episode from another of his books, *Citizen Soldier*. Ambrose spoke extensively about the nature of friendship, which was so evident in the relationship between Lewis and Clark and clearly the element that gave them the strength to endure the hardships they faced as they worked together to cross this continent as the first explorers ever to do so. It made me appreciate the deep and lasting friendships that have been so much a part of my life, and to realize how important friendship has been in achieving the things people accomplish. I hope you find this passage from the book worthwhile and wish for you true friendships with the people with whom you share your work.

"Friendship is different from all other human relationships.

Unlike acquaintanceship, friendship is based on love. Unlike lovers and married couples, friendship is free of jealousy. Unlike children and parents, friendship knows neither criticism nor resentment nor rebellion. Friendship has no status in law. Business partnerships are based on a contract, as is marriage. Parents are bound by the law as are children.

"But friendship is freely entered into, freely given, freely exercised. Friends never cheat on one another, or take advantage, or lie. Friends do not spy on one another, yet they have no secrets. Friends glory in each other's successes and are downcast by their failures. Friends minister to each other. Friends give to each other, worry about each other, stand always ready to help. At its height, friendship is an ecstasy. For Lewis and Clark, it was an ecstasy and the critical factor in their success."

Warren Benis & Patricia Ward Biederman

Organizing Genius by Warren Benis and Patricia Ward Biederman presents a marvelous case for why groups so dramatically outperform individuals and is one of the strongest testimonials I've found for why you invest in long-cycle strategies. Benis teaches at USC, writing extensively on leadership. I've met him several times and find his thoughts quite fascinating. Biederman writes thoughtfully and provocatively for the LA Times.

Benis and Biederman discuss how great stuff gets accomplished through "Great Groups," using organizations like Disney, Xerox PARC, Apple Computers during the development of the MacIntosh, Lockheed's Skunkworks, even the Manhattan Project that developed the atomic bomb to illustrate their points. They focus on the dynamics between teams of people who accomplish great things. I found enormous resonance with teams I've worked with when everything is really "clicking." So often over the years, I've heard every member of a team as they wrap up a project which has gone particularly well describe the experience as "the most fun they've ever had; like not working at all" even after they've committed incredible amounts of time and energy, putting forth the best work they've ever done.

Benis and Biederman use case studies to explore the dynamics that have yielded that sort of atmosphere. I found their analysis to be so consistent with my own observations. I've often wondered about what created the "magic" and wished I could find ways of recreating that environment over and over. To the degree we're able to do this, we all have more fun, feel more fulfilled, grow and learn more richly.

One of the principles described is the value of finding meaning in the work the team is doing; a little like that old story about the three masons who were asked what they were doing. The first said, "I'm setting stones." The second said, "I'm building a wall." The third remarked, "I'm building a cathedral." Guess who went home with a smile on his face? To quote from the book, "Without meaning, labor is time stolen from us. . . [Steve] Jobs and the others also understand that thought is play. Problem solving is the task we are evolved for. It gives us as much pleasure as sex." Well, I'm not sure I'd go that far. They say, "What happens in a great group is always in Technicolor. What happens afterward may seem as drab as a black-and-white movie." But his point is well illustrated in example after example describing teams that truly believe in the importance of what they're doing and the impact that attitude has on both the quality of work accomplished and the excitement and satisfaction of the group members.

They note that a great group is made up of a few great people; not just good, but great; a group that thinks of itself as elite, for whom it's an honor to have been chosen to participate. "Told he was the best to be had, each recruit tried to live up to [the leader's] faith in him." Leaders of great groups are not superstars. They tend to be the ones who are able to effectively recruit or select great and compatible team members, filtering out people who "don't play well together." They coach, they keep the big idea or great cause visible, they shield from bureaucracy and other destructive influences, they help the group avoid and excess perfection syndrome, recognizing that the group will only be successful if it "ships product," and they create an environment where everyone can do their best. "Great groups tend to be non-hierarchical. Members make contributions based on talent, not on role."

Optimism (a characteristic which for me has been a key filter when recruiting) turns out to be a strong factor in both individual achievement and success for great groups. A couple of quotes from the book: "the optimists, even when their good cheer is unwarranted, accomplish more. They do better in school, for example ... the people most likely to succeed are those who combine reasonable talent with the ability to keep going in the face of defeat." To cap it off, a quote from Henry Ford puts it nicely: "If you think you can't, you're right. And if you think you can, you're right."

Benis and Biederman use several examples to illustrate the benefit of a team feeling as if they are underdogs and mavericks acting outside restrictive corporate bounds. My favorite story revolves around Apple's MacIntosh team: "Jobs promised them they were going to build a machine that would 'put a dent in the universe.' They were not engineers or marketers; they were buccaneers, cunning underdogs, going up against the Establishment in the name of excellence and innovation. 'It's better to be a pirate than join the navy [referring to IBM]!' Jobs urged in one of his trademark epigrams, and they raised a skull and crossbones over Bandley [the team's building]."

"The tendency of great things to be accomplished in dreadful spaces should give architects and decorators pause. There is something about the controlled chaos of a garage, the joyless interior of a Quonset hut that seems to spur the imagination. Perhaps the charmlessness of these places forces people who work in them to turn inward, where problem solving takes place. Certainly these environments offer few distractions, including comfort. For reasons still to be discovered, creative collaboration seems to be negatively correlated with the plushness of the office or the majesty of the view." Now that's provocative, suggesting an entirely new design approach to enhance the performance of work teams.

The final chapter lists the characteristics of Great Groups:

1. Greatness starts with superb people.

2. Great groups and great leaders create each other.

3. Every great group has a strong leader.

4. The leaders of great groups love talent and know where to find it.

5. Great groups are full of talented people who can work together.

6. Great groups think they are on a mission from God.

7. Every great group is an island - but an island with a bridge to the mainland.

8. Great groups see themselves as winning underdogs.

9. Great groups always have an enemy.

10. People in great groups have blinders on.

11. Great groups are optimistic, not realistic.

12. In great groups the right person has the right job.

13. The leaders of great groups give them what they need and free them from the rest.

14. Great groups ship [they deliver a product or service on time and on budget].

15. Great work is its own reward.

Ernest L. Boyer and Lee D. Mitgang

Building Community: a new future for architecture education and practice by Ernest L. Boyer and Lee D. Mitgang is a must read for anyone aspiring to be an Architect for the next millennium, and the thoughts contained in it are a rich source of considerations for the future of any profession. Others will probably want to pass on this book unless you're interested in comparing the introspections of the profession of architecture compared to your own professional field. While it was sponsored by Carnegie Mellon University as a research paper into the state of the profession and the educational system that supports it, Boyer and Mitgang are generous with their philosophy and recommendations for change and their thoughts are profound.

They present Seven Essential Goals for the profession:

1. An enriched mission setting forth the architect's mission as building for beauty, building for human needs, building for urban spaces,

and preserving the planet.

2. Diversity with dignity proposes that true learning for this or any profession takes place through a range of methods and curricula; there is no one right process, and we must sustain learning throughout the profession.

3. Standards without standardization suggests that architectural schools are short changing students by not meeting the National Architectural Accreditation Board's standards which may be too explicit anyway. Although it supports NAAB's approach to evaluating curriculum, it proposes a mission of lifelong learning describing four headings for the accumulation of knowledge: discovery of knowledge, integration of knowledge, application of knowledge and sharing of knowledge.

4. A connected curriculum discusses the need for architecture programs to break out of the isolation found in schools today and engages in a dialog with teaching in other disciplines.

5. A climate for learning makes some healthy suggestions for change in atmosphere, at schools and in practice. It begins with: "Healthy learning communities share certain unmistakable characteristic— openness, fair play, clarity of communication, inclusiveness, tolerance, caring, joyfulness and commonly held purposes."

6. A unified profession calls for the development of a strong connection between the university, the internship process and the practice of architecture (this was echoed strongly by the deans of the architectural schools in Miami).

7. Service to the nation speaks to the role of the architect as citizen.

It's an impressive work and a thoughtful digest of the profession today. While academic, it creates a platform for the development of specific response and action from the universities and the profession. Read it and discuss it in the office. It's a strong baseline of thought for the development of the profession and our practice.

Jim Collins

In *Good to Great: Why Some Companies Make the Leap ... and Others Don't*, Collins continues the research into themes explored in *Built to Last: Successful Habits of Visionary Companies*. These are mandatory "reads" for anyone interested in the long-cycle ideas discussed in this book.

Max Depree

Max Depree, former CEO of Herman Miller, provides a marvelous anecdotal primer on leadership entitled *Leadership is an Art*. It contains some wonderful stories of Depree's experiences over the years and will help you to understand what leading looks like, up close and personal. This is easy reading and I've given out many copies over the years to people on a quest to figure out how to be good leaders. This isn't all there is to say on the subject, merely the first things that need to be understood. Give it to that young aspiring leader in your organization.

Joe Florian

A book for that young, aspiring leader in your organization, *Writing in the Information Age* by Joe Florian, provides some of the best writing advice I've seen. Florian makes the case that succinct and compelling business writing is more important today than ever before. We are inundated with information that is so poorly written that material constructed in a crisp, compelling fashion can have a profound impact on readers. He also shows us that good writing is not rocket science and gives some excellent methods that you can apply right now to make your writing easier and better.

The Gallup Organization

Three books have come out of The Gallup Organization that I have found completely compelling in guiding an enterprise to high value. Each builds a case for a strengths based organization that treats people as individuals, capitalizing on their talents. All three merit your attention. The second and third provide a website for you to profile your own strengths and impact on your organization:

1. *First, Break All The Rules—What the World's Greatest Managers Do Differently* by Marcus Buckingham and Curt Coffman

2. *Now, Discover Your Strengths* by Marcus Buckingham and Donald O. Clifton, Ph.D.
3. *How Full Is Your Bucket? Positive Strategies for Work and Life* by Tom Rath and Donald O. Clifton, Ph.D.

Malcolm Gladwell

What is the sequence of events leading to major change in a business, a community or the world? *The Tipping Point: How Little Things Can Make a Big Difference* explores eloquently how change comes about and how minute the event might be that shifts a major system.

His new book, *Blink*, pursues the topic of intuition. Where do our quick, instinctive responses to situations and people come from, what value do they have and should we follow them? These are both "light" reads but filled with wonderful insights to why things happen the way they do.

Charles Handy

Charles Handy is prolific and one of my favorite authors on changing cultures in our society and the impact they're having on our work lives. To understand what your employees are going to be like and what it's going to take to attract and retain them, spend some time with Handy. Following his much acclaimed *The Age of Unreason*, he wrote *The Age of Paradox*. The First book took us through a transition in work life that radically shifted my thinking about who's going to be occupying all this office space around the world in the coming decades - and it's not conventional large corporations as we know them. He wrote of a new array of not-for-profit enterprises taking on the role of government services, of individual entrepreneurs replacing commitment for life relationships in large corporations and generally described a society which is in dramatic transition. In the second book, he wrote extensively of the dismemberment (downsizing) of large, vertically integrated companies and the creation of virtual enterprises where people rely on the talent, skill and knowledge they accumulate throughout a career to come together for a specific purpose then break apart and reconfigure for a new mission. At the end, we're left with many mysteries about how to manage an organization under these circumstances.

Beyond Certainty is a collection of essays in which Handy explores "Federalism," where real power resides with individual work teams which still yield some authority to a central entity for better leverage and wiser long term decisions. This is a discussion of interdependence which he believes works for nations as well as organizations. For those of us who continue to try to understand how our world is going to feel and what paths our careers are likely to take, these books are a fine and provocative collection of thought.

Handy continues with *The Hungry Spirit* to be one of the most interesting speculators about the evolution of our society. The subtitle, *Beyond Capitalism, a quest for purpose in the modern world,* is a good descriptor of Handy's explorations. If you're interested in value systems in work and family life, you'll find this wonderfully thought provoking. This is a book you'll want someone else you know to read as well. It deserves discussion. I certainly found myself wanting to talk to someone about the implications of Handy's speculations. While perusing any of his works is provocative and filled with insight, reading these four in sequence helps you to see how he's built his thoughts over the years.

Oren Harari

Leapfrogging the Competition, Five Giant Steps to Market Leadership by Oren Harari, a professor of management at the University of San Francisco provides wonderful insight into how to lead quantum change in response to an ever-changing world. The book is filled with easily understood conceptual ideas about how to thrive in this era of staggering change (a quote from the book, "half of the Fortune 500 companies listed in 1983 are no longer around"), backed up by pragmatic methods to structure your organization to excel. While the concepts are straightforward, the things you have to do are easier said than done. So, while it's a great how-to book, it won't be very easy for most enterprises to undertake enough of the "giant steps" to make a difference. Herein lays the opportunity.

Jerry Jellison

Jerry Jellison teaches at USC and, long before his book *Overcoming Resistance: A Practical Guide to Producing Change in the Workplace* was published, spent time with Gensler leading workshops on why people resist change and how to overcome that resistance to build an organization with common purpose. Jellison's techniques are easy to learn and apply. Many of his aphorisms became reminders for us when encountering objections to the direction we were headed. They also helped us to work more effectively with clients. Give this book to your managers to help them learn how to deal with organizational resistance.

John Kotter

I'm often asked about leadership: What makes a good one? Can I learn to be one? What can I read to help me understand leadership? An excellent source immediately comes to mind: *A Force For Change: How Leadership Differs from Management* by John Kotter explores a broad array of characteristic behaviors which distinguish leaders from managers in an organization.

More than any other book I've read, it discusses personal histories of leaders and how the personality and style of a leader is formed. It is profound in its endorsement that both management and leadership are part of an effectively functioning organization. Each is necessary and important; we need to celebrate and appreciate both roles as different career tracks. The "Peter Principle" of someone rising to their own level of incompetence is captured by the observations of great managers who think that they can only be successful if recognized as great leaders but never get there because this is not their strength.

David Maister

I often assigned "homework" before a retreat as a platform for discussion of issues that formed the underlying agenda. *True*

Professionalism: The Courage to Care About Your People, Your Clients and Your Career by David Maister was one such assignment and is a "must" for anyone in a service enterprise. The term "one-firm firm," which we adopted to describe our goal for Gensler as a single integrated and collaborative enterprise across broad geographical and service boundaries, was coined by Maister in an essay that was later republished in another terrific book entitled *Managing the Professional Service Firm.*

This book is entirely accessible and, while Maister's work is generally thought to be most appropriate for law firms and accounting firms, this work might as well have been written for anyone in a service business. From designing your own career, and being a "true professional"—"believe passionately in what you do and never knowingly compromise your standards and values ...aiming for true excellence"—to the importance of having fun in what you do, and developing a personal career strategy, this book is extraordinarily important for everyone thinking through long-cycle strategies.

This book is certainly more appropriate for people in service businesses, particularly ones that have enduring relationships with their customers. But even product companies are migrating in this direction. So, if you find your relationship with your customer looking more and more like a consultative one or if your customer's relationship with your product is going to last a long time, read this book.

Maister's new book, *The Trusted Advisor*, continues and updates his themes.

Gordon MacKenzie

Orbiting the Giant Hairball by Gordon MacKenzie, a former creative director at Hallmark in Kansas City, MO, is a simple collection of mini-essays about survival in the corporate world. The metaphor sounds strange but is actually a good one when I think of how often I've watched people (even in my own organization where we tried to dismantle the "hairball" of internal bureaucracy and politics on a daily basis) get tangled in that mess of corporate life that pours giant buckets of cold water on creativity and innovation, where the idea of actually having fun at what you do can seem like a distant memory connected only to the school play yard of our youth.

The concept of orbiting this hairball of entanglement and frustration is a good one—stay in the gravitational field of the organization, have fun and be creative without pushing the limits of propriety too far and flying away (getting fired or acting so much out of alignment with the organization that you lose your value or viability as a member of the enterprise).

The last two chapters are wonderful teachings for life. Don't miss it if anyone has ever talked about your organization as being a bit too "corporate!"

Neil Rackham

I was having dinner a while back with a very good friend, Ava Abramovitz. The subject of how architects interact with clients came up and we digressed to the subject of "selling." She mentioned a body of research and a book by her husband, Neil Rackham, entitled *Spin Selling* (SPIN is an acronym for Situation-Problem-Implication-Need/Payoff), which sounded fascinating. She subsequently sent me a copy, and I found it most worthwhile. Its dominant theme is the differentiation between selling small stuff and big stuff, between selling impulse items and complex services.

For better or worse (according to the book, much worse), the techniques which have been taught for qualifying a customer, discussing their problems and closing a sale are fine for small items but actually work against selling services to clients. Some of the advice in the book is pretty intuitive to design professionals, but much of it is completely contrary to the various tapes, books and seminars I've experienced in my career about how to sell something, whether it be selling services to a client or someone who has to say "yes" for your work to proceed after you've been hired

Don Miguel Ruiz

My wife gave me a book that I found compelling in its simplicity and message. *The Four Agreements* by Don Miguel Ruiz calls itself "A Practical Guide to Personal Freedom," exploring the wisdom of the Toltec, developed thousands of years ago in southern Mexico.

Briefly, the four agreements are:
• Be impeccable with your word—speak with integrity, say only what you mean.
• Don't take anything personally—learn that nothing others do is because of you.
• Don't make assumptions—finding the courage to ask questions.
• Always do your best—avoiding self-judgment, self-abuse and regret.

Seems simple, maybe even simplistic, but Ruiz' development of these ideas will change your life. I highly recommend you take a look. It's a small book, accessible in form, easy to understand but frustratingly difficult to implement. I've read it three times now and have become a student.

Peter Schrag

Paradise Lost: California's Experience, America's Future carries all the strength and fear which Cadillac Desert delivered about our water system. Except it's focused on our system of governance.

Schrag takes the position that where California goes, so goes the rest of the nation. We who live in California may be a little closer to the future than we'd like, but it's pretty important for those of you from other parts of the country to see what's happening. The book surveys the change in the way budgets have been determined since the advent of Proposition 13, the infamous Jarvis-Gann Tax Limitation initiative passed in the early 70s. It takes us through the impact on government that has resulted from the increased use of the initiative process in California to severely limit the ability of legislative and executive branches of our government to function.

A case is made, illustrated by the fact that an initiative may be passed by a simple majority but takes a "super-majority" or two-thirds of the votes to overturn. Our governance system has been taken over by lobbyists who have made a business of dreaming up causes to fuel their enterprises. This removes legislative debate from the process of making laws and results in bad laws. Many initiatives voted on in California are admitted to be "probably unconstitutional." The result has been expensive court challenges with the judicial branch ultimately defining legislation. Judges making laws based on initiatives written by lobbyists was not what our founding fathers had in mind.

Peter Schwartz

The Art of the Long View is the primer for anyone wanting to understand how to undertake scenario planning in their organization.

Peter Senge

The Fifth Discipline: The Art & Practice of the Learning Organization gave structure to a great deal of my thinking about how to implement and inspire programs that make your enterprise a "learning organization." While the case for continuous learning has been thoroughly made in the last few years, few books deliver methodology as well as this.

Jack Welch

Jack Welch wrote *Jack – Straight from the Gut* just after he retired as chairman of General Electric. What is it about corporate leaders and intestines? *Guts* is the title of Bob Lutz's book about his years at Chrysler—must be a male way of getting in touch with your intuitive side.

The story is as much about General Electric as it is about Welch. GE has been by far the most consistently successful company measured by growth of stock value, size, profits, quality and globalization over Jack Welch's 20-year tenure. Known as the "people factory," GE has produced a steady flow of top-notch business leaders in the last 20 years, many of whom have gone on to lead other global companies. The book is a marvelous study of a truly remarkable business and businessman. His style is curt and to the point, consistent with stories about him as head of GE. The book includes an interesting insight into the transition to a new CEO, Jeff Immelt.

For those of you interested in different leadership styles, there is some sage advice. For those of you who want to know the real facts behind the headlines of issues and events involving GE, the book reads like *Barbarians at the Gate*. If you're just interested in a fascinating personality who's become an icon in management and leadership throughout the world, you'll find *Jack* a unique study.

I got a good swift kick in the pants about some things I could have done faster and better. Even in stressful times, Welch cuts you no slack. He tells you how to stay focused and grow even when things are bad. Despite the recent discrediting of Welch in his retirement, the book remains a marvelous and instructive read.

On Sustainability

Ray Anderson
In *Mid-Course Correction: Toward a Sustainable Enterprise*, Ray Anderson, the chairman of Interface Carpets and a very dear friend, discussed the epiphany that set him on a new course: to build a company that does not deplete natural resources and leaves no waste. It's a daunting challenge for any enterprise to say nothing of a major carpet manufacturer dependent on petrochemicals, energy and water.

Ray has been a good friend and an idol of mine for many years. His thoughts, concerns and ideas for sustainability are an inspiration. Since writing the book and embarking on this path, Interface has made astounding progress, dispelling the notion that being good stewards of our planet costs more. They remain highly competitive and have by and large paid for every new sustainable program with the cost savings from earlier initiatives.

Janine Benyus
I had the great pleasure of hearing Janine Benyus speak, so I was excited to read her book, *Biomimicry*. The term, which she coined, is the man-made emulation of something that occurs in nature.

Biomimetic refers to something that characterizes this property.

Biomimicry makes all of the efforts we're making in sustainable design seem like Model "T" Ford stuff. While I'm enormously proud of the progress Gensler made in sustainability in its work (as proud as Henry Ford was of his "any color you want as long as it's black" transportation revolution), the examples cited in Benyus' book are like being transported onto the Starship Enterprise. I was inspired by the many strategies being undertaken throughout the world to model processes that nature has evolved over millennia, from sustainable agriculture that imitates the natural prairie offering opportunities for equivalent crop yields from cultivated fields and without pesticides, topsoil loss or irrigation to adapting photosynthesis to the generation of electricity.

The book has some highly technical sections so to the non-scientific person can be a challenging read. But even if you skip over some of the complex sections, I encourage you to visit this book. *Biomimicry* is the wave of the future and the path to true sustainability. I subsequently spent a weekend in a Biomimicry workshop with Janine and was amazed by the application not just of elements and constructions found in nature, but also processes and systems, including the management of an organization.

Jared Diamond

Curiosity is the most energizing human characteristic I know of and I'm blessed with an insatiable appetite (which is perhaps why I receive an occasional comment about having a high energy level). I'm always wondering why things are the way they are. I recently finished a book that answered a whole array of questions I'd thought about from time to time and a few more that had never occurred to me.

Jared Diamond, author of *Guns, Germs & Steel, The Fates of Human Societies*, is a historian of a whole new dimension. As a professor of physiology at the UCLA School of Medicine, Diamond explores the development of human civilizations by synthesizing the work of archeologists, geologists, paleontologists, linguists, epidemiologists and others from the physical and social sciences to create a broad and sweeping history of the evolution of human societies.

Have you ever wondered why, how, when and where humans developed speech and writing? Why, when and where did man begin domesticating plants and animals? Why did such developments take place in some regions and not others? Why is the history of human invention so Euro-centric? Did you know that when the first Spaniards set foot in the Americas, there were as many people in North, Central and South America as there were in Eurasia (approximately 20 million)? How is it that within a few years, 95% of the inhabitants of the Americas were dead (hint: it wasn't the Conquistadors who killed them)?

Diamond's book lays to rest once and for all the grounds for racist theories of history by analyzing the development of human societies on different continents. He reveals the real reasons for the great differences in the speed and configuration with which human cultures and societies evolved over the last 13,000 years. Once you start reading it, you won't be able to put it down.

And now, Diamond has written *Collapse*, a journey through a variety of civilizations who have confronted over-population, resource depletion and environmental abuse both successfully and unsuccessfully. The book is filled with lessons for our current civilization about the future we're facing, what collapse looks like and what we'll need to do to survive.

Thom Hartmann

Hartmann's profound book, *The Last Hours of Ancient Sunlight*, explores the way in which we're using our hydrocarbon reserves—namely oil, gas and coal which he defines as ancient sunlight—although he makes a few references to other mineral and water resources and, of course, America's largest export (topsoil) most of which continues its steady flow out the mouth of the Mississippi River. His case is strong for a true crisis in energy supplies within a very short period of time and for the need to change our point-of-view in the consumption of these resources now. You'll find resonance between Hartmann's research and findings, Jared Diamond's *Collapse* and Marc Reisner's *Cadillac Desert*. You'll find some encouragement in Janine Benyus' *Biomimicry*.

Paul Hawkin

Paul Hawkin's *The Ecology of Commerce* is the book that inspired Ray Anderson's epiphany about sustainable commerce and is the original manifesto for reorientation of our thinking about our businesses. This is not a tree-hugging radical-thinking call for a return to tribalism or nature, but a hard hitting and important (even today) treatise on why and how sustainable commerce makes good business sense.

Daniel Quinn

There are many books out there about sustainability, but most of them focus on applications. These books are about "why." I can't think of a less likely vehicle for a philosophy discussion than a gorilla as a teacher, communicating with a man who wants to learn how to change the world. But Daniel Quinn's book, *Ishmael*, is a brilliant treatise on where our civilization is going, how we got this way and what we need to learn. This book had been around for a while by the time I read it (two sequels have been written, *My Ishmael* and *Beyond Civilization*) so several people at Gensler asked, "Where've you been?"

Ishmael is a brilliant essay, worthy of your time. I also recommended *Biomimicry* in this bibliography and only wish I'd read *Ishmael* first. For those of you who are interested in sustainability, how our civilization is evolving and what can be done about it, I recommend these two wonderful books. One will make you uncomfortable, the other will give you hope. If you are on the three week vacation plan instead of two this summer, take along a third book I recommended, *Guns Germs and Steel*, and read it before the other two. You'll come back with a whole new perspective on life and the world around you. I guarantee it!

Marc Reisner

Cadillac Desert: The American West and Its Disappearing Water
sent me into apoplexy. Having been a sustainable design advocate
throughout most of my life, I'd always suspected that water (both
fresh and waste) was going to be a serious problem in our lifetimes.
Having grown up in California and watched the water debates
between the northern and southern halves of the state and having
lived through a few droughts, I thought I knew something about the
subject. As old as this book is, it provides an important digest of the
history of water policy and problems in the U.S. Its projections aren't
far off and the problems described haven't gone away. Today they're
simply closer to us.

On Design

Stewart Brand

If you're about to embark on a building project for your organization, you must read this book. In *How Buildings Learn*, Stewart
Brand helps us look at the cycle of the use of buildings, describing
"high road" buildings (those that are built for a unique purpose
and that tend to remain intact over long periods of time, sometimes
merely as shrines if the use for which they were built no longer
exists) and "low road" buildings (those that are more generic in
character and that adapt over and over as their uses change). There
are clearly many more "low road" buildings on our planet than
"high road," yet most architects aspire to creating edifices that will
remain unchanged by their users. In fact, many are offended if their
work is modified in any way.

     This is an excellent journal for anyone undertaking a con-
struction project, providing terrific insights into the decisions you'll
be making about materials, systems and the character and quality of
the spaces in and around the building you're making. Every building has components that should be designed to survive differing life
cycles. And the configuration of the space contained in the building

as well as its connections to the community into which it's integrated should be carefully considered with an eye to how easily it will be adapted to future, as yet unknown, uses.

Betty Cornfield & Owen Edwards

I refer often to *Quintessence, The Quality of Having It* by Betty Cornfield and Owen Edwards, a delightful, if a bit oblique, little book which I've had for years. This thin volume defines through a series of examples like a paper clip, a classic Coke bottle or a Mont Blanc pen, the quality of "quintessence," that characteristic of an object when it is the perfect exemplar of what it is and does. We can do no more than to strive for quintessence in the work we do, to do projects which are so perfectly suited for the purpose for which they are designed, that everyone who experiences them finds them intuitively satisfying and perfect for their use. An example would be a Japanese tea house, so perfect in scale, proportion, detail and materiality that it brings serenity to anyone who uses it, consistent with the ceremony performed.

The quality of quintessence can also be applied to organizations and, in my opinion, is the highest achievement that one can ascribe to an enterprise: it is the perfect manifestation of what it needs to be for its vision and mission.

Tom Kelley

A friend gave me a great book the other day, *The Art of Innovation*, by Tom Kelley of IDEO. Tom's brother, David, founded this renowned product design firm in Palo Alto, California, and remains the CEO. I have come to know David very well over the years and, through his stories about designing everything from the first computer mouse to the squeeze containers for Crest toothpaste, have great respect for the creativity and innovation that continually emerges from their firm.

Tom explores the organization and processes IDEO incorporates into their work. The descriptions of their brainstorming methods and theories about office design and planning are particularly compelling. It's a fast and enjoyable read; I read most of the book on a flight home from the East Coast. It's a "must" for all designers and most enjoyable for any enterprise as it thinks about how to stimulate and manage creativity.

Robert A. Lutz

Bob is a motorcycling buddy of mine and has been referred to as "the ultimate car guy" so I couldn't wait to read his book when it came out. *Guts: 8 Laws of Business from One of the Most Innovative Business Leaders of our Time* didn't disappoint, capturing his swashbuckling character as he recounts his history with Chrysler, BMW and other automotive companies over the years. His insights on the importance of design and its connection to the emotional buying decisions we all make are tremendously insightful. I've long respected the automotive industry for the long-cycle issues in product development, marketing, sourcing and managing that it must grapple with on a global basis. This book will be compelling for anyone, car buff or not, who is interested in the career of a fascinating guy, his insights and frustrations in large corporate structures. Give this book to your product development team.

William J. Mitchell

Bill is currently dean of architecture at MIT and taught at UCLA for many years where I came to know him. He continues to be one of the profound thinkers about the effects of technology on our lives. His book, *City of Bits: Space Place and the Infobahn*, was, I believe, the first to be published simultaneously in hard copy and on the Internet. If you visit the Internet site, you'll find a number of hot links between subjects mentioned in the book and more detailed information on the issue as well as comments from readers. Is this the future? It certainly makes this book much more robust.

The book explores the implications of various technological developments on architecture and the nature of communities. I won't spoil your enjoyment by repeating anecdotes but urge you to read this text. It will rock your boat as you consider the likely lifespan of some of the things we're designing into our buildings as our lives are changed through technology.

As a footnote, keep a dictionary by your side. Mitchell is British by birth and uses a vocabulary that is rich and often arcane.

Cesar Pelli

I recommend *Observations for Young Architects* for architects of all ages or anyone interested in the process of making a building. Cesar explores the history of modern architecture in a thoughtful and comprehensible way. Having known him for many years, I found his comments on place making particularly appropriate. He spends some special time on a discussion of design in context and the making of cities. In discussing the importance of restraint and context in building design, he says: When we first become architects, we are delighted to be given a piece of a city or a landscape to design—however small it may be. As we seek to create the best possible design, we face the sometimes conflicting goals of making the building relate to its place or to our favorite forms. I believe that cities and landscapes are more important than any building, and that the building is more important than any architect.

In architecture, each building has a role to play, expressing its particular nature and its place in the city or the landscape. It may be helpful to keep in mind that the best actors, the artists of acting, are those who enhance the whole cast and most completely express each particular role, surmounting their own personalities, rather than those who steal the show and always play themselves.

Keep that in mind when you're thinking about your next building project.

Bill Stumpf

Want to know where trust and other characteristics of relationships we used to enjoy have gone? *The Ice Palace That Melted Away*, subtitled *Restoring Civility and Other Lost Virtues to Everyday Life*, presents some wonderful thoughts about one of my favorite topics: civility (or what it is about the places we most enjoy or the behaviors of people we find most pleasurable to be with that is slowly disappearing from our world and what we should be doing to recapture it). You may recognize Bill Stumpf as the designer of some of the best chairs Herman Miller (or any other manufacturer) has made. He quotes Antoine de Courtin from his *Rules of Civility*, "Civility being nothing but certain Modesty and courteous disposition which is to accompany us in all our actions …Civility is a Science that teaches us to dispose our words and actions in their proper and just places."

Stumpf is a designer. I found great resonance in his point of view. He defines design as "the process both physical and mental by which people give an order to objects, community, environments and behavior. It aims to make our existence more meaningful, connect us to natural realities, infuse serious work with playful humor, extend human capacity—physical, emotional and spiritual. Designers make ideas into things." Great! And if you've read this far, I hope I've convinced you that being a designer is not a privilege granted to an anointed few. You have the capacity to attune your senses to take responsibility for the things and events in your life.

The book rambles a bit and most of the quotes that introduce each chapter are pretty oblique, but Bill synopsizes each section eloquently. An example is a chapter which describes an aspect of civility best exhibited by D. J. DePree, the founder of Herman Miller who had a penchant for always leaving any place he'd been a little better than he found it. He always cleaned up after himself (and others, too). Think about this the next time you walk away from the kitchen or pantry in your office, leaving dirty cups and glasses in the sink or spilled coffee on the counter, whether it's yours or not. Stumpf's close: "A caretaking relationship is necessary for us to survive, much less prosper. Nothing will change until we take personal responsibility for caretaking not just what we own, but what we all share."

Stumpf also makes some choice comments about architecture. "Hugh Hardy once lamented to me a few years ago that the most disturbing characteristic of young graduate students applying for work was that they had more interest in designing a building than actually building it. This kind of thinking has given design a tinge of effete uselessness. Design is much more than talk or sketches or plans, which almost any person can engage in. Design, like music, offers up its true meaning and significance only in its performance." I couldn't agree more.

Where will clients be?

Richard Florida
Where, geographically should you be doing business and why? No book I've ever read has given me as many insights into the way cities and communities are going to evolve as *The Rise of the Creative Class*. Florida is a thoughtful researcher exploring how rapidly knowledge work is migrating to creative work, how important creative thinkers are becoming to organizations and how the psychology of these creative types is going to drive their location decisions, affecting entire regions either positively or negatively.

The book is filled with statistical data on specific communities throughout the U.S. analyzing why their culture is attracting or driving away those people who will be most important to every company's future. If you're thinking of locating a business, investing in a market that you're currently not in, merging with or acquiring another business, read this book first!

Thomas Friedman
The Lexus and the Olive Tree: Understanding Globalization describes the broad changes that are occurring in our world as barriers to trade, and particularly money flows dissolve. There is no better primer than this to help you understand why entire businesses and the jobs that go with them are migrating around the world. Tom Friedman, a columnist for *The New York Times*, uses his broad perspective from covering stories around the globe to connect the impacts of this change to our day to day lives. I found his observations about the influence of Standard and Poors, the bond rating agency, on human rights to be of particular note, pointing out how much stronger the impact of the private sector is on governance and

policy issues in countries than outside governments or the United Nations.

Friedman's new book, *The World is Flat*, continues his exploration of the global context in which all of us do business today.

B. Joseph Pine II & James H. Gilmore

Every business needs to understand the principles explored in this book. *The Experience Economy, Work is Theatre & Every Business a Stage* examines our journey from a "goods" economy to a "service" economy, into an "information" economy and beyond to an "experience" economy. The premise is straightforward: goods are easily commoditized; a service can make the goods themselves more valuable. Information in itself is intangible but can assume a value far greater than the goods or services alone. An experience can have the most value as it is transformative. It can entertain, educate, and provide high emotional content esthetically or through escape from your current world. It's participatory and involving.

The authors explore numerous examples of how companies have taken their offerings from commodity to customization, from undifferentiated to differentiated and from irrelevant to the needs of customers to intimately relevant. It's a "must read" for all of us as we shape our own service offerings and the experience we deliver to our customers. Have you asked a customer lately how much they enjoyed the experience of working with you or going through the process of buying your product or service or getting something built? The future lies in reshaping our working methods to bring excitement, fulfillment and enrichment to our customers, not just through the built product, but through the experience they have while working with us, a tough challenge in any business.

P. J. O'Rourke

In *Eat the Rich*, P. J. O'Rourke explores economies and economic theory from around the world in a way that is wonderfully humorous, more than a little cynical but quite informative. You'll understand a lot more about how different economies of the world function and why most of them are so completely screwed up. And, no, you don't have to be an economist to understand this book. In fact, if you were an economist you'd probably have nightmares about how a newspaper columnist can make such enormously complex things, which you've spent your life taking way too seriously, so marvelously simple.

The book takes the reader through the U.S. economy, explaining why unfettered capitalism and free markets don't always work (Albania is the example). He then uses examples of socialism that work and don't work (Sweden and Cuba), contrasts Hong Kong and Shanghai, tells all about Russia and finally explains what really works. It's a lighter more digestible version of globalization than Tom Friedman's *The Lexus and the Olive Tree*. You'll have to read through to the very last paragraph to understand the title. And don't jump ahead as it won't mean anything to you until you've read the entire book. Have fun!

Michael J. Silverstein & Neil Fiske

If you're selling anything in the retail world, *Trading Up: The New American Luxury* will give you a completely new insight into the buying patterns of today's consumer. Silverstein and Fiske connected many dots for me, describing why people will pay so much for a BMW (making it the most profitable car company per unit in the world) or why a carpenter still making payments on his pick-up truck will pay out his entire discretionary budget on a full set of Calloway golf clubs. If you're in the retail business, this book will help you find the emotional connection to your customer of today. And probably the foreseeable future as I think this trend is just beginning.

Lester Thurow

The third book I've recommended on globalization, *Fortune Favors the Bold: What We Must Do to Build a New and Lasting Prosperity*, will let you know how important I think this subject is to business today. While protestors continue to rail against globalization, the impacts as described by Thurow are, by and large, positive. I wish I could get anyone participating in such a rally to read this book.

Thurow carries the conversation deeper than Friedman or O'Rourke, discussing the deep concern among economists for our widening trade deficit. While politicians continue to put their heads in the sand, the magnitude of this problem, as of this writing in excess of $660 billion per year that we spend outside this country in excess of what others spend for American goods and services, is likely to come to a screeching halt at some point in time. Thurow describes why the impacts will be far greater for third-world countries than for the U.S., predicting a slide backward in the improvement of income and quality of life in the poorest nations. But there is hope in the form of some clear, if difficult, recommendations to our governments for actions to change this pattern.

On the future

Roger Bootle

See Chapter 2 for a discussion of *The Death of Inflation: Surviving and Thriving in the Zero Era.*

Michael Dertouzos

What Will Be by Michael Dertouzos explores developments in technology, both hardware and software, in a fashion which is both accessible and grounded. He helps us understand what research is underway and which products and services are likely to impact our lives in the near future while debunking much of what is often presented as being "just around the corner." One clear message: it's no good being a Luddite, sticking your head in the sand and expecting that you can live your life ignoring the effects technology is having daily on our work, and home lives. More importantly (from the liner notes), he describes "what areas of our society will never be altered by technology and offers an inspiring blueprint for how new technologies could bridge the centuries old gaps between reason and the spirit."

Larry Downes & Chunka Mai

Since Internet companies are here to stay, I refer you to a great book entitled *Unleashing the Killer App* by Larry Downes and Chunka Mai. These two able authors deliver a 12-step program for any company to build a "killer application," a business strategy to kill the competition. It's a wonderful digest for considering a new business start-up but its greatest value is for companies that find themselves competing on unstable ground in an ever changing marketplace. It will also help you understand what technology start-up companies in the 90s were trying to accomplish.

Michio Kaku

Michio Kaku stretches us very far into the future in *Visions*, taking us on a broad ranging tour of research underway as well as directions which are likely to be taken in three key areas: The Computer Revolution, The Biomolecular Revolution, and The Quantum Revolution. Kaku leads us on a carefully structured tour of worlds which none of us in our normal course of life would ever find, describing the most likely developments in each area between now and 2020, the most likely directions from 2020 to 2050, and then speculations from 2050 to 2100 and beyond. This is the most far-reaching yet most plausible and thought-provoking book on these issues I've ever read. The third segment of each chapter becomes quite spiritual and philosophical as it debates questions about the limits of technology (will humans become obsolete?), the genetics of a brave new world and the quantum potential of becoming masters of space and time.

For those of you who, like me, enjoy speculating about the future in order to create scenarios to help guide our lives today, this is a "must read." If you just like to do a little old fashioned fantasizing, you'll enjoy the speculations about a wild future, some of which you're going to experience in your lifetime (although if you accept some of Kaku's predictions, some of you younger folks are going to have some longer life times than we've known in the past).

One of the most remarkable and provocative aspects discussed is the incredible short time frames in which enormous change is going to happen. In the millenial scheme of things, a couple of hundred years isn't even a blink of the eye, and 20 years is just around the corner.

Abraham Maslow

In college while in a psychology class, I was inspired by *Toward a Psychology of Being* and Maslow's pyramid model of human needs. Over the years I've used Maslow's thinking to develop a number of business and market analogs, particularly in the retail sector. A testimony to the durability of this book is that, although it was originally published in 1968, it was reprinted with a marvelous new introduction in 1998. This is not an easy read and should only be undertaken by those that are prepared to dig deeply into psychology. The introduction in the new edition is all you'll need to understand Maslow's needs hierarchy. But it's a powerful concept worth understanding as you seek to get closer to your customers' and employees' motivations.

Kerry Mullis

I'm very fortunate to have a lot of friends who recommend books to me. I guess it helps to let people know that I read a lot. It saves me from reading bad books. *Dancing Naked in the Mind Field* by Karry Mullis was such a referral. When I read Arthur C. Clarke's (author of *2001:A Space Odyssey*) liner note: "One of the most mind-stretching and inspirational books I've read for a long time. It is also very funny and, I hope that - before it gets banned - myriads of copies will infiltrate all the legislatures, colleges, and high schools of the U.S.," I had to dive right in, setting another book aside. It was worth it. It is irreverent, entertaining and provides an insight into a person I would love to get to know personally. Mullis won the Nobel Prize in chemistry and is a surfer, not necessarily in that order. He debunks several myths about science and life in general while delivering a delightful look with a most unique personality and life-style. It's not for everyone (his life-style that is; I don't think I would have survived it and I've been out at the edge quite a bit), but you'll enjoy reading about it and probably change a few of your preconceptions about the world around you. This book is just plain fun and a good thing to read simultaneously with your young teenaged kids.

Steven R. Quartz & Terrence J. Sejnowski

Liars, Lovers and Heroes—What the New Brain Science Reveals About How We Become Who We Are takes us into the realm of brain science, bringing new clarity and scientific research to the age-old "nature vs. nurture" question. For any parent wondering how the infant mind forms intelligence to all of us wondering what happens to our brain and our intelligence as we age, this book is extraordinarily enlightening.

I found the discussions of intelligence gained through socialization particularly applicable to organizational design. My take is that organizations build real value through the ways in which the people in them interact and learn, further reinforcing my argument that you lose true intelligence and therefore organizational intelligence and value when people who have been nurtured by your enterprise leave.

Julian Simon

The State of Humanity (see Chapter 2 for a discussion of this book)

Ben Wattenburg

Values Matter Most (see Chapter 2 for a discussion of this book)

Available from Östberg...

How Firms Succeed: A Field Guide to Design Management
James P. Cramer and Scott Simpson

A hands-on guide to running any design-related business—from a two-person graphics team to middle-management to CEOs of multi-national firms—offering advice on specific problems and situations and providing insight into the art of inspirational management and strategic thinking.

"How Firms Succeed is a fountainhead of great ideas for firms looking to not just survive, but thrive in today's challenging marketplace."

—Thompson E. Penney, FAIA
President/CEO, LS3P Architecture, Interior Architecture, Land Planning and President, American Institute of Architects, 2003

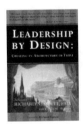

Leadership by Design: Creating an Architecture of Trust
Richard N. Swett

Ambassador Richard Swett's groundbreaking new book investigates the unique civic leadership strengths of the architecture profession. Leadership by Design is an eloquent plea to architects, leaders and citizens alike to expand the tool chest as we seek new leadership to design new solutions for the complex challenges facing our nation and the world.

"This book reveals that the 'citizen-architect' has always been in our midst and begins an important dialogue about how that role should be designed for the future."

—Robert A.M. Stern, FAIA
Robert A.M. Stern Architects and Dean, Yale School of Architecture

Almanac of Architecture & Design
James P. Cramer and Jennifer Evans Yankopolus, editors

The only complete annual reference for rankings, records, and facts about architecture, interior design, industrial design, landscape architecture, planning and historic preservation.

"The reader who uses this book well will come away with a richer sense of the texture of the profession and of the architecture it produces."

—Paul Goldberger, The New Yorker

The Next Architect: A New Twist on the Future of Design
James P. Cramer and Scott Simpson

The Next Architect takes a fresh look at our fast-evolving profession, focusing on how new design technologies and processes are changing not just what we do, but how we do it. This book challenges the next generation of design professionals to make full use of their talents to build a better, healthier, more prosperous world. (NEW)

Value Redesigned: New Models for Professional Practice
Kyle V. Davy and Susan L. Harris

In Value Redesigned, Davy and Harris reveal a vivid landscape where innovative new models for professional practice are already beginning to flourish, showing firms avenues of escape from the vicious cycle of commoditization and low prestige that is epidemic within the architecture and engineering community. Aligned with the dynamics of the emerging knowledge-based economy, these new models of practice offer bold value propositions, combining new ways of creating value with innovative pricing strategies.

"Value Redesigned is a timely and important book for all professionals and professional firms involved in the built environment projects. This is a must read for any one who cares about the future of their own firm and the future of the industry."

—Al Barkouli, PE
Executive Vice President, David Evans and Associates, Inc.

Design plus Enterprise: Seeking a New Reality in Architecture & Design
James P. Cramer

Using specific examples, Design plus Enterprise illustrates how using business principles architects can create better design services—and thereby, a better society. It also demonstrates how smart design can drive economic success.

"This is must reading for every architect...It clearly points out how design and the designer are enriched by recognizing that the profession of architecture is both a business and a way of enhancing the environment"

—M. Arthur Gensler Jr., FAIA
Chairman, Gensler Architecture, Design & Planning Worldwide

Communication by Design: Marketing Professional Services
Joan Capelin

How to communicate—and, especially why—to clients, prospects, staff, and the public is the basis of this powerful book. It is targeted to business principals as well as anyone who aspires to a leadership position in a firm, association, or business joint venture.

" Capelin offers thought-provoking practical lessons in marketing leadership—illustrated by interesting insights and implementable ideas. Read this book, put her advice into action, and your firm will flourish."
—Howard J. Wolff
Senior Vice President/Wimberly Allison Tong & Goo

DesignIntelligence

The Design Future Council's monthly "Report on the Future" provides access to key trends and issues on the cutting edge of the design professions. Each month it offers indispensable insight into management practices that will make any firm a better managed and more financially successful business.

"We read every issue with new enthusiasm because the information always proves so timely. No other publication in our industry provides as much useful strategic information."
—David Brody Bond LLP

Change Design: Conversations About Architecture as the Ultimate Business Tool
NBBJ and Bruce Mau Design

Change Design explores how traditional "form-driven" architecture is falling before a new approach that integrates design with business performance.

Highlighting journeys of visionary leaders who are transforming their organizations by leveraging design, and filled with interviews, essays, methodologies, metrics and project case studies, Change Design provides a road map for business leaders and designers alike to build transformative, effective, and competitive organizations. (NEW)

Order online at www.greenway.us, by phone at 800-726-8603, or by using the order form on the next page.

FORM

How Firms Succeed: A Field Guide to Design Management	$39.00		
Communication by Design: Marketing Professional Services	$34.95		
Leadership by Design: Creating an Architecture of Trust	$39.50		
Value Redesigned: New Models for Professional Practice	$39.50		
Architecture, Seriously	$28.95		
Design Plus Enterprise: Seeking a New Reality in Architecture & Design	$29.00		
Almanac of Architecture & Design 2006	$49.50		
Almanac of Architecture & Design 2000 – 2006 Library	$219.00		
Change Design: Conversations About Architecture as the Ultimate Business Tool	$88.00		
2006 DesignIntelligence Compensation Survey	$69.95*		
DesignIntelligence (1 year subscription)"	$365.00		
The Next Architect: A New Twist on the Future of Design	$39.95		

*GA residents add 6%

Shipping: $4.95 for first item; $1.00 each additional item

' A PDF version of the 2006 DesignIntelligence Compensation Survey may be downloaded immediately from our Web site at www.greenway.us for only $49.95 (a $20 savings off the print edition).

" 2 year (US and Canada) subscriptions $547. International subscriptions are available for $395 per year.

Subtotal

Shipping

Tax*

Total

❑ Check ❑ Credit Card

Card Number   Exp. Date   Signature

Name   Title

Company

Address

City   State   Zip

Telephone   Fax

Email

Your completed order form may be faxed to us at 678.879.0930 or mailed to:
Greenway Communications
25 Technology Parkway South, Suite 101
Norcross, GA 30092

All our publications can also be purchased online at www.greenway.us.

östberg ™

Library of Design Management

Every relationship of value requires constant care and commitment. At Östberg, we are relentless in our desire to create and bring forward only the best ideas in design, architecture, interiors, and design management. Using diverse mediums of communications, including books and the Internet, we are constantly searching for thoughtful ideas that are erudite, witty, and of lasting importance to the quality of life. Inspired by the architecture of Ragnar Östberg and the best of Scandinavian design and civility, the Östberg Library of Design Management seeks to restore the passion for creativity that makes better products, spaces, and communities. The essence of Östberg can be summed up in our quality character to you: "Communicating concepts of leadership and design excellence."